The Northern Frontiers
of Roman Britain

For Brian Dobson

The Northern Frontiers of Roman Britain

David J. Breeze

BATSFORD ACADEMIC AND EDUCATIONAL LTD   LONDON

Photoset in Monophoto Sabon by
Servis Filmsetting Ltd, Manchester
and printed in Great Britain by
The Anchor Press
Tiptree, Essex
for the publishers
Batsford Academic and Educational
a Division of B.T. Batsford Ltd
4 Fitzhardinge Street
London W1H 0AH

ISBN 0 7134 0345 4

Contents

Plates

Maps and Diagrams

Acknowledgments

The author and publisher wish to thank the following for permission to reproduce the photographs and plans appearing in this book: *Scottish Development Department Ancient Monuments Branch*, plates 1, 9, 10, 18, 19, figure 25; *Royal Commission on the Ancient and Historical Monuments of Scotland*, plate 4; *Cambridge University Committee for Aerial Photography*, plates 2, 3, 5, 6, 12; *Newcastle Museum of Antiquities*, plates, 7, 11; *National Museum of Antiquities of Scotland*, plates 13–17; *Mr Peter Connolly*, plate 8; *Society for the Promotion of Roman Studies*, figure 5; *Mr C.M. Daniels*, figures 17, 36, 37.

The jacket illustration, of a watch-tower on the Gask Ridge, has been kindly prepared by Mike Moore.

A Note on Terminology

Modern political divisions complicate life for the ancient historian. The Romans knew no such place as Scotland. They called the whole island *Britannia*, and the only distinction within that was the geographical territory of the British tribes. However, Tacitus, writing of the campaigns of his father-in-law Agricola in the first century, spoke of *Caledonia*. Unfortunately it is not clear whether this refers merely to the tribes inhabiting the Highlands, or to all the tribes north of the Forth-Clyde isthmus. For that reason, and because its usage by the Romans will have changed over the years, this term is eschewed. That part of Britain north of the Tyne-Solway isthmus is referred to throughout this book as north Britain. Areas within that area are related to modern geographical names or to ancient tribes.

The Romans called the people living beyond the empire, barbarians, a term they had inherited from the Greeks, to whom they had once been barbarians. The term is frequently used below in relation to the northern tribes: it does not imply any slur upon their state of civilisation, but merely emphasises that they were not Roman.

Preface

Hadrian's Wall holds a perennial fascination, as the visitor numbers to such important sites as Housesteads and the considerable success of Chesterholm-Vindolanda demonstrate. However, Hadrian's Wall is only one of several Roman frontiers in Britain, which survive to greater or lesser extent. In Scotland the Antonine Wall, though much less well preserved, has been well known for centuries, while recent research has cast light upon Agricola's lost frontier on the Forth-Clyde isthmus and its apparent successor in Perthshire. All these frontiers are the subject of this book, leaving aside only the Saxon Shore along the south and east coast of England, which has recently been discussed in detail in two monographs.

These Roman frontiers did not stand in isolation. They were built in reaction to something – or rather someone: the native peoples of north Britain. The northern tribes – the Caledonians and their successors the Picts – therefore form as much a part of this book as the Roman frontiers and the soldiers who manned them. It is unfortunate that we know so little about the enemies of Rome, largely because no written record of theirs has survived, and much of what we do know emanates from Roman sources, hardly an unbiased point of view. However, archaeology can go some way towards redressing the balance.

It is important also to place the British frontiers within the overall setting provided by the Roman empire. Hence this book commences with a look at the rise of Rome and a discussion of the conquest of Britain. An examination of the northern tribes in Britain at the time of the Romans forms the body of the next chapter. The northern frontiers are then discussed in chronological order: Agricola on the Forth-Clyde isthmus, the 'Gask frontier', Hadrian's Wall and the Antonine Wall. The next chapter deals with the history of the northern frontier following the abandonment of the Antonine Wall, while a final chapter draws together the various themes of the book. At all stages an attempt has been made to interweave the Roman and native material to create a meaningful story, reflecting not only the building, occupation and abandonment of the frontiers, but their development and their impact upon the native peoples living in their vicinity and the barbarian tribes to the north.

No book is the product of one man. One person may write it, but he has previously assimilated facts and beliefs brought to his attention by others, some of which are bound to be incorporated, consciously or subconsciously, into the book. I am pleased to acknowledge one major and formative influence on this book: the teachings of the Department of Archaeology in the University of Durham. In particular I owe a considerable debt to Eric Birley, John Mann and Brian Dobson who first encouraged and nurtured my interest in Roman Britain and in Roman military studies, the last not least serving as my research supervisor through five years and two theses. I would also like to acknowledge my debt to other members of the 'Corbridge School': John Gillam, Charles Daniels, George Jobey, Valerie Maxfield and the late Jock Tait. While none would agree with all the views expressed in this book, and some would regard many as downright heretical, these scholars have nevertheless wittingly or unwittingly helped to create and mould those views. Finally I must thank the adult students who have attended my courses, and especially those on the Hadrian's Wall course run jointly with Brian Dobson and Valerie Maxfield, for asking difficult questions, offering solutions to difficult problems and generally forcing me to think again (and again) about different aspects of the frontier.

This book has been read in draft by Brian Dobson, Iain MacIvor and Anna and Graham Ritchie. To them I offer my grateful thanks for all their suggestions and comments aimed at improving the text. I would also like to thank John Barber, Gordon Barclay and Ian Hodgson for discussing various problems with me, Tom Borthwick for preparing figs 1, 2, 7, 11, 12, 21, 28, 35 and 39, Mike Moore for executing the reconstruction drawings (figs 9, 14–16, 18, 22 and 24), Charles Daniels for generously making the drawings of Housesteads and Wallsend available in advance of publication, W.S. Hanson for similarly allowing me to use the plan of Croy Hill, and all who so kindly provided photographs. Thanks are also due to Graham Webster and Peter Kemmis Betty for inviting me to write this book. Finally, my best thanks must go to my wife who has had to live with Hadrian's Wall and the Antonine Wall for far too long.

Edinburgh
March 1981

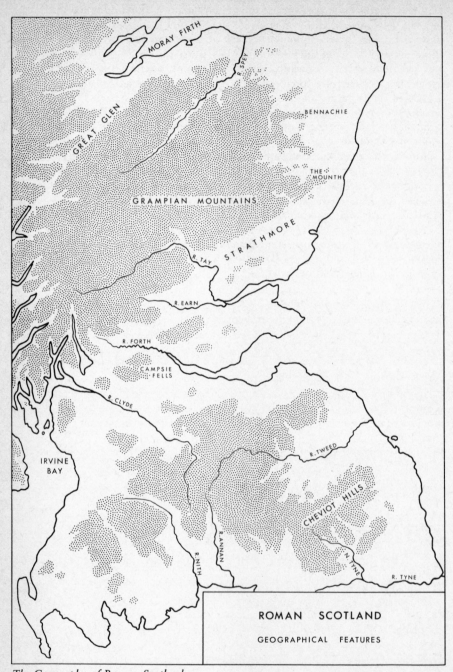

The Geography of Roman Scotland

Romans

The arrival of Roman armies in north Britain in the 80s AD coincided with the establishment of the first frontiers in the Roman empire. Before that time the empire, of course, had boundaries but not frontiers in the sense of patrolled and defended lines of control or, as they were to become in the second century AD, barriers. The construction of these frontiers reflected a changing attitude on the part of the Romans to the extension of their empire. The possibility that their empire might not continue to expand indefinitely was first recognised, para-doxically, in the testament of the greatest expansionist of them all, Augustus. The construction of the lines of control in the 80s was the second step, and the hardening of these into linear barriers a third. But throughout these years, and beyond, the empire was still expanding, though not in the grand way of previous centuries. Claudius, Nero, Vespasian, Titus, Domitian, Trajan, Antoninus Pius, Marcus Aurelius, Septimius Severus all expanded, or attempted to expand, the Roman empire, and it was the advent of the civil wars in the mid-third century and the swing in the balance of power against the Romans that led at first to a halt to this expansion and then a gradual, and long drawn out, contraction; long drawn out, for the Roman empire did not end until the fall of Constantinople in 1453. Within this time scale the frontiers of the Roman empire such as Hadrian's Wall and the Antonine Wall had a very short life. Further, while ostensibly reflecting the might of Rome, viewed against the background of the twenty-two centuries from the traditional foundation of Rome to the fall of Constantinople in 1453, they may be regarded as expressions of failure.

The expansion of Rome

Patrolled lines of control along a frontier had no place in the early history of Rome. The city's first concerns were to rid herself of the oppression of her foreign masters, and then to defend herself against her neighbours. Through successive struggles with the peoples of Italy Rome gradually came to control the whole of the peninsula: by the end of the third century BC all Italy lay within her grasp. What drove Rome on was fear of her enemies, fear of being conquered and subdued by them. During the course of these struggles Rome perfected a military machine, a vehicle which eventually was to bring her to the control of the whole Mediter-ranean basin. This vehicle was the legion. Copied from the Greek phalanx this body of 4,000–5,000 men was rendered more flexible by its organisation into three lines, each advancing through gaps in the line ahead to present fresh troops to the enemy. The Romans were also prepared to learn from other peoples: the Greeks might provide one example but weapons and armour were also adopted from the Gauls. The legion was primarily an infantry unit; the cavalry element in the army was provided by Rome's allies.

The legion was fully incorporated into the Roman state. It was formed from the citizens of Rome and the farmers of its territory; its commanders were drawn from the ruling oligarchy of Rome. However, these men were not a separate military caste: when not fighting they were civil magistrates and administrators. Thus military affairs permeated the whole Roman state, and was not a distinct and separate element in society.

Her skill in warfare and administration, the loyalty and resilience of her people, were to stand Rome in good stead in her fiercest fight, that against the Carthaginians. Over half of the sixty years 264–204 BC were spent fighting this people. Again the war grew out of fear, fear that the only other major power in the western Mediterranean would come to subjugate Rome unless prevented by forceful action on the part of Rome herself. However, in this war Rome moved first and carried out a pre-emptive strike by crossing the Straits of Messina into Sicily to occupy the city of Messina which she believed was about to be occupied by the Carthaginians. Menacing activities by her enemies were to be used again and again as an excuse for war by Rome even against the weakest foe: she always liked a *casus belli*, even if this was a patent fabrication. The first Punic war ended with the victory of Rome and the acquisition of its first overseas territory, Sicily – which was quickly followed by Sardinia and Corsica. The victorious conclusion of the second Punic war saw the absorption of the Carthaginian territories in Spain into the Roman orbit.

So far as possible the new provinces were left to govern and administer themselves, and this was to be a continuing feature of Roman provincial administration. The new territories were already divided among city states and Rome perpetuated this organisation, later creating new cities where necessary. To govern each province a magistrate was sent out from Rome. His duties included administering the law, raising taxes and keeping the peace. In carrying out such functions he would have assistance, from, for example, a financial secretary (also sent out from Rome annually), and from the army. However, unless these provinces were troubled by bandits, as in Sardinia, or an external enemy as in Spain, army units were not usually permanently stationed in them: there was no need to control the local cities by a military presence, for they could be controlled by the mere existence of the army. A serious revolt within a few years of the establishment of a new province was a regular accompaniment of the expansion of the empire, but thereafter for the most part the provincials settled down peaceably under their new masters (though internal disturbances and insurrections broke out occasionally in both the Republic and the Empire).

The second Punic war by chance also brought Rome an interest in the eastern Mediterranean. Macedonia had declared war on Rome after Hannibal's victory at Cannae and thus drew on herself the wrath of Rome after her success over the Carthaginians. Thus was Rome drawn into the maelstrom of eastern politics. At first she seemed to be content merely to hold the ring, but this changed in the middle of the second century BC when, losing patience, she destroyed Carthage, incorporated Africa and Macedonia into her empire and then proceeded to expand further in the eastern Mediterranean by the simple expedient of inheriting kingdoms from childless monarchs. Eighty years after the destruction of Carthage practically all the Mediterranean basin was in Roman hands – Egypt was the only major exception – and Rome was turning her attention to its hinterland.

This era of expansion brought new tensions to Rome. Now a permanent field army was required. The conscription of men from Rome and Italy on an annual basis and for a limited number of years was no longer tolerable or efficient. The old ways, the old Roman army, ended for ever when in 107 BC Marius enrolled volunteers for the war in north Africa. A new problem was created in turn, for these soldiers owed their allegiance not to the Roman state but to their commanders. Further, the state was finding it increasingly difficult to control overweening and unscrupulous nobles. These strains tore the republic apart and resulted in the creation of the principate under Augustus' guidance. Through these years, however, the empire continued to expand. The best known war of conquest was conducted by Julius Caesar in Gaul – best known because he left his own record of his exploits. The Gallic War reveals clearly the Roman military machine, Roman strategy and tactics and Roman diplomacy at work.

The conquest of Gaul was unprovoked. The Romans, of course, had their excuse for intervention – the migration of the Helvetii, then the presence of Germans in Gaul (who had incidentally, as Caesar records, been invited there by one of the Gaulish tribes), and finally the reaction of the Gaulish tribes to the Roman intervention. But the main purpose of Caesar's war was to enable him to keep an army in the field, and as a result increase his power (he gained important prestige through his triumphs) and obtain booty for his army. When Gaul seemed to have been subdued, Caesar turned his attention to Britain and led two expeditions there. He also reconnoitred across the Rhine. In both cases he had excuses for intervention and might well have gone on to further conquests but for insurrections in Gaul and then a changed political situation in Rome which led to his interests being directed elsewhere. When he actually became master of Rome, Caesar significantly did not return to Britain but turned his attention towards Parthia.

The fighting in Gaul was carried out by legions supported by troops raised from the less civilised parts of the empire or from the Gallic allies. The number of legions steadily increased from four to 11, new ones being raised from Italy when required. Support – or auxiliary – troops included Cretan archers, slingers from the Balearic islands, light armed infantry from Numidia in north Africa, Gaul and, in later years, Germany. An important element in the army was the Gallic cavalry, in total something over 4,000 men, raised from friendly or allied tribes, even during the rebellion of Vercingetorix from German allies. This force was of great value in reconnoitering and raiding, as well as supporting the legions in battle. The cavalry occasionally fought engagements by themselves, and in a set-piece battle served an important function in following up the victory won by the legions: Caesar lamented that the lack of cavalry in Britain in 55 BC prevented him from achieving his usual success.

Caesar was a civil magistrate as well as a military commander during his governorship of Cisalpine Gaul (actually north Italy), Transalpine Gaul (southern France: modern Provence) and Illyricum (the west coast of Yugoslavia). Each winter he returned to his provinces to supervise their administration and dispense justice. In the spring he gathered his army together and set out on campaign. The fighting and diplomacy during these campaigns was carried out at Caesar's behest: he never appears to have consulted the Senate in Rome on any matter, though he sent regular dispatches and justified his actions retrospectively. Some of the Gallic tribes were allied to Rome and Caesar was quick to exploit the jealousies and differences between the tribes and indeed within each tribe. He controlled all the tribes, both friendly and hostile, by taking hostages from among their chief men and by the presence of his army and himself – or by the threat of his presence (though this did not always prevent revolts from breaking out). Caesar does not mention the construction of a single permanent fort in Gaul during the eight years of campaigning there and none of this date have been found by modern archaeologists working in France. At the end of each season the army returned to winter quarters. At first all the legions were placed together close to the existing province, but later they were split into separate groups, though never less than a legion in size, and quartered in the territory of newly conquered tribes. During the summer the army lived off the land as much as was possible and then laid in supplies for the winter months. The winter quarters, temporary timber huts, were protected from attack by a rampart and ditch and such camps were also constructed on campaign.

The situation in Gaul in the years following Caesar's conquest is far from clear. When the position becomes clearer, early in Augustus' reign, the army units are found on the Rhine: it seems probable that legions were first stationed there permanently between 16 and 13 BC. Here the units were poised for intervention either in Gaul, where insurrections might break out – as in 12 BC, or in Germany, which was to be the scene of the next step forward.

The bringing of new order to the empire by Augustus resulted in new order on the frontiers. As soon as Augustus had achieved an internal settlement, with the establishment of the principate in 27 BC, he turned his attention to the problems of the frontiers. It is possible that Augustus' activities, which at first sight appear to have no thread or purpose, in fact were carefully considered and executed according to a coherent plan.

In the years 27–13 BC Augustus concentrated on trying to impose lasting settlements on all the frontiers of the empire except the northern. He reorganised the remaining African kingdoms by annexing Numidia and moving its king, Juba, to Mauretania. Shortly afterwards, in 25–24 BC, he sent an expedition into Arabia, during which Aden was sacked, and probed up the Nile: it was clear that nothing was to be feared from these quarters. Internal dissensions in Parthia led to success on the eastern frontier merely by threatening invasion: sabre rattling by Tiberius on the frontier in 20 BC led to the return of all Roman prisoners and captured standards in a truly cheap victory. At the same time Augustus ratified Antony's re-organisation of the local client kingdoms. Meanwhile in western Europe Augustus completed the conquest of Spain, which had been dragging on for nearly two centuries, subdued the Alpine tribes, organised the affairs of Gaul (which seem to have been left untended since Caesar lost interest) and achieved some sort of diplomatic settlement with Britain. During these years minor campaigns were fought elsewhere, in Illyricum, Pannonia and Moesia, along the Danube and in Asia Minor. The assimilation of the tribes up to the Danube was achieved by 15 BC, though, as often happened, serious revolts broke out some years later. Most of this military and diplomatic activity was carried out by Augustus himself, by Tiberius and Drusus his stepsons, or by Agrippa, his closest friend and later his son-in-law.

The successful settlements on all the frontiers except the north left Augustus free in 13 BC to consider the conquest of Germany. It has been argued that Augustus saw the conquest of Germany as imperative for the security of the empire. Whether Augustus would have stopped on the Elbe, which was seemingly the initial objective, is uncertain. The Romans at this time thought the world was limited in extent and Augustus could well have considered that the subjugation of Germany was merely the first step towards the control of all the world beyond the Danube. Augustus had many excuses for invading Germany, for since Caesar's time there had been several forays into Gaul by the Germans.

Starting in 12 BC Drusus conducted four campaigns into Germany as far as the

Elbe. After his death in 9 BC Tiberius and L. Domitius Ahenobarbus took over, the latter even crossing the Elbe. At the same time the North Sea coast was explored as far north as the northern tip of Jutland. Periodic revolts by the tribes living in the provinces immediately south of the Danube accompanied the campaigns of these years. In AD 6, while Tiberius was attacking the Marcomanni, who had given no offence to Rome save by maintaining a well equipped and trained standing army, a most serious revolt broke out in Pannonia and Illyricum which led to the abandonment of the campaign and the start of fierce fighting in the Danube provinces. No sooner was this revolt put down than P. Quintilius Varus was defeated in Germany: his army of three legions and an unknown number of auxiliaries were massacred in the Teutoburg Forest. Augustus was now an old man in his seventies. He lacked the resilience of earlier years and these two events – the Illyricum revolt and the loss of the legions in Germany – resulted in a loss of faith, retrenchment and the famous advice to his successor not to extend the empire any further (advice which he had signally failed to follow himself).

The Varan disaster of AD 9 has clouded the Augustan achievements in Germany up to that date. It is clear, however, that Roman strategy and tactics in conquering and organising a new province were no different now from what they had been forty years before under Caesar. Following the *casus belli*, taken up in 12 BC, Rome had first conquered the German tribes and then set about reducing the land between the Rhine and the Elbe to the status of a province. During the course of these operations reconnaisance expeditions crossed the Elbe just as Caesar had crossed the Rhine and the English Channel, and treaties were concluded with the tribes beyond the river. An altar and cult of Augustus was established at Cologne on the Rhine to be the focus for provincial unity and loyalty, in emulation of an earlier establishment at Lugudunum for the Gallic tribes. Later another altar to Augustus was erected on the Elbe. Cities and markets sprang up, Germans joined the Roman army and the country appeared to be largely pacified. However, even now, in AD 9, there were few forts in Germany. Timber forts constructed along the Lippe, the main route into Germany, were possibly not occupied all year. Other forts in the new province are mentioned by Roman writers, but these have not been located and it is probable that they were only occupied during the summer, for still the main body of the army retired each winter into Roman territory, as Caesar had done while conquering Gaul. By AD 9 the pacification of Germany was so far advanced that taxation and Roman law were being imposed on the new provincials. Whether this action, Varus' temperament or simply German restlessness led to the subsequent – successful – revolt is difficult to determine. Certainly the situation in Germany followed that in other provinces: initial Roman success, revolt(s), eventual Roman victory, often after bitter and protracted fighting. The important difference now was that Augustus was too old to recover from the blow and preferred to retreat, abandon the forts across the Rhine, and re-establish that river as the empire's frontier.

The methods used to defend that frontier, and others, were simple and straightforward. The five or six legions on the Rhine were placed so that they could intervene in either Gaul or Germany. The forces were concentrated in large army groups. Only four military bases dating to the years before 12 BC have been found on the Rhine, though others may have existed. These bases were all, with possibly one exception, apparently capable of holding two legions, though they may not all have been occupied at the same time. They were usually placed beside access routes into Germany. The auxiliary units were stationed at, or close to, the legionary bases, though a few guarded important points such as river crossings. Such dispositions continued, with the modification of an extra base at Cologne on the Rhine and forts along the Lippe and possible elsewhere in Germany, until the Varan disaster. It was only after AD 9, or possibly AD 16, when Germanicus was recalled, that new forts were established on the Rhine, in positions indicating that they were more concerned with defence than offence.

This situation was reflected elsewhere in the empire. In the east, for example, the army units were not spread out along the frontier, but placed astride the great trade routes, which of course also served as invasion routes, so that they could not only control the local population within the empire but also move out against the adjacent kingdoms. The main base on the eastern frontier lay at Antioch where three or four legions were stationed at the western end of the caravan route into Parthia.

The second method of defence was by means of client kingdoms, a device long used in the eastern Roman world. Much of the eastern Mediterranean was controlled through client kingdoms, Rome often preferring to establish a new king when one died without an obvious heir rather than to incorporate the kingdom into the empire. The client kings were responsible for maintaining law and order within their own territory and for defending their states from external agression: in many ways they were useful buffer states for Rome. At Rome's behest they would have to provide troops for Rome's armies, but they were not allowed their own foreign policy and if they demonstrated too much independence they were simply replaced. In this way Rome controlled great areas with the minimum of trouble and cost. Augustus' own statement of his achievements, the *Res Gestae*, makes it clear that Rome regarded the client states as subject to her and therefore part of the empire.

Rome's defence was thus her latent power, supported by the visible expression of the force behind that power, her armies. Client kings could be kept under control by the threat of Roman intervention: diplomacy – and the payment of subsidies – to such kings and to peoples beyond the empire, was cheaper than military intervention. Order was maintained within the empire, and the frontiers defended by troops placed at strategic points, usually close to but not actually on, the frontiers of the empire. Army groups stationed at such points were also in a position to move forward to conquer new lands as and when necessary: there was no point in stringing the army units out along the frontier simply because there was no permanent frontier, there was only the boundary of this year, or this decade, and before long the unconquered Roman army would move forward again and incorporate new tribes and cities within the empire. And indeed this happened regularly up until AD 9. The Varan disaster brought about a pause in Rome's expansion, a pause which was to last throughout the remaining years of Augustus' principate and, with the exception of Germanicus' abortive and costly campaigns in Germany, throughout the twenty-three years of Tiberius (14–37), and, in spite of the preparatory moves and gestures of Gaius (37–41), was not to end until AD 43 when Claudius (41–54) began the conquest of Britain.

The thirty years between the Varan disaster and the invasion of Britain saw a number of changes in the Roman army, changes partly resulting from the inertia of those years. The army was gradually settling down to a life on the frontier and adapting itself to that life. By AD 43 no soldier in the army, apart from a few long serving centurions, would have known the days of expansion and exploration under Augustus: those days were now over a generation ago. The army of Claudius, although in theory similar to that of his great-uncle, was subtly modifying itself to suit its new role. This process can first be seen in Germany.

In the years following the recall of Germanicus in AD 16, the virtual end of Roman pretensions in Germany (at least for two generations), there was a move away from the garrisoning of two legions together in the same base. In the army of lower Germany the two-legion base at Cologne was abandoned, the garrison being provided with separate fortresses elsewhere, though two legions remained at Vetera. In the army of Upper Germany two legions remained at Mainz, but the other two legions were split between separate fortresses. Now also there was a move to fill, at least in part, the gaps between the legionary fortresses along the Rhine by auxiliary forts, linked by a road along the river and connected in certain areas by fortlets. This was accentuated in Upper Germany after the withdrawal of the legion at Strasbourg for service in Britain in 43. This move was compensated for by the establishment of auxiliary forts spread over a wider area, but still not abandoning the principle of military strong-points for a linear arrangement. In Raetia (modern Bavaria), further to the south-east, under Claudius there was, however, a move towards the establishment of a linear defensive system along the Danube. Here, for the first time, the south bank of the Danube was defended by the construction of a series of forts – ten have so far been assigned to these years – and this probably reflects the abandonment of Roman designs on the tribes beyond the river.

The conquest of Britain

The change in military thinking can perhaps best be seen in Britain for here the system of defence and control started *de nouveau* in 43 and is not obscured by earlier dispositions. The real reason for the invasion of Britain in 43 is probably given by the Roman writer Suetonius: Claudius required a triumph. Claudius had come to the throne in 41 after the murder of his nephew Gaius (better known by his nickname Caligula), in not too auspicious circumstances. There was a rebellion a few months later, quickly put down, but Claudius, who had no military experience, and indeed had had to wait until the age of 47 before being made consul, required military prestige – so necessary for an emperor – to strengthen his position. He chose Britain, long considered a legitimate Roman sphere of interest, presumably considered not too difficult a task, and for which he had a pretext – the expulsion of a king, Berikos (almost certainly Verica of the Atrebates), by his brother. Further Claudius could be seen to be emulating the actions of his ancestor, the great Julius Caesar, while the conquest of land considered by the Romans to be at the end of the world would bring its own mystique.

The invasion force consisted of four legions, *II Augusta*, *IX Hispana*, *XIV* and *XX*, with probably an equivalent number of auxiliary soldiers. The main opponent was the kingdom ruled by Caratacus and Togodumnus, sons of King Cunobelin, who had died about three years before. Their realm embraced the tribes of the Catuvellauni and Trinovantes in central southern England and Essex. The Roman army dealt with the opposition expeditiously, though not without some hard fighting, and in one skirmish Togodumnus was killed. Claudius himself arrived for the final blow against Colchester, capital of the kingdom. The vanquished sued for peace, Caratacus fled westwards, and other tribes submitted. Claudius in Britain was hailed as Imperator, the senate voted him the title of Britannicus, and awarded him a triumph. Claudius had indeed won his military prestige and was not challenged by rebellion during the remaining eleven years of his reign, though he did use other means to strengthen his position, such as his marriage to Agrippina.

Following the return of Claudius to Rome Aulus Plautius, the governor of Britain, was left to conquer 'the rest', a meaningless phrase which is incapable of interpretation: it could imply the completion of the conquest of those parts of the island designated by Claudius as the province, or the rest of the island, excluding the client kingdoms, which it was felt in time would be incorporated within the empire. Plautius' army quickly overran the south and midlands of England. Little is known of these operations. Vespasian, later to become emperor, was legate of II Augusta at this time and fought thirty engagements and captured more than twenty *oppida* (probably mainly forts rather than towns) in southern England, including the Isle of Wight. Otherwise the strength of the opposition to the Roman armies is not known: the hints in the relevant Roman literature suggest that opposition was not great – Vespasian's achievements were recorded only because he later became emperor.

Although little evidence survives concerning Roman campaigning methods in Britain during the early years of the conquest a clear picture of campaigning in Britain does emerge when the various comments in the books of Tacitus (in particular his biography of his father-in-law the Flavian governor, Gnaeus Julius Agricola) are gathered together. The pattern that emerges when these various statements, often made almost as throw-away lines, are combined to form a continuous narrative, is little different from that provided by Caesar's *Gallic War*.

At the beginning of the campaigning season the governor concentrated his army and marched out to try to locate the enemy, a task in which he was not always successful. Intelligence was gathered from a variety of sources, including merchants, and this information included details of the tribes to be attacked, their political organisation, their strongholds, the lie of the land and landing places and harbours where appropriate. Where an excuse for attack was needed a pretext was manufactured. In 43 there was a fugitive British prince in Rome and while Agricola was considering the possibility of invading Ireland he had an Irish prince to hand. His excuse for attacking the Caledonians a year later was that he had heard of threatening movements made by the tribe. It was only after the Roman invasion that the northern tribes 'without provocation' – a statement very reminiscent of that concerning a similar incident in the Gallic war – attacked a Roman fort.

Much time on campaign was clearly spent fighting the terrain and weather rather than the enemy. Each night the army defended itself from attack by the construction of temporary camps, a device shown to be of special value in Agricola's sixth season when, after he had divided his army into three divisions (a move approved by modern military tacticians), one division was attacked. It might take several seasons to defeat the enemy, but Roman generals were used to such problems and more than one governor of Britain had experience of mountain warfare in more difficult parts of the empire.

At the end of each campaigning season the army retired into winter quarters, which, until the enemy was subdued, always lay within the province. It was only after the defeat of the enemy that forts were built in his territory; until then it was controlled by the army's presence, or threat of its presence, and by the taking of hostages as recorded in the second season and after Mons Graupius. After its defeat the enemy, or rather the new provincials, would be disarmed. Finally, it may be noted that campaigning was only the summer's activity. In the winter the governor, as had Caesar, turned to the problems of administration and justice in the more settled parts of the province.

The main distinction to be drawn between Tacitus' account of campaigning and Caesar's, lies in the nature of the winter quarters. Caesar, each winter, divided his army into groups never less than one legion strong, and generally two or three legions in strength. These were placed either in friendly territory or in the area of newly conquered tribes in order to intimidate and control them. The position in Britain is not clear during the very early years after the invasion but when a pattern does emerge it is not of such concentrations. On the contrary, the units are now spread between a large number of forts, echoing the pattern apparently developing at the same time in Germany. In part this reflects the increasing importance of the auxiliary regiments, which for the first time in the Flavian period (69–96) formed a battle-line without help from the legions.

The arrangements made by the first governor of Britain, Aulus Plautius, for the organisation of this province are fairly clear. Certain tribes – the Catuvellauni, Trinovantes, Coritani, Dobunni, Durotriges and Dumnonii – were formed into the province. Each tribe was organised into the north-west European equivalent of the city state prevalent in the Mediterranean basin, the tribe being translated into a *civitas*. The *civitas* consisted of the territory of the tribe, possibly modified from pre-conquest days, with the chief urban centre of the tribe forming the city of the *civitas*. Much controversy surrounds the question of the strict definition of the *civitas* and it is not possible to be sure whether the Romans saw the organisation as essentially a city with a surrounding territory, on which lay lesser settlements, or as a tribe with a town chosen to be its administrative and religious focus: so far as one can tell the former is more likely to be nearer reality. These *civitates* would take some time to create and it is possible that in the early years, while the local aristocracy was being introduced to Roman ways, each was governed by a prefect sent out by Rome. When this period was over the *civitates* would be left to govern themselves within the administrative, legal and financial framework provided by the governor and procurator of the province.

After the conquest not all tribes were incorporated into the province. Some were made, by treaty, into client kingdoms. These were the Iceni in East Anglia, the Atrebates in Wessex, and the Brigantes in northern England. These client states extended the area under Roman influence to the later provincial boundary, though with the notable exception of Wales. They were a device frequently used by Rome when incorporating new territory into the empire, partly, no doubt, in order to relieve pressure on the army in those early days. Certainly Rome would have regarded them essentially as parts of the empire and felt free to intervene in their affairs at will – as she was later to demonstrate in her dealings with the Iceni in 47 when the governor sent troops to disarm the tribe and with the Brigantes on a number of occasions. These tribes were, however, for the most part left to run their own affairs, and, so far as can be seen, left ungarrisoned by Roman troops. As the client kings died, the treaties between them and Rome lapsed and were either renegotiated with their successors (though there is no evidence for this) or their kingdoms were incorporated into the province. Thus on the death of Prasutagus of the Iceni in 60, apparently with no male heir, his kingdom was taken into the province; this led, as was so often the case when client kingdoms were absorbed by Rome, to a bloody revolt. Ten years later the expulsion of Queen Cartimandua from her Brigantian kingdom resulted in the incorporation of that client state into the province. The kingdom of Cogidubnus of the Atrebates was also presumably absorbed into the province on his death and was divided into possibly as many as three *civitates*.

The tribes who submitted to Rome and were formed into the province had to be controlled and defended from attack. Little is known of the disposition of the auxiliary units in these early years, so it is not possible to determine whether or not they were grouped round the legionary fortresses in the concentration of forces still found at this time on the continent. The placing of the legions is rather more certain. One was established at Colchester, the former capital of the kingdom of the Catuvellauni and Trinovantes, and now to become the capital of the new province. A second legion was placed in the south-west, a third in the northern part of the province, the east midlands, while the fourth presumably lay somewhere in between in the west midlands. It is possible that in some areas legionary detachments were garrisoned away from the main legionary fortresses, though this would be unexpected in view of the situation still pertaining elsewhere in the empire. The discovery of a fort at Verulamium, the main town of the new *civitas* of the Catuvellauni, suggests that military units, presumably auxiliary units, may have been stationed at all the new tribal centres in the early years after the conquest.

The army must soon have started the construction of roads to link the new forts. One of these roads, the Fosse Way, ran from Exeter to Lincoln. This has been described as the first frontier in Britain, but in reality it is merely a road connecting the forts situated in a broad zone along the western and northern boundaries of the province and no more. The boundary of the province at this time would presumably have been the western and northern boundaries of the tribes which submitted to Rome. There would have been no point in defending such a boundary; rather the troops would be placed in the most convenient geographical positions in order to intercept any attacks on the province. Furthermore, there is no need to envisage these forts as being occupied throughout the year. In the summer, as the contemporary accounts of activity in Britain make clear, the army would be out on campaign. The strategy behind the disposition of the military forces was not to change throughout the many fluctuations in success. The main factors governing the position of forts were that they should be so placed that the army could control the local population and defend it from attack, units in the 'front line' being supported by others placed on the roads leading into the interior of the province.

Military affairs in Britain did not proceed smoothly. After the initial flurry, culminating in suitable prestige for Claudius, his interest seems to have flagged and for the remaining twelve years of his reign the only recorded recurrence of his interest was when Caratacus was captured and paraded through Rome. Britain also appears to have been left in a backwater during the early years of Nero's reign (54–68). When, in 57, he took up the reins of government himself he at first seems to have considered abandoning the province – no doubt after securing a suitable settlement in Rome's favour. In the end he decided to retain control and press forward the conquest of the island, commencing with the Welsh tribes. This advance lost some impetus when Nero's new governor, Quintus Veranius, died after only a year in office, and then ground to a halt in 60 when the Iceni revolted during their absorption into the province following the death of Prasutagus. Britain again reverted to being a backwater through the remaining years of his reign and during the succeeding civil war; this was reflected in the withdrawal of *legio XIV* from Britain in 66. The accession of Vespasian (69–79) brought to the throne a soldier who had previously served in Britain. He replaced the withdrawn legion and initiated an advance in the island which culminated in the defeat, fourteen years later, of the final major enemy in Britain, the Caledonians.

The erratic way in which events proceeded in Britain was due almost entirely to the interest and involvement of the emperor. When he was actively concerned to deal effectively with frontier problems, they were dealt with expeditiously; at other times they were left as a running sore. Under the Flavians, Vespasian and his two sons (69–96), no other events intervened for thirteen or fourteen years to slow up or stop the forward progress of Roman arms in Britain. During this time the size of the province was almost doubled.

In Britain the major task facing Vespasian was the recovery of Roman influence in Brigantia after the expulsion of Queen Cartimandua by her consort Venutius during the Roman civil war. The kingdom was invaded by the new governor Petillius Cerealis, Venutius and the opponents of Rome were defeated, and the construction of forts commenced. The next governor, Julius Frontinus, plucked out the thorn which had long been in the side of the Roman forces in the west of Britain by conquering and garrisoning the Welsh tribes. The activities of both generals could be seen, in some ways, as the completion of unfinished business. It was not until the next governorship, that of Julius Agricola, that the Roman army pushed forward into new lands.

It is under the Flavian governors that the pattern of the military occupation of Britain first becomes clear. The legions were widely spaced as before, though all were moved at this time. Under Petillius Cerealis *IX Hispana* was moved from Lincoln to York and under Julius Frontinus *II Augusta* was established at Caerleon in South Wales and *II Adiutrix* transferred to a new base at Chester. *XX Valeria Victrix* appears to have remained at Wroxeter for some time, but took *II Adiutrix*'s place at Chester when that legion was sent to the continent probably in 86. These legions were carefully placed for effective action. *II Augusta* could oversee the Silures in south Wales, with *XX Valeria Victrix* poised to provide support, and to keep watch on the Ordovices in north Wales. *II Adiutrix* was positioned so that it could intervene either against the Ordovices or the Brigantes where it would be able to support *IX Hispana*, whose sphere of activity would include defence of the northern frontier.

While the legions were concerned with larger strategy the local situation was covered by the auxiliary units based on a network of forts connected by roads. So little is known about the internal layout of these forts, or their garrisons, that it is not possible to determine if normally one unit was assigned to each fort, or if units were divided between a number of forts, or combined in other instances. An added complication is that units may not have become fully standardised in size and internal organisation. In the only widely investigated fort of this period, Pen Llystyn, there were twelve barrack-blocks suggesting either the brigading together of two small cohorts, or the existence of a large unit of double size not attested anywhere else. There are peculiarities too in the barrack-blocks within the Scottish 'type-site', Fendoch, which may imply that the fort was not built, as is generally assumed, for a thousand strong infantry unit. What is clear, however, is that the forts are not specially grouped round the legions in preparation for offensive protection or advance, but are spread across the country, concerned rather with the strategy of control: there was of course in Wales no enemy beyond the province poised to attack.

The Roman army in Britain

The nature and size of the force charged with keeping peace in the province and protecting it from attack also becomes clearer in the Flavian period. The four legions each contained something over 5,000 infantrymen with a small detachment of 120 cavalrymen, Roman citizens all. Each infantryman wore articulated plate armour, known as the *lorica segmentata*, an iron or bronze helmet and carried sword, dagger, two throwing spears, or *pila*, and a large shield; the cavalryman probably wore mail, but otherwise was similarly armed. Well armed, the legionaries were also highly trained and disciplined. They were used to fighting the set-piece battle but also carrying out major building programmes: each legion contained its own engineering corps, building and maintenance staff, medical service and artillery corps. The legion was divided into ten cohorts, subdivided in turn into six 80-strong centuries, with the exception of the first cohort, which in some, possibly most, legions was composed of five double-sized centuries. The century was commanded by a centurion, usually a soldier who had risen from the ranks: these professional officers formed the core of the army. The cohort had no administrative organisation, though it had an important tactical role in battle, and sometimes served as a conveniently sized detachment for duties away from base. The senior officers of the legion were drawn from the aristocracy of the empire, the legate and the senior tribune, his second-in-command, from the senatorial families and the prefect of the camp and the junior tribunes from the equestrian nobility.

The other main branch of the provincial army was the *auxilia*. This was originally formed from the friends and allies of Rome to give support to the legions, but now auxiliary units were raised from the frontier tribes of the empire and thereafter locally recruited. The term *auxilia* covered a variety of units of different sizes and organisation. There were three basic types of unit: the infantry cohort of six centuries, the cavalry *ala* of 16 troops and the mixed cohort of six centuries and four troops. In the Flavian period a double-sized unit of each type was introduced. Although the units were in theory double in size – milliary as opposed to quingenary – in fact they were not quite so large, the infantry cohort containing ten centuries, the *ala* 24 troops and the mixed cohort ten centuries and eight troops. Epigraphic evidence allows the strength of this branch of the British army to be closely defined in the early second century. During the reigns of Trajan and Hadrian (98–138) the minimum number of auxiliary units in Britain seems to have been as follows:

The '*Auxilia*' in Britain during the reigns of Trajan and Hadrian (98–138)

	number	total strength
ala milliaria	1	800
ala quingenaria	14 + 1 ?	7,000 + 500 ?
cohors milliaria equitata	4	4000
cohors milliaria peditata	1 + 1 ?	800 + 800 ?
cohors quingenaria equitata	23 + 1 ?	13,800 + 600 ?
cohors quingenaria peditata	14	6,720
	57 + 3 ?	33,120 + 1,900 ?

It seems unlikely that the strength of the *auxilia* in Britain in the Flavian period was less than the above total of between 33,000 and 35,000 men. There were losses from the British army between the retirement of Agricola and the second century, for

Tacitus records the presence of four Batavian cohorts at Mons Graupius while only one is later attested in Britain. There were certainly a number of occasions when troops could have been withdrawn from Britain, but none when new units are likely to have been sent to the province, in the late first century or early second. Furthermore, a number of units are attested in Britain, but not in the Trajanic-Hadrianic period so the above total is most probably on the conservative side.

The table clearly demonstrates that the most common unit in the British army was the *cohors quingenaria equitata*, the smaller mixed unit, about 600 men strong. The *ala quingenaria*, 500 men strong, and the similarly sized cohort, the *cohors quingenaria peditata*, were present in approximately equal sizes. The milliary, thousand strong units, of all types were rare now as always: there was only one *ala milliaria* in this, or any other, province. The auxiliary century seems to have contained the same number of men as the legionary century – 80, while the cavalry troop was 32 men strong. The infantry centurion and the cavalry decurion were soldiers risen from the ranks, and the commanding officers, prefects and tribunes, were members of the equestrian nobility. The auxiliaries were armed in a similar manner to the legionaries, though they wore mail rather than plate armour. Auxiliaries were not Roman citizens, but awarded that honour on retirement.

The Roman army was, in the main, a volunteer army, though conscription was on occasion employed. A tolerably good level of regular pay was a powerful inducement to recruiting. Legionaries and auxiliaries both served for twenty five years, though centurions and decurions had no set length of service. The senior officers served for much shorter periods, generally about three years and had much less military experience than the men they commanded. Provincial governors such as Agricola had only acquired about six years service before commanding an army of about 50,000 men. It is indeed remarkable that with commanders of such limited military experience the Roman army did not lose more battles!

2

Barbarians

This book is concerned with the frontiers which Rome built in Britain along its northern boundary – or perhaps boundaries would be more accurate as the line fluctuated – over a period of sixty years from the end of the first century to the middle of the second. The enemy which these successive frontiers faced was primarily the Caledonii and their successors the Picts who lived north of the Forth. There is no evidence that the tribes of the Scottish Lowlands ever gave the Roman army any serious cause for concern, yet as these people were those more immediately close to the longest-surviving Roman frontier in north Britain – Hadrian's Wall – it is essential to consider their archaeology and history, as well as the Caledonians', and also their relationship to Rome.

The tribes of north Britain

The earliest surviving description of the tribes of Scotland is by the Alexandrian geographer Claudius Ptolemaeus writing in the mid-second century AD. He wrote two books, the *Almagest* and the *Geography*. It is the latter which contains the references to Britain and it is simply a list of geographical features, tribes and places with their latitudes and longitudes. As such the *Geography* is an incomparable source, but it suffers from three defects so far as Scotland is concerned. Firstly, Ptolemy made a basic error in his measurements in relation to north Britain and as a result Scotland north of the Forth is twisted round at 90°. Secondly, it is possible that Ptolemy had no astronomical data from the British Isles, locations being determined by measurements from Marseilles. Finally, Ptolemy probably simply read names off a map, placing in his list under the tribal heading those place names which appeared on the map in the general area of the tribe. This map has not survived but it was probably also used to provide the basic information in the later document known as the *Ravenna Cosmography*. As a result of these defects many places mentioned by Ptolemy cannot now be identified, and even when a name appears under the heading of a tribe the possibility that it has been wrongly attributed by Ptolemy cannot altogether be dismissed. One final general point should be mentioned: it is not clear whether the place names listed by Ptolemy in northern Britain are native sites or Roman forts or even camps. (The places listed in Ireland clearly cannot be Roman forts, so there is equally no need for all the places in Scotland to be Roman sites.)

South of the Forth Ptolemy lists four tribes: the Votadini of eastern Scotland, the Selgovae in the centre, the Novantae in Dumfries and Galloway, and the Damnonii or Dumnonii who occupy the Clyde basin and spread northwards through Strathearn into south Strathmore (fig. 1). The location of the Votadini and the Novantae is not in doubt, but there are problems concerning the territory of the Selgovae and the Damnonii. Four places, probably all Roman forts, are placed within the territory of the former. Only one of these places can be identified,

Trimontium, Newstead in the middle Tweed basin. However, the co-ordinates of the other three places suggest that they are further west and one ought to lie at the mouth of the Nith, where there is a fort known, Ward Law. It seems improbable, though not impossible, on geographical grounds that the same tribe should occupy the middle and upper Tweed valley and also Annandale and Nithsdale. Further, if *Trimontium* were a Selgovian seat this would be a salient pushed into Votadinian territory which included not only the coastal plain from the Tyne to the Forth but also some of the valleys in the hinterland of that plain including Redesdale. *Trimontium* is placed at the end of the list of Selgovian places and it seems possible that Ptolemy has simply got his tribal attribution wrong and the fort really lay in Votadinian territory.

The second point of doubt concerns the territory of the Damnonii. This stretched from Irvine Bay in Ayrshire across the Clyde, through Menteith and the upper Forth valley into Strathmore. Again this might seem improbable on geographical grounds, reinforced in this case by the political history of the area for Strathmore later undoubtedly fell within the southern division of the Picts. Ptolemy clearly made a mistake with one of his northern tribes, the Vacomagi, as he assigned them places in Angus and the Mearns and in Banff and Moray. In fact it seems more probable that this tribe should be placed in the more northerly position on the south shore of the Moray Firth. It is possible that Ptolemy also made a mistake with the Damnonii and assigned them the territory and places of two tribes, one, presumably the Damnonii, occupying the Clyde basin, and the other, whose name is now unknown, lying north of the Clyde in Strathmore: equally possibly a tribal name has slipped out of Ptolemy's list in later copying.

North of the Forth there are similar problems concerning tribal areas: one has already been noted. The general outlines are clear, however. The Caledonii occupied the Great Glen and the central Highlands, the Vacomagi probably the Moray plain, the Taezali the modern Grampian Region, and the Venicones Fife. The populous area of Strathmore was, according to Ptolemy, assigned to the Damnonii. Along the western and northern littoral of Scotland there were a further eight tribes, their names only appearing in Ptolemy and none of the later sources, unless some are the garbled names in the Ravenna Cosmography.

Some of the place names listed by Ptolemy can be assigned to known Roman forts. The best example is *Trimontium*, the modern Newstead, beside the three Eildon Hills. Others include *Uxellum*, also assigned to the Selgovae and which ought to be Ward Law at the mouth of the Nith, and *Bremenium*, High Rochester on Dere Street, in Votadinian territory. But considerable doubt surrounds the identification of the remaining 19 'places'. In certain cases, even when the approximate location of the 'place' can be determined, there is no known Roman fort in the area to qualify for the name: thus *Vindogara* must lie in the vicinity of Irvine though no Roman fort has been recognised there. One final interesting point remains concerning these place-names. Ptolemy includes within the territory of the Votadini *Curia*, in the land of the Selgovae *Coria*, and amongst the Damnonii *Corda*. These all appear to derive from the same Celtic word, *curia*, meaning hosting, and by extension hosting-place or meeting place, and may refer to the capitals of those three tribes. It is unfortunate that the location of none of these places can be determined, though the Selgovian *Corda* would appear to lie in Upper Annandale, or less likely Upper Nithsdale, while the Votadinian *Curia* seems to be on the southern shore of the Firth of Forth and may lie at or towards Traprain Law.

It is probable that Ptolemy and his sources, one of whom was Marinus of Tyre,

1 *The tribes of north Britain in the first century (after Ptolemy)*

CORNAVII

SMERTAE

LUGI

CAERENI

CARNONACAE

DECANTAE

VACOMAGI

TAEXALI

CREONES

CALEDONII

?BORESTI?

VENICONES

EPIDII

DAMNONII

V O T A D I N I

●Traprain Law

Eildon
Hill ●
North

SELGOVAE

NOVANTAE

B R I G A N T E S

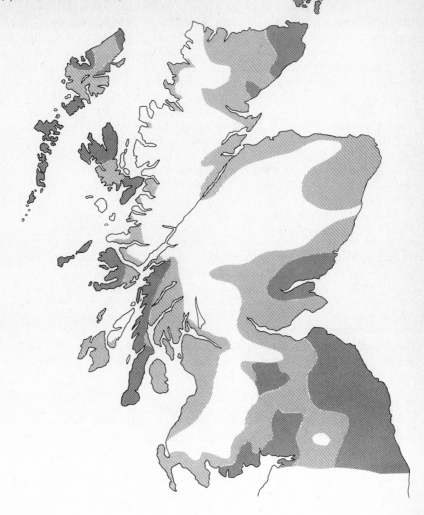

2 *The distribution of Iron Age monuments in north Britain (after Childe and Gillam)*

acquired most of their information from the records of Agricola's campaigns and voyages in Scotland in the 80s. Tacitus, in his accounts of Britain, mentions very few place-names, and several of these, such as Mons Graupius and Portus Trucculensis, cannot now be identified. He records an otherwise unattested tribe, the Boresti. We are not informed where these people live, but Agricola marched into their territory after Mons Graupius and returned thence to his winter quarters: it seems to be not impossible that the Boresti were the lost tribe of Ptolemy and were located in Strathmore, though it is also possible that they should be placed in the Moray plain.

The names of two northern tribes in Ptolemy's list, the Damnonii of the Clyde valley and the Cornavii of Caithness, are also found in England. The former inhabit the south-west peninsula, where they are termed the Dumnonii, while the latter, here the Cornovii, occupy the west Midlands. It has been suggested that the occurence of the same tribal name in southern Britain and in Scotland points to a northward movement of people, presumably on a fairly substantial scale for the tribal name to be maintained, possibly as a result of the Roman invasion. Support for this hypothesis has been sought in the discovery of artefacts imported from the south.

This folk movement, or at least contact, has also been extended to Ireland, for three tribal names appear here as well as in western England. The Brigantes are found in south-east Ireland as well as northern England; the Gangani, recorded in the *promontorium Ganganorum* of Caernarfonshire, are also found in Galway; while the Lagin appear to have given their name to Leinster and Lleyn. The recurrence of so many tribal names may point to the existence of a cultural province round the Irish Sea, as has been recognised at other times, or at least regular contact.

There is, however, more than one interpretation of both forms of evidence, documentary and archaeological. Tribal names do recur among the northern and western fringes of the empire. The name Brigantes, beside appearing in north England and Ireland, occurs as Brigantii in Raetia, while the Parisi are found in east Yorkshire and – as the Parisii – in the Seine valley in Gaul. There is no known connection between the Brigantes of the British Isles and the Brigantii of the upper Danube, but the occurrence of similar burial rites in the territories of the Parisi and Parisii has been taken to imply a close connection between these two tribes, possibly even a common origin. This suggestion is, however, incapable of proof. A further difficulty lies in the nature of the documents used by Ptolemy in compiling his Geography. His source material depended essentially upon the interpretation of a Roman scribe writing down the names of unfamiliar tribes. It seems not impossible that when hearing a name which sounded familiar the scribe, perhaps unconsciously, wrote down that known name, or one similar to it. This itself may be significant, but without supporting evidence, which may be difficult to identify, the connections drawn out of the identification of tribal names should be treated with caution.

A small number of imports were certainly entering Scotland throughout the Iron Age. Some seem to have been transported up the west coast, and include finger rings, glass beads, dice, querns and crucibles. Elsewhere imports were generally high-status goods. They include the Torrs pony cap and horns, probably manufactured in central England in the second century BC, a gold torc terminal with East Anglian parallels, and horse-trappings from East Anglia: other objects have been considered to have connections with Ireland. In no case is the way by which the object found its way north definitely known. Some may have come as a result of trade or plunder, others with craftsmen or refugees. The Middlebie hoard in Dumfriesshire includes objects almost certainly imported from East Anglia and others made locally either by or for the owner of the imports. There is no documentary evidence for refugees, though elsewhere it is known that some fled before the Roman advance. In each case, however, the refugee was a king or noble: Commius fleeing from Caesar and Caratacus from Claudius, for example. This may reflect the inadequacy of our sources, or may correctly demonstrate that it was only the aristocracy who had the wish, freedom and means to escape: refugee craftsmen were probably unusual.

A further complicating factor is that so many of the late Iron Age objects have demonstrable Roman connections. This may take the form of the inclusion of Roman objects in hoards of native Iron Age material, such as the Carlingwark Loch hoard from Kirkcudbrightshire or the Blackburn Mill hoard in Berwickshire which contained a second century Roman *patera*: both hoards were almost certainly votive deposits in a pool or loch. Other Iron Age hoards or collections containing imports have been found near to Roman forts, such as the Middlebie hoard, which was buried less than a kilometre from the first century fort at Birrens. It is difficult to determine the part the Roman army, rather than native refugees, craftsmen or traders, played in the distribution of this material.

North-east Scotland saw a flowering in metalwork in the late first century and extending into the third century. This was clearly the result of closer contact between this area and the south but with no known predecessors in the area it would be difficult perhaps to postulate that the massive terrets, armlets and snake bracelets now manufactured were made by local craftsmen influenced by external styles rather than that incoming smiths introduced new items or adapted local styles. In fact the range in size and variation in quality of both types of armlets have led to the suggestion that the objects were first made by incoming smiths and were then copied by local craftsmen. However, the place of origin of the incoming smiths is a matter of debate, both northern England and Ireland having been suggested. It seems further possible that insufficient allowance had been made for the innovatory skill of the local Caledonian craftsman.

In summary, there is no definite proof of northward folk movement in the immediate pre-Roman Iron Age which would account for south British tribal names reappearing in the north, and little for individual refugees fleeing before the Roman advance. Certain artefacts, however, point to direct contact with schools of metalwork elsewhere and it seems possible that this contact was through refugee craftsmen and nobles, though the number of refugees seems to have been small. The Roman army also played a considerable part in introducing material from the southern part of the island to the northern tribes. Indeed when all the hoards with possible Roman connections are removed from the distribution maps remarkably few collections remain, suggesting less contact between northern and southern natives than often assumed.

There was in north Britain a distinctive division between the tribes north and south of the Forth. This great estuary was to become the southern boundary of the Picts, as is clearly demonstrated by the distribution of 'pit' place names and Pictish symbol stones as well as historical documentation (fig. 39 and pl. 18–19). Yet earlier the Forth also appears to have been a boundary, for in Neolithic times the distribution pattern of carved stone balls is very similar to that of Pictish symbol stones. In the Iron Age the distributions of brochs, duns and timber-laced forts all emphasise the position of the Forth as a cultural division. Further, the Forth also appears to have been a linguistic divison for the tribes of Lowland Scotland spoke a P-Celtic language while those to the north spoke a different, or rather two different languages. Here, it has been suggested, the mass of people spoke a pre-Celtic, non-Indo-European language, while later arrivals, settling mainly along the coast between the Forth and south-east Sutherland, spoke a Gallo-Britonnic language similar to, but not the same as, the P-Celtic spoken further south. This division was to be reflected in the Roman frontier organisation.

One later source, the Anglo-Saxon historian Bede, mentions a distinctive feature concerning the Picts. He stated that 'whenever doubt arises they choose a king from the female royal lineage rather than from the male: which custom, as is well known, has been observed among the Picts to this day'. The lists of Pictish kings demonstrate that, apart from two possible cases towards the end of the Pictish kingdom, no son succeeded his father, though brothers followed one another; this appears to support Bede's statement. This form of succession is not known in Celtic nations and it is possible therefore that Bede is describing a pre-Celtic practice surviving here, uniquely, in Britain.

Roman accounts of the barbarians

The Celts had long been known to the Romans and many accounts of them appeared in Roman literature, though few have survived. The differences between the various tribes were distinguished by some writers – by Caesar, for example (not that the people of the three areas of Gaul that he conquered differed from one another in language, law and customs). Roman descriptions of Celtic practices in continental Europe can therefore only be transferred to Britain with extreme caution, not least because the Celtic settlement of the island is primarily a matter of deduction based on archaeological and philological evidence: the only historical reference to the migration of Celtic peoples to Britain is Caesar's description of the emigration of Belgic tribes from Gaul. Nevertheless it is worth considering Roman comments on Celtic society for they help paint a general picture, in broad outlines relevant to Britain.

In Gaul, Caesar noted, each tribe was divided among rival factions, each headed by a member of the warrior aristocracy. These men, called knights by Caesar, formed one of the two leading classes of society, the other being the priests. Below these were the common people. These had no say in the governing of the tribe but, oppressed by debts or taxation, were bound to the service of the knights: Caesar comments that they were treated little better than slaves. The craftsmen were highly regarded and seem to have fallen between the aristocracy and the free peasants in the social hierarchy. Slaves may have existed but there is no clear evidence for them.

Inter-tribal fighting was a regular pursuit. Wars took place in Gaul nearly every year, with the knights taking the field at the head of their retainers: the size of his following was the main indication of a knight's status. Later Irish literary sources support the accounts of classical writers. According to these medieval traditions cattle raiding and feuding were important aspects of Celtic life, being followed by the warrior aristocracy as a way of life.

The priestly class also possessed considerable power. Not only did they officiate in religious affairs, but they also acted as judges and were the main repositories of tribal knowledge and traditions. Eloquence was highly valued in the Celtic world and in an heroic society the bards served an important role in lauding the achievements of the warriors. Britain was said to be the main centre of Druidic learning, but there is no evidence either now or later for Druids in Scotland. One gruesome practice linked warriors and priests: head-hunting. Enemies' heads were collected as trophies and suspended over house entrances. This also had a religious significance for the human head was believed to contain powers of good which would ward off evil. Heads fashioned out of stone are another manifestation of this cult. It may be noted that head-hunting was not restricted to the Celts, for it was also practiced by the soldiers of the Roman army, as is amply demonstrated by Trajan's Column.

Women do not appear to have had an equal place with men in Celtic society, at least according to Caesar. In Britain wives were shared between groups of ten or twelve men, especially between brothers and between fathers and sons, but the offspring of such unions were counted as the children of the man with whom a particular woman first cohabited. In Gaul husbands had powers of life and death over their wives and children. Against this may be set the existence of two British queens, Boudica of the Iceni and Cartimandua of the Brigantes.

Caesar's description of the Britons is clearly only relevant to the southern part of the island, and cannot be extended to the northern tribes. He stated that the Britons dyed their bodies with woad, which had a blue colour, giving them a more terrifying appearance in battle, but this cannot be connected with the possibility that the name *Picti* derives from the fact that the northern tribes tattooed their bodies – though it may hint that the warriors fought naked or semi-naked, as did a famous group of Gaulish mercenaries in the second century BC.

Tacitus in the *Agricola* furnishes the first account of the peoples of north Britain. He provides the only description of the physique and complexion of the Caledonian: he had large limbs and red hair, in contrast to the Silurian of south Wales who had a swarthy complexion. Tacitus' account of the nature of British society is strongly reminiscent of Caesar's earlier description. The main strength of the British tribes lay in their infantry. Some tribes also fought from chariots, a practice long abandoned on the continent, and the account of Mons Graupius reveals that the Caledonians fought in this way. The chariot was driven by a nobleman who was supported by his dependants on foot. The warrior aristocrats drove up and down between the rival armies, challenging their enemies to fight, but after these individual contests, when the serious fighting began, the charioteers retired from the field to return and fight on foot.

Obedience to kings, states Tacitus, had given way to rivalry between tribal factions headed by chieftains. This rivalry extended to the tribes themselves, as in Gaul in Caesar's time, and Tacitus wryly notes that it was unusual for two or three states to unite to repel a common danger, and in this way they were easily overcome by the Roman armies. The affinity of institutions between the tribes of southern England and Gaul was noted, but this does not necessarily imply that those of the more northerly tribes were much different.

Tacitus also discussed the climate of Britain: it was objectionable with frequent rains and mists, but there was no extreme cold. The shortness of the night in the north was noted, no doubt during the voyage round Britain at the close of Agricola's seventh season. The soil is fertile and can bear all produce, except the olive, vine and other species native to warmer climes. Crops are slow to ripen, but quick to grow, both facts due to the extreme moistness of the climate.

The most detailed account of the northern tribes is by Dio in the preface to his discussion of the Severan campaigns in the early third century and it seems probable that the position described at this time was very similar to that pertaining 120 years before. The passage is worth quoting *in extenso*.

There are two principal nations of the Britons, the Caledonians and the Maeatae, and the names of the others have been merged in these. The Maeatae live by the wall which divides the island in half and the Caledonians beyond them. Both inhabit wild and waterless mountains and desolate and swampy plains, and possess neither walls, cities nor cultivated land, but live on their flocks, wild game and certain fruits, for although the stocks of fish are limitless and immense they leave them untouched. They live in tents, unclothed and unshod, possess their women in common and bring up their children together. Their government is for the most part democratic and because they are very fond of plundering they choose the bravest men to be their rulers. They fight both in chariots with small swift horses, and on foot, when they run very fast and also stand their ground with great determination. For arms they have a shield and a short spear with a bronze apple on the end of the shaft which they can shake and clash to terrify the enemy; and they also have daggers. They can endure hunger and cold and any form of hardship; for they plunge into the swamps and exist there for many days with only their heads above water, and in the forest they live off bark and roots; and for all emergencies they prepare a certain kind of food and when they have eaten a portion of this the size of a bean they do not become hungry or thirsty.

Dio also mentions a conversation between the wife of a Caledonian Argento-coxus, possibly a hostage, and the Empress Julia Domna, consort of Septimius Severus, in about 210. In reply to a comment by the Empress on the freedom of Roman women to have intercourse with whom they pleased, the Caledonian replied that, while Roman women allowed themselves to be seduced in secret by the worst of men, the Caledonian women had intercourse openly with the best men. This could be connected with the matrilinear succession recorded by Bede: in a society with free sexual practices, succession through the female line will have been an advantage.

Herodian's account of the northern barbarians includes many items already recorded by Dio, but also some new comments:

> . . . most of Britain is marshland because it is flooded by the ocean tides. The barbarians usually swim in these swamps or run along in them submerged to the waist: they are practically naked and do not mind the mud. They are unfamiliar with the use of clothing but decorate their waists and necks with iron, valuing this metal as an ornament and as a symbol of wealth in the way that other barbarians value gold. They tattoo their bodies with various patterns and pictures of all sorts of animals. Hence the reason why they do not wear clothes, so as not to cover the pictures on their bodies. They are very fierce and dangerous fighters, protected only by a narrow shield and a spear, with a sword slung from their naked bodies. They are unaccustomed to breastplates and helmets, considering them to be a hindrance as they cross the marshes. A thick mist rises from the marshes, so that the atmosphere in the country is always gloomy.

Archaeology and the northern tribes

Many items in the above accounts are clearly myths or travellers' tales. Archaeology has amplified and amended the picture of the northern tribes as painted by the Roman writers. In spite of the tribal and linguistic differences dividing the peoples of the Scottish mainland on the eve of the Roman invasion their life styles were not materially different.

The ubiquitous form of dwelling in southern and eastern Scotland was the round timber house. The houses varied in diameter from about 6 to 15m though the average size was about 9m across. They were built in a variety of styles. Generally, however, the houses seem to have had low walls of wattle and daub or logs and high conical roofs of thatch or skins. The main weight of the structure rested on a circle of principal uprights but in some instances these were supplemented by central posts. Some houses were divided internally into rooms. Cooking was normally carried out on open fires placed more-or-less centrally. Sometimes houses were placed on natural or artificial islands or platforms in a lake or river. This form of settlement, the crannog, was popular in certain parts of Scotland until the medieval period.

A single family might occupy one or two houses, thus forming a farmstead: analysis of the population of similar modern houses in Africa and elsewhere suggests that on average between five and nine people might occupy a house about

10m in diameter. Sometimes several families grouped themselves together in a village or homestead, containing perhaps up to twenty houses, often defended by ramparts and ditches. The slight nature of such defences emphasises that many must have been simply to keep out wild animals – wolves and bears roamed Scotland at this time – but some were clearly built against warring neighbours and can be fairly termed forts. Such forts might have two, three or even four rows of ramparts and ditches. In certain cases the defences were strengthened by extra outworks or other measures at the entrances. One particular form of extra defence was the *chevaux de frise*, a series of small projecting pointed stones or stakes set in the ground and intended to break an infantry or cavalry charge.

Forts, often placed on top of hills, abound in the Borders. Most are less than half a hectare in area but the size of some – about 8 hectares and above – is such that they have been suggested as the strongholds of tribal chiefs or chieftains. It is not possible to relate these major forts closely to the known tribes or to use them to suggest divisions within the tribes. However, Traprain Law in East Lothian is generally recognised as one of the chief seats of the Votadini if not their capital: it is the only known hill fort in southern Scotland to have continued in occupation through the Roman period and furthermore it survived, seemingly, with its defences intact. Another major hill forts in the Borders was that on Eildon Hill North, by Newstead (Pl. 1). Nearly 300 hut platforms are still visible within the 10 hectares enclosed by the defences and it has been calculated that the population of the 'town' might have been between 2,000 and 3,000 people. Nevertheless it is possible that such hill forts were not occupied all year round. Some may have been refuges or strongholds to which the local population, possibly with their herds, could retire when attacked. They may also have been the 'castles' of the aristocracy. In view of the account of the Celtic way of life with endemic warfare, raiding and feuding, this may not be too fanciful a picture. The warrior aristocrat in his fort may have controlled an area, the people of that area paying taxes to him, helping in the construction of his 'castle' and forming his following in battle.

Hill forts are not only found in the Lowlands, but also north of the Forth in eastern and north-eastern Scotland, though in smaller numbers. Many of these were built in a distinctive manner, with timber-laced ramparts. This form of construction is found mainly in the area between the Forth and Moray Firths and along the west coast from Galloway to Cape Wrath, but there are outliers elsewhere. These distinctive ramparts owe nothing to the Romans, or even the Gauls, for some were built as early as the seventh century BC.

In the far north and west of Scotland different forms of settlement are found (figs. 32–33). Here stone was more plentiful, or perhaps simply more easily won, and as a result many settlements were constructed of this material. Stone houses were built as early as the fourth millennium BC in northern Scotland but in, or shortly before, the second century BC a new form of dwelling appeared in north Scotland, the broch. Brochs are dry-stone built towers, with small, low entrances, and no other openings on their external elevations. The highest surviving broch is on an island in the Shetlands and is 13m high. Brochs were clearly used as dwellings, but they are so small that animals could not be brought in as well with any degree of comfort. They are also clearly defensive, but who was the enemy? It used to be considered that they may have been built against Roman slave raiders, but as they have now been shown to originate well before the arrival of the Romans that theory is no longer tenable.

There are very few brochs in Argyll on the west coast of Scotland, but here as elsewhere in the western islands are found many small stone-walled forts or duns.

Duns vary in shape and in internal area, though most are up to 375 square metres in floor area, and have lower walls than brochs; many indeed were probably little more than stoutly defended houses. The majority of duns have been found on the west coast but there are also groups in the central valley of Scotland and in the far south-west. The large forts found in south and east Scotland generally do not appear in north and west Scotland and while this undoubtedly to some extent results from variations in topography it may also suggest a rather different social organisation.

The people of the Scottish tribes carried out a mixed farming economy. They reared cattle and sheep, hunted wild animals, especially deer, fished, collected wild berries, shellfish and fruit and also grew cereals. Barley has been found in archaeological contexts dating to the fourth millennium BC, and wheat (emmer) has also been found in prehistoric settlements in Scotland. Farming implements survive from at least the second millenium BC, and marks made by the plough or ard have been recognised in archaeological contexts. The deterioration in the climate of the British Isles some centuries before the beginning of the Christian era may have made cultivation of cereals in Scotland more difficult. During the first half of the first millenium BC rainfall increased and the temperature fell, though it was still probably a degree or two higher than the average temperature today. In the later Iron Age in many parts of Scotland the temperature may have been insufficient during the summer months to ripen the grain, and this may have led to the abandonment of existing fields, which in some areas became overgrown by peat. Other fields no doubt reverted to pasture for herds and flocks. Nevertheless some fields associated with settlements of this period may have been used for cultivation while there is evidence for ploughing in the Iron Age. Plough marks have been found below several sites on Hadrian's Wall, though in no case is the ploughing dated. It seems improbable that all date to the years immediately before the construction of the Wall in the 120s, and perhaps unlikely that all are Bronze Age in date: some or all could date to the Iron Age. One site in particular must have been inhospitable then as it is now, for the ploughing at Carrawburgh is on an exposed hillside with a clay subsoil. If such land could be cultivated then it seems likely that agriculture at this time was more widespread than usually considered. Indeed evidence for ploughing in the Iron Age has recently been discovered on Arran. Parts of two ploughs have also been found in Lowland Scotland. Near Lochmaben in Annandale was found in 1870 a wooden beam from an ard, now dated by radio carbon analysis to the second or first century BC. Excavations at Milton Loch Crannog in Kirkcudbrightshire have revealed an ard head and stilt, possibly a votive deposit, again dated by radio carbon analysis, but in this instance to the fifth century BC. Part of a rotary quern was also found at Milton Loch, and quern stones and barley grains have been discovered in Iron Age contexts elsewhere. Grain could have been traded like any other commodity but it seems probable at this time that cereals continued to be grown in certain favoured situations.

The previous clearances of forest in the Neolithic and Bronze Ages had been to some extent temporary for as the land became exhausted through cultivation the farmers moved on and the woodland was allowed to recolonise. The major and more or less permanent deforestation appears to have started in the late pre-Roman Iron Age in the north and have continued through the Roman period. It was probably mainly in order to provide more pasturage for animals, though other factors in certain areas will have played a part: the construction of stockades and also timber-laced forts will have required considerable quantities of timber. On the eve of the Roman advance into Scotland then the landscape would still have been well forested with clearings, most containing pasturage for cattle and sheep, but some with fields for cereals such as wheat and barley. The animals would have provided a wide variety of raw materials in addition to food. These included wool, skins and leather for clothing, leather for containers of all kinds, fastenings and bindings, hair for ropes, fat for food, cooking, lamps and soap (used by the Celts in Gaul according to Roman writers), horn and hoof for glue, artefacts and possibly medicine. Some animals, cattle especially, may have been used to measure the wealth and status of their owners, though no Roman writer mentions this.

The domesticated animals were not·of course the modern improved breeds. Generally they were smaller than modern specimens. Cattle were of the Celtic shorthorn variety, the closest modern representative today being the Kerry breed and the Welsh Black. Sheep were slender legged animals similar to Soay and Shetland sheep, with less meat and wool than modern improved breeds, though an improved breed was probably introduced to Britain either before or during the Roman period. The pig was a more agile type than modern specimens, being left free to forage in scrubland rather than kept in farmyards or the in-fields. Horses too were small by modern standards; the animals that pulled the war chariots were little bigger than today's ponies. At the Roman fort at Newstead the bones of two types of ponies were recovered during the excavations early in this century: the unimproved native British breed similar to the modern Shetland pony and the small slender limbed pony such as the Exmoor or the 'Celtic' pony of Iceland. Both types were under 12 hands high. Also found were the bones of larger ponies between 12 and 13 hands high and the bones of horses from just under 14 to nearly 15 hands.

Cattle bones are usually more numerous than the bones of sheep, pig or wild animals on late Iron Age sites in north England, so it seems probable that beef formed the major part of the meat diet here and presumably further north. In northern England it was possible to keep animals over the winter, demonstrating that there was no problem of winter fodder. The majority of cattle and sheep at one settlement were slaughtered between 12 and 30 months of age, when a moderate weight would have been achieved.

Archaeology too has clothed the barbarian warrior described by Tacitus, Dio and Herodian. The sword of the barbarian generally appears to have been rather longer than the auxiliary cavalryman's *spatha*, as Tacitus implies. It was of iron with a distinctively Celtic tang and its scabbard was usually of wood or leather, sometimes decorated with bronze fittings. Spears were often of ash with leaf-shaped iron tips. The rectangular shield depicted on the second century AD Bridgeness distance slab and other Roman and Pictish sculpture probably represented the shield carried by the Caledonian and his allies (pls. 17 and 19). It was probably constructed of wood and leather with a central boss, usually of iron.

Chariot burials dating to the Iron Age have been found in East Yorkshire and although cemeteries similar to those in East Yorkshire have been discovered in Scotland no chariot burials have yet come to light. However, examples of horse equipment do survive. Terret rings and snaffle-bits were both probably used on chariot horses rather than cavalry mounts. Terrets were mounted in pairs on the yoke to guide the reins: sets of five indicate a double harness. Such items of horse equipment were sometimes highly ornamented with enamel.

The warrior himself will also have worn elaborate ornaments. Armlets and torcs, in one case of gold and imported probably from eastern England, are known and a single example survives of an elaborate collar of bronze, though this probably belongs to a period contemporary with the Roman occupation of Scotland. Herodian states that the Caledonians fought naked and this is not impossible as Polybius records that Gaulish mercenaries fought naked at the battle of Telamon in 225 BC. Roman writers testify to the noise created by the Celtic army preparing for battle. The whoops of the charioteers joined with the yells of the infantryman to form a deafening cacophany. Human voices were supplemented by the war trumpets. Part of one such trumpet, the Deskford Carnyx, from Banff, survives. It was in the form of a boar's head with, originally, a moveable wooden tongue and eyes. No doubt each army would have possessed several trumpeters leading each warrior's retinue.

Little is known about the clothing worn by the Caledonian. Wool, leather and skins were available and presumably used: Caesar specifically mentions skins, while Dio describes Boudica as wearing a thick plaid over a voluminous patterned cloak. A type of check woollen cloth was popular in the Roman period in north Britain and may have been worn earlier. The woollen cloak with a hood, the *cucullus*, known on sculpture, and the longer, heavier cape, the *byrrus Britannicus*, recorded in Diocletian's edict on prices, may have had a respectable, but unknown history in northern Britain. Certainly spindle whorls from prehistoric contexts attest the spinning of wool before the arrival of the Romans, while even woollen textiles have occasionally been found. Pins and brooches, usually of bronze, for fastening clothing are known. Bone pins survive, and also bone combs. One final decorative item may be mentioned, the finger ring.

It is too easy to depict the Caledonian as a wild and savage barbarian, devoid of political organisation and prey to internecine strife. There are, fortunately, reminders that this is a false picture. The splendid tomb of Maeshowe, constructed over 2,500 years before the Roman conquest, bears witness to the architectural skill and achievement of the northern peoples. The broch tower of Mousa, which has weathered 2,000 years of storms and a Norse siege, is testimony not only to the barbarian's prowess in design and building technique but also to the existence of itinerant architect-engineers, the economy to support such craftsmen, and the social organisation to order the construction of these dwellings.

The Caledonian peoples and their allies must have enjoyed a profit-making agricultural economy for many generations. Agricultural surplus would have had to have been produced to support not only the architect-engineers, but miners, smiths and presumably the aristocracy. Little is known of religion in Scotland at this time, though what there is demonstrates affinity with practices in the mainstream of the Celtic world. Several ritual deposits in pools emphasise the veneration of springs and rivers, while the cult of the human head – which in Celtic eyes was symbolic of divinity – also seems to have been current. It is not impossible therefore that a priesthood, which we have already met in the Druids in Gaul and southern Britain, existed in Caledonian society and if so would have required to be supported by the community at large.

The political sophistication of the tribes is a more difficult area to probe. There is no reason to believe that the northern tribes were not ruled by kings who manifestly existed in southern Britain. Certainly, too, in the face of the common Roman enemy, the barbarian tribes were capable of sinking their differences and combining their forces against that enemy. Tacitus records that in preparation for meeting the Roman army at Mons Graupius the northern tribes negotiated treaties with each other in order to field as large a force as possible, and, it would appear, chose one of the many tribal leaders to be their general. The accounts of the

Agricolan and Severan campaigns abound with references to the barbarians' strategic skill and their military intelligence. For example, they knew which division was the weakest in Agricola's sixth campaign when the army was divided into three columns, while their tactics in the face of Severus' overwhelming numerical superiority were clearly carefully thought out and executed, even though not successful. In such a fight the odds were heavily stacked against the more wayward Celts.

Even the recording of their customs, as we have seen, was in the hands of their enemies and the final indignity is undoubtedly their anonymity. The best known Caledonian, Calgacus, leader of the northern tribes in their fight against Agricola, was possibly named by the Romans, leaving only Argentocoxus, whose wife met the Empress Julia Domna about 210, and Lossio Veda, grandson or nephew of Vepogenus, a Caledonian, who dedicated a votive plaque at Colchester in the reign of Severus Alexander (222–35).

3

Agricola and the first frontier in Britain

Agricola

The career of Gnaeus Julius Agricola, governor of Britain for almost six and a half years, is better known than that of any of his colleagues. This is simply because he had the good fortune to have the historian Cornelius Tacitus as his son-in-law. Tacitus wrote a biography of his father-in-law, which is one of the few such works to survive from Roman times. The biography naturally extolled the virtues of its hero and can hardly be considered an unbiased account of the events of these years. Nevertheless in spite of this, and in spite of the paucity of geographical names in the *Agricola*, the work provides an invaluable account of events in Britain for forty years from the conquest to the recall of Agricola.

There is one outstanding problem concerning the governorship of Agricola. Tacitus does not give the dates of his term of office and they have therefore to be calculated from other evidence. The governorship began in either 77 or 78: both dates have their followers and it is not possible on present evidence to be sure which is correct. For the sake of convenience therefore the events of Agricola's governorship will be related to the year of his governorship and not absolute dates.

Agricola was an unusual governor of Britain in that he had previously served twice within the province: it was not unusual for a man to have two of his three or four military postings in the same province, but Agricola is unique in having all three of his in the one province. The reason for this is probably connected with the general political situation in the empire. In 68 and 69 there was a bitter struggle for the throne following an abortive coup, a rebellion which nevertheless caused Nero to commit suicide. Agricola espoused the cause of the eventual victor, Vespasian, even before he had been proclaimed emperor. This action was to bring him suitable rewards, including an accelerated career and, four or five years later, elevation to patrician rank. As a loyal supporter of the Flavian dynasty Agricola was a safe man to put in charge of one of the three largest provincial armies, even though he might have acquired many contacts there as a result of his previous service in the island. It was also equally safe to leave him there for an unusually long term of office. The dislike – even fear – of Agricola by Vespasian's son Domitian, recorded in the *Agricola*, may well be overplayed by Tacitus as Domitian did award Agricola triumphal ornaments, the most prestigious battle honours, on the completion of his governorship of Britain, which he himself allowed to extend to six years, while it was Agricola who excused himself from the governorship of Asia, not Domitian who refused it him. Tacitus may be purposefully distancing Agricola from the tyrant Domitian who after his death had his memory damned. In the days of Trajan's reign, when the *Agricola* was written, it would have been embarrassing to have been too closely associated with Domitian and that emperor's natural act of regularly enquiring after Agricola, an old family friend, during his last illness, as Tacitus faithfully records, may have been wilfully re-interpreted in a more sinister light in the changed political situation.

Agricola's close relationship with the Flavian dynasty was to colour – and cloud – his whole career. It is impossible to say how successful he might have been if Nero had lived, but it seems unlikely that he would have enjoyed the governorship of Britain for six years nor have acquired the reputation of being a great general. As it is, through his unusually long governorship, defeat of the major Scottish tribe, and posterity's blind belief in the words of his son-in-law, Agricola has acquired a reputation which he may not have altogether deserved.

Agricola's career, up to his governorship of Britain, was normal. He served in Britain as a military tribune on the staff of the governor Suetonius Paulinus at the time of the Boudican rebellion. His next position was as quaestor (financial secretary) of Asia and two appointments in Rome followed. Vespasian sent him back to Britain at the beginning of his reign as legate of *legio XX Valeria Victrix*. The governorship of Aquitania followed, then the consulship in 77, at the age of 37, well below the official minimum of 42. In 77 or 78 Agricola returned to Britain for the third time, as governor.

Agricola arrived in Britain late in the year and spent the latter part of the summer quashing a revolt of the Ordovices in north Wales. Tacitus does not name the area where Agricola campaigned in his second season but it is usually considered to be northern England – the territory of the Brigantes. Petillius Cerealis, governor in the early 70s, had conquered this tribe, but may not have had time to consolidate his victory by the construction of a full network of forts. It is clear that Agricola fought no battles in this season but was concerned to mop up local resistence and complete the fort-building programme started by Cerealis. As Tacitus records that several tribes submitted to Agricola, it is possible that his activities extended beyond the Tyne-Solway isthmus, beyond Brigantian territory. As it is only in the next season that he ventured into the territory of new tribes, it is possible that Cerealis had already made contact with the tribes who were incorporated into the province in Agricola's second season.

In his third season, his second full season, for the first time Agricola passed beyond the limits of earlier campaigning. Moving through the territory of new nations he reconnoitred as far as the river Tay. His route is not known but he must have moved either up the east coast, probably following the line of the present A68, or up Annandale and down Clydesdale – the route of the present A74 – or both. He passed through the territory of several tribes, but Tacitus states that the enemy did not attack the Roman army and devotes some space to discussing the appalling weather of that summer. He goes on to remark that there was even time to construct forts that year: clearly the Lowland tribes gave Agricola little trouble.

In 79 the Emperor Titus was acclaimed *imperator* for the fifteenth time as a result of the achievements of Agricola in Britain. It is not possible to be certain whether the occasion for the acclamation was the results of the second or third season of campaigning: an equally good case can be made out for both years. The move north was also commemorated in another way for a Caledonian bear appeared at the opening of the Colosseum in Rome in June 80.

Tacitus opens the discussion of the following season, Agricola's fourth, with a remarkable phrase: if the valour of the army and the glory of Rome had allowed it, a halting place would have been found within the island. He then goes on to state that the neck of land between the Forth and Clyde estuaries was secured by a line of garrisons. This is the first known suggestion in the history of the province of Britain that a frontier might be established within the island: in other words this is the first known explicit rejection of the idea of total conquest of the island. Previously, expansion of the province had moved forward erratically, but there had been no hint that any of the halting points had been intended to be permanent. It seems probable that the line of forts established now was intended to be the permanent boundary of the province, and the peculiar phraseology of Tacitus may merely reflect (as he knew with hindsight) that the boundary was not in fact permanent as the army moved on two years later. However, there is another consideration. Roman governors generally served for three years at a time, and this was Agricola's fourth campaigning season in the province – towards the end of the year he would have passed the third anniversary of his arrival in Britain. Roman emperors carefully controlled the activities of their governors and no doubt Agricola had been sent to the province with specific instructions. Usually, it would appear, in these years emperors provided their governors with tasks which might be expected to last three years. Thus Petillius Cerealis, the first Flavian governor of Britain, was charged with subduing the Brigantes, while Julius Frontinus, his successor, completed the conquest of Wales. Agricola's task would seem to have been to complete Cerealis' work in north England and then move on to take another convenient grouping of tribes into the province. He had successfully completed this by the end of his third season and in that year and the following he moved on to the second stage of the operation, namely the control and protection of the newly conquered tribes by the construction of forts. He then, it may be presumed, had completed the task he was sent out to do. The construction of forts across the Forth–Clyde isthmus may or may not have been part of his original instruction: almost certainly they were not.

Tacitus' mention of a halting place on the Forth–Clyde isthmus emphasises that this line of forts was unusual. During the course of his third season Agricola had reached the Tay and from there he will have seen the Highlands barring his passage to the north. Word of the country ahead must have been brought to him by the scouts habitually employed by the army and no doubt more information was obtained from the local tribesmen and captives. Agricola may have realised the difficulties of operating in that mountainous terrain and advised the emperor, Titus, of this. In that case Titus, acting on the intelligence received from Agricola, may have decided to halt the expansion in Britain on a convenient line. It seems unlikely that Agricola wished to advance further north but was held back by Titus and Tacitus gives no hint that his hero's ambitions were thwarted at this time only to triumph two years later. Agricola had not only completed the tasks allotted to him by the Emperor Vespasian but gone as far in Britain as the Romans now intended to go.

Little is known of Agricola's frontier on the Forth–Clyde isthmus, but before examining the surviving remains it would be better to consider the overall pattern of the occupation of northern England and southern Scotland at this time. This pattern was largely dictated by the geography of the area. On either side of the Pennines a road led north, connecting the forts along the route, and where appropriate these major lines of communication were linked by roads across the hills. At this time two new legionary fortresses were constructed. In the east *legio IX Hispana* was moved up from Lincoln to York, while in the west Wroxeter was abandoned and *legio XX Valeria Victrix* established at Chester, where it was strategically placed for intervention in either Wales or north England. On either side of the Pennines the auxiliary units were placed in forts about 20–30 kilometres apart, approximately a day's march. These forts generally appear to have varied in size from 1.5 to 2.5 hectares: the forts on the roads across the hills were usually smaller at about 1.2 hectares. Little is known of the garrisons of these forts. Each of the smaller stations was presumably garrisoned by the smallest auxiliary unit of the Roman army, the 480 strong infantry unit, the *cohors quingenaria peditata*. No doubt many of the other forts were garrisoned by its sister unit, the *cohors quingenaria equitata*, which contained a cavalry complement of 120 men in addition to the 480 infantry.

Forts were established at other points beside these, at Brough-on-Humber, for example, in the territory of the Parisi, and at Malton, north-east of York. One area does not appear to have had troops placed within it at this time, the present-day Lake District. No forts seem to have been established here until the early second century.

In southern Scotland too geography dictated routes and many troop dispositions. The eastern and western roads continued north. The eastern road, Dere Street, stayed close to the line taken by the modern A68 while the western road followed the line of the modern A74 up Annandale and down into Clydesdale. Again these two main roads were linked by cross routes, one running westwards from Newstead towards Irvine Bay, and the other south-westwards from Newstead into Annandale and Nithsdale.

In each of the major river valleys there was placed a large fort, usually about 3 hectares in size and containing a composite garrison (fig. 4). In the Tyne valley lay a large fort, about 10 hectares in extent. This was found on trial examination to contain some store-houses and it may be that this was a base or depot rather than a fort proper. Further north lay Newstead in the Tweed valley, Camelon on the Forth, Milton in Annandale, Dalswinton in Nithsdale, while in Clydesdale was constructed Castledykes. Elsewhere there were smaller stations: forts capable of holding a single auxiliary unit such as Oakwood or Easter Happrew, small forts such as Crawford acting as the bases for units which had men posted elsewhere, and fortlets like Birrens or Gatehouse of Fleet containing a detachment of 80 men or thereabouts. These forts and fortlets were also generally about 20–30km apart, though the distances varied considerably depending upon the topography.

The forts and fortlets and the road connecting them formed the sort of network which might be expected in any territory recently conquered by Rome, the idiosyncracies dependent on the topography. The only unusual feature was the line of forts built across the Forth-Clyde isthmus. Although Tacitus records the construction of these stations few have been recognised archaeologically. The major fort at Camelon in the Forth valley is strategically not one of these stations. On the other side of the isthmus the fort at Barochan, rediscovered in 1972, lies on the low hills overlooking the Clyde and may or may not be one of the forts specifically built to guard this neck of land. In between in 1977 a new small fort was located at Mollins about 4km south of the Antonine Wall. Excavation in 1978 confirmed a late first century date for this 0.4 hectare fort and it seems most likely therefore that it was one of the stations built under Agricola.

Two other fortlets on the line of the later Antonine Wall have been assigned to Agricola: the enclosures under the forts at Croy Hill and Bar Hill. Excavations in 1975 at the former site demonstrated conclusively that this structure dated not to the governorship of Agricola, but to the reoccupation of Scotland in the 140s. Examination of part of the enclosure under Bar Hill fort failed to produce any first century artefacts while the filling of the ditch would argue for an early Antonine rather than an Agricolan date.

No other structure on the Forth-Clyde isthmus can be assigned to the governorship of Agricola, but it seems not improbable that more may yet come to light through the medium of aerial photography. Artefactual evidence, however, may play a part in determining the position of Agricola's forts. Glass and samian pottery dating to the first century has been found at Castlecary and Cadder, two forts on the Antonine Wall (fig. 21). First-century bronze coins have come to light at Mumrills, Castlecary, Balmuildy and Kirkintilloch, all on the line of the Antonine Wall: first-century bronze coins had a short life so it is possible that these sites were occupied in the Flavian period. Finally, pre-Hadrianic, and possibly Agricolan, coarse pottery has been recorded at Mumrills, Castlecary, Balmuildy and Old Kilpatrick. These artefacts may suggest that all or some of the forts of Mumrills, Castlecary, Kirkintilloch, Cadder, Balmuildy and Old Kilpatrick were the sites of Agricola's stations being garrisoned by Roman forces, large or small, but to date no structural evidence has come to light to support these chance finds, and the possibility that many of the finds were brought by the later Antonine builders should not be ignored.

Agricola would normally have expected his governorship to end after three years and, as discussed above, it seems probable that his term of office was planned with that in mind. However, he was to continue as governor for a further three years, thus achieving an unprecedented – for Britain at least – governorship of over six years. The two final seasons of Agricola's governorship were spent campaigning and fighting north of the Forth, but the year before, Agricola's fifth season, was spent elsewhere. The operations began with a sea voyage, clearly in the west of Britain for Agricola drew up his troops facing Ireland, and involved the subduing of tribes hitherto unknown. It has been suggested that Agricola moved down into Ayrshire and Galloway to conquer the Novantae who, because of their isolation, had been by-passed on the march north, or sailed across the Clyde to campaign in Argyllshire, or perhaps carried out both operations during that season. A further possibility, proposed by Mr W.S. Hanson, is that the reference to the sea voyage may imply that Agricola sailed, from his winter quarters, perhaps at Chester, to Scotland at the opening of the campaigning season.

It seems a reasonable assumption that the main campaign of this season was into south-west Scotland: this is the most appropriate part of north Britain to be described as facing Ireland. Further, it is quite possible that this area had been ignored in the move north through the Scottish Lowlands in the same way as earlier Agricola had by-passed the Lake District. The route taken by the army is not known, but if it moved directly from its winter quarters it may have passed along the north shore of the Solway, the route at present taken by the A75. The only physical indication of its presence may be a marching camp at Girvan in south Ayrshire.

Tacitus records that Agricola considered the possibility of conquering Ireland. He had a fugitive Irish prince with him, who would provide a pretext for intervention, and strategic reasons – or excuses – in that, as Ireland was considered to lie between Britain and Spain, it would provide better communications between those two parts of the empire and also extinguish the torch of liberty beyond the frontier. There is a further possibility, not recorded by Tacitus. Agricola had been ordered to stay in Britain but may not have been given any specific task. He may have been collecting information on Ireland in order to offer it as a possible area of expansion, possibly for his successor rather than himself, now that the intention of conquering northern Scotland had been abandoned. It may be that Agricola went so far as to prepare a report for the emperor; certainly he gathered intelligence on harbours and landing places, the climate and the tribes, and calculated how large a force would be required for the subjugation of the island – a legion and a few auxiliaries. This estimate is generally considered to be too low, but it may not have been too far wrong for in 1315–16 Edward Bruce conquered Ireland with a similar sized army.

However, Ireland was not to be brought within the Roman empire. In the following year Agricola turned north, crossed the Forth and began an operation which ended with Roman victory at Mons Graupius a year later. Tacitus records the pretext: the enemy gave provocation. The relevant passage in the *Agricola* deserves close examination for it records that Agricola 'feared a rising of the northern tribes' and so moved across the Forth; only then did the enemy retaliate and 'without provocation' attack a Roman fort. The *Agricola* is unmistakable: the first move was by the Romans, who moved to prevent a real or imagined threat (though it is hard to see how the Caledonians could seriously have threatened Rome). This was the sixth year of Agricola's governorship and whichever dating system is adopted was certainly within the reign of the Emperor Domitian (81–96). It is noteworthy that this emperor commenced his reign with warfare on another frontier, for in Germany he fought a war with the Chatti. This probably commenced in the spring of 83, at first under the direction of Domitian himself. The Roman sources do not state the reason for the war and it is possible that the emperor wished to demonstrate his military prowess, having lived for so long in the shadow of his elder brother Titus. The advance in Britain may have been for the same reason; it was certainly not in response to unprovoked aggression by the northern tribes.

Agricola spent two seasons campaigning north of the Forth (fig. 3). He advanced by land and by sea, using the fleet to supplement his army weakened by withdrawals for service elsewhere, but also to reconnoitre the harbours. In the first season he failed to bring the Caledonians to battle but was attacked himself, nearly losing a third of his army, including *legio IX*, in a night assault on their temporary camp. He also had to suffer a mutiny by a regiment recently raised in Germany and still undergoing basic training in Britain. In the next season he was more successful. He brought the Caledonians to bay at Mons Graupius and soundly defeated them. This is the only battle between the Romans and the Caledonians (or the Picts) described in ancient literature and it is therefore worth examining in some detail.

In this season Agricola sent his fleet ahead to plunder and spread consternation among the enemy while the army marched light. Agricola and his army met the Caledonians at Mons Graupius (the Graupian Mountain) where the barbarians were drawn up on ground of their own choosing. The northern tribes had made careful preparations for the battle. They had put aside their differences and entered into treaty relationship with each other so as to be able to assemble the full force of all the tribes – an action worthy of special note in view of the statement by Tacitus that seldom did the British tribes combine together to fight the Romans. The barbarians mustered, according to Tacitus, more than 30,000 men and these were arranged on the hillside, with the van on the level ground at the bottom and the rest riding up the gentle slopes behind.

The Roman army was drawn up in front of their camp. In the van lay the auxiliary infantry, and on the flanks the cavalry, while the legions were kept in reserve. Tacitus does not give a total for all the Roman forces present, but he does state that there were 8,000 auxiliary infantry and 3,000 cavalry in the battle line, while an additional 2,000 cavalry were kept in reserve. Included within the infantry

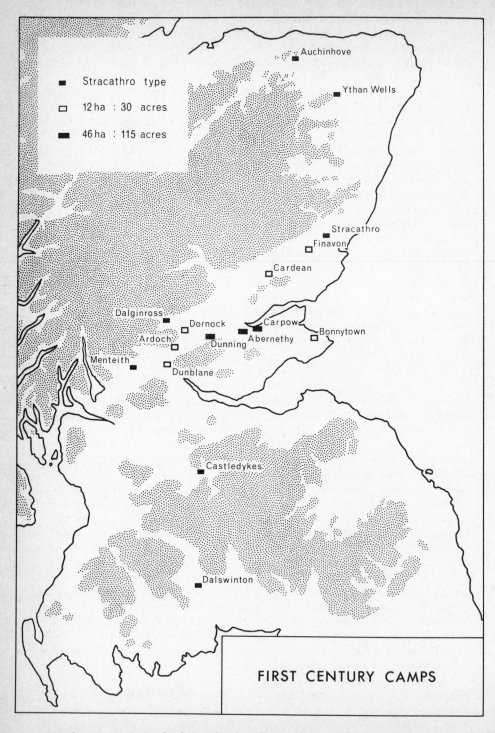

3 *Marching camps in Scotland considered to date to the Agricolan campaigns*

were four cohorts of Batavians and two of Tungrians, though it is not known whether these were 500 or 1,000 strong. The army also contained soldiers recruited in Britain and it seems probable that these were serving in the auxiliary units. Presumably all four British legions were present at Mons Graupius, but none were at full strength. While nominally 5,200 strong, headquarters staff, recruits and training officers would no doubt have remained at base. In addition, however, detachments from all the legions were at this time serving elsewhere. A single detachment, probably 500 or 1000 strong, from each legion had been sent to the Rhine for service in the Chattan war, while an extra detachment from *IX Hispana* was also operating in the same area. The legionary strength, in theory something over 20,000, may therefore have been reduced to 15,000 or even less. Agricola's army is unlikely to have numbered more than 28,000 men, and may have been considerably smaller.

Tacitus' description of the battle includes preliminary set-piece speeches by the two commanding officers. It is not known whether speeches were actually made, though it seems probable that Agricola did address his men in the usual Roman manner, but the speech of Calgacus, the Caledonian leader, as relayed by Tacitus is clearly merely Roman rhetoric put into the mouth of Rome's enemy. Calgacus made a classic anti-imperialist speech, dwelling on the freedom of the Caledonians and the success, albeit limited, of other opponents of Rome, and included the famous phrase that the Romans created a desert and called it peace. Agricola referred to the bravery of the Roman army and the cowardice of the enemy, emphasising that this was the final victory they required to complete the conquest of the island.

Before the battle commenced the Caledonian charioteers rampaged up and down between the two armies. In the face of such a substantial force Agricola spread his battleline dangerously thin, but this was to prevent being out-flanked. The battle itself began with an exchange of missiles. Then Agricola ordered the Batavian and Tungrian cohorts to advance. Now the Caledonians were at a disadvantage. The Romans were armed with short stabbing swords and protected, in addition to their normal armour, by large shields. The Caledonians, on the other hand had smaller shields and long slashing swords unsuitable in close encounters. The Roman auxiliaries, stabbing with their swords and pushing with the bosses of their shields, routed the enemy on the plain and pushed on up the hill, quickly overcoming the men on the lower slopes. They were now joined by the cavalry who had been seeing off the chariots. The very speed of the initial Roman advance, however, nearly proved to be their undoing, for now, faced by the main body of the Caledonian force and the rough hill-slope, their advance ground to a halt, while the presence of cavalry amongst the Roman infantry led to disarray in the ranks. The Caledonians on the higher ground began to advance and threatened to envelop the rear of the Roman army, so Agricola set this cavalry reserve of four regiments against them and broke their attack. The Caledonians were now faced by the Romans on both sides and broke rank, being driven back to some woods. Here they rallied, but the Roman infantry and the dismounted cavalry ringed the wood and drove forward, pushing back the Caledonians. Seeing no chance of victory the barbarians turned and fled, pursued by the Romans. Night brought an end to the fighting and when the Romans counted the dead they found, according to Tacitus, that only 360 Romans had fallen as opposed to 10,000 Caledonians.

According to the account of Tacitus there was only one point when the battle seriously turned against the Romans, and then the situation was saved by the timely action of Agricola in throwing in the cavalry reserve. The legions, also kept in reserve, were not required, the whole brunt of the fighting falling on the auxiliaries; as a result not a drop of 'Roman', that is legionary, blood was shed. In only using his auxiliaries Agricola was not innovatory. Exactly the same tactic had been used by Petillius Cerealis fifteen years before during the Batavian revolt. This action was part of the increasingly important role played by the auxiliary units in different aspects of military affairs. It is clear, however, that Agricola kept a close control over the movement of the battle and, of course, was successful in achieving victory. The Caledonians fell before the superior weapons, armour, discipline and tactics of the Romans.

The day following the battle Agricola sent scouts to search for the enemy. However, finding that they had all fled, he made no attempt to pursue them further but made preparations for returning south. He led his army into the territory of the Boresti, an otherwise unknown tribe, and there collected hostages. He ordered his fleet to sail round Britain (during the voyage they discovered the Orkney Islands and sighted Thule), while he marched south with his army.

One major problem concerning the battle of Mons Graupius is that its location is not known. Tacitus makes no attempt to locate the site: it would appear to lie beside the Boresti, but, as this tribe is otherwise unknown, this piece of information is of little value. The battle clearly lay north of the Forth and the line of first-century marching camps appears to stretch as far as Auchinhove in Banffshire. It seems possible therefore that Mons Graupius lay beyond the Mounth, the point where the Highlands nearly reach the sea at Stonehaven. Various locations have been suggested for the battle. One argument would place it near the later battle of Culloden, for here the Caledonians would have been compelled to fight for the same reasons as the Jacobites: if they had retreated further the army would have split into different sections as the tribes fell back on their homelands, north, south and west of Inverness. More recently the hill of Bennachie, 32 kilometres north-west of Aberdeen, has been proposed as the site of the battle. While many of the topographical features support this allegation there are still some discrepancies. In fact it is most unlikely that we will ever know the exact site of the battle and the most that can be said is that it probably lies north of the Mounth.

Agricola's achievements were welcomed in Rome and he was awarded the ornaments of a triumph, the highest honour a general could receive as the triumph itself was reserved for members of the imperial family, and the erection of a statue. Agricola, having served over six years as governor of Britain, soon after Mons Graupius, it would appear, retired, handing over his province to his successor. Thereafter he was to hold no public office, declining even the offer of the prestigious proconsulship of Asia.

Agricola's governorship is the longest known in Romano-British history. However, it seems unlikely that this was due to any special military merit on his part. Agricola's loyalty to the dynasty rendered him a safe candidate for the governorship of a major military province like Britain, and even an extended governorship, though this was probably the result of the 'accident' of the death of the Emperor Titus. The duration of the governorship was the equivalent of two more normal-length governorships and this may not have been coincidental. Such long terms of office were rare at this time though the Emperor Tiberius fifty years before had kept some governors in post for as long as 10 and 25 years, while Didius Gallus had been governor of Britain for five or six years in the 50s and Trebellius Maximus for six years in the 60s. Two emperors died during the course of

Agricola's governorship: Vespasian in the middle of either the first or second full year and Titus at the end of either the third or fourth. Of these two deaths the more important was that of Titus, for it fell about the time when Agricola might normally expect his governorship to end: it may have been easier for Domitian to leave Agricola in Britain than immediately find a replacement. Whichever date is prefered for the commencement of the governorship it will still have been Titus who ordered the halt on the Forth and Domitian the advance two years later. Agricola's task was to implement the policies initiated by his emperor, though he could of course recommend a course of action himself, as he may have been preparing to do in his fifth season when he drew up his troops facing Ireland. Agricola was duly rewarded for faithfully and successfully obeying his orders.

The award of the ornaments of a triumph to Agricola suggests that the conquest of Britain was now considered to be completed – the great triumphal monument at Richborough was probably erected at this time and points to the same conclusion. The position of the most northerly marching camps attributable to the campaigns of Agricola on the south shore of the Moray Firth would allow it to be said that Agricola had reached practically the end of the island and he had certainly defeated his major foe. There is no hint in the *Agricola* that during these last two campaigning seasons Agricola built any fort north of the Forth. The most northerly forts recorded in the biography are those on the Forth-Clyde isthmus, unless the fort attacked in the sixth season lay in Strathmore or Strathearn. It would not be unusual for the mopping-up operation following a battle such as Mons Graupius to be left to his successor. It seems probable therefore that all, or at least most of, the forts now built north of the Forth were the work of Agricola's successor. It is possible that the position of some had already been determined by Agricola himself, but that is speculation; there is no need to consider that Agricola viewed himself indispensable in the matter of British affairs: such decisions could be left to his successor.

The aftermath of Mons Graupius

There are two main groups or lines of forts north of the Forth (fig. 4). The outer line hugs the edge of the Highlands, the forts usually being placed within the very mouths of the glens. Seven forts are known in the line, eight if Barochan on the Clyde is included. The forts stretch north-east from Drumquassle at the south-east corner of Loch Lomond through Malling at Menteith, Bochastle at Callander, Dalginross at Comrie and Fendoch at the mouth of the Sma' Glen to the legionary fortress at Inchtuthil. The inner line lies in the centre of the valleys Strathearn and Strathmore, following the line taken by the Roman road leading north from Camelon. The first fort in the series may be presumed to have lain at or near Stirling guarding the crossing of the Forth: it is as yet undiscovered. Beyond there were forts at Ardoch (pl. 4), Strageath, Bertha, Cargill, Cardean and Stracathro: the extra-long gap between the last two sites suggests that another fort remains to be discovered.

The forts on both the inner and the outer line follow an interesting pattern of alternating small and large enclosures. The smaller forts vary from about 1.5 to 1.8 hectares in size while the larger ones cover about 3 hectares. Most of the smaller forts will have held only one auxiliary unit, though it seems that Strageath may have been garrisoned by a force in excess of a single regiment. The larger forts will no doubt usually have contained more than one unit: Ardoch may have been

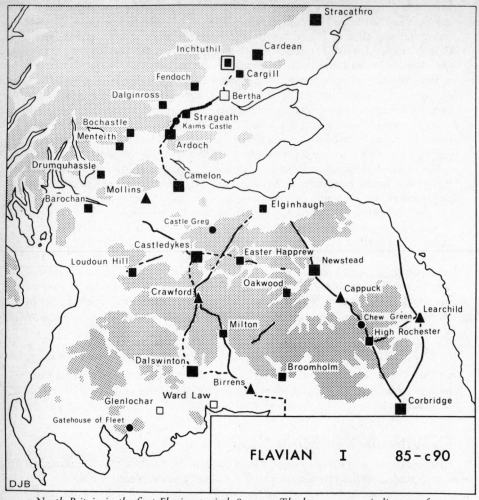

4 *North Britain in the first Flavian period, 85–c.90. The larger square indicates a fort 2.8 hectares (7 acres) or excess in area, the smaller square a fort of 1.4–2.4 hectares (3.5–6.5 acres), the triangle a small fort of about 0.4 hectares (1 acre), the larger circle a fortlet, while the Gask towers are marked as small circles. Inchtuthil is denoted by a double square. An open square indicates occupation uncertain*

garrisoned by an auxiliary unit and a legionary detachment. This arrangement obviously reflects a carefully planned use of manpower and resources: as the same arrangement was adopted for both lines it may suggest that the outer line had no special significance.

It appears that none of the forts north of the Forth were occupied for long. None could have been constructed before Agricola's third season, 79 or 80, when he first reached the Tay, while pottery evidence points to the abandonment of all forts north of the Forth-Clyde isthmus by about 90. Further, the legionary base at Inchtuthil was abandoned before it was completed while excavation at two of the auxiliary forts, Fendoch and Cardean, has demonstrated that they were given up after brief occupations. Thus the construction, occupation and abandonment of at least 12 forts, two with two phases of occupation, have to be squeezed into a period of no more than ten years, and possibly less. No literary sources survive for this period and epigraphic and numismatic evidence is slight: purely archaeological dating methods cannot be refined so closely as to distinguish between the occupation of forts within five or even ten years. In the light of these difficulties the history of the area north of the Forth in these years has to be determined by reference to 'historical' and 'logical' arguments rather than literary documentation and concrete fact.

It is not possible to determine the exact sequence of events; all that can be done is to suggest the probable pattern, or patterns, in the knowledge that the truth will never be known. More than one explanation, on present evidence, is possible and, where appropriate, will be discussed. One final problem remains to be mentioned. It seems possible that the Roman network of forts north of the Forth was never completed. Thus we are trying to link together not just the pieces of a partially surviving jigsaw, many fragments having been lost through the passage of nearly 2000 years, but the pieces of a jigsaw which was never complete.

Agricola first reached the Tay in his third season, 79 or 80. However, the frontier line established in the following season lay on the Forth-Clyde isthmus. It is possible therefore that he built no forts north of the isthmus. On the other hand in the discussion of his sixth campaign, the first against the Caledonians, it is recorded by Tacitus that a Roman fort was attacked, and it is usually presumed that this lay north of the Forth. There is no warrant for this assumption, for the Caledonians clearly had the mobility to attack a fort on, or even south of, the Forth-Clyde isthmus. Nevertheless, for what it is worth, this passage may imply that one or more forts had been built during or before the sixth season north of the Forth. The obvious candidates are those on the road to the Tay. At two of these forts, Ardoch and Strageath, two phases of occupation in the first century have been discovered. The first may date to Agricola's third season, though equally possibly both phases may fall within the years following Agricola's retirement.

In fact it is probable that no forts were constructed by Agricola north of the Forth. No fort building is mentioned in the *Agricola* during the last three seasons when Agricola drew up his troops facing Ireland and campaigned against the Caledonians. The last fort building recorded in that book was in the governor's fourth season when he consolidated his hold on the Lowland tribes and placed a chain of garrisons across the Forth-Clyde isthmus (though perhaps too much reliance should not be placed on the essentially negative evidence of Tacitus). During his last two seasons Agricola was concerned with the conquest of the Caledonians and it was only after that tribe and their allies had been defeated that attention would have turned to the construction of forts in their territory. As Agricola did not have time to do this – he seems to have left Britain immediately after Mons Graupius – the work was left to his successor.

The construction of forts north of the Forth by Agricola's unknown successor ties in well with other evidence from Inchtuthil. The legionary fortress at Inchtuthil was still being built when it was abandoned (fig. 5). The reason for this change in plan must have resulted from the withdrawal of *legio II Adiutrix* from Britain. The exact date of this is not known but evidence from the continent points to the winter of 85/86 or 86 as being the most likely time. Inchtuthil, in common with a number of other Scottish forts, Camelon, Strageath, Stracathro, Crawford, Newstead and possibly Cramond, Castledykes and Barochan, has produced a number of *asses*, coins, of 86 in unworn condition, demonstrating that it – and the other forts – was

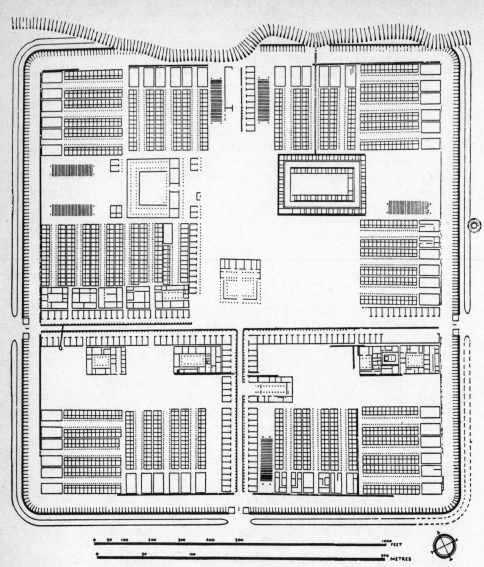

5 *The legionary fortress at Inchtuthil. The fortress contains sufficient barrack-blocks for the 10 cohorts, but granaries for only 6, a small headquarters building in the centre, hospital and workshop behind. No house for the legate had been built and only 4 of the 7 senior officers' houses. (Drawn by I.A. Richmond)*

garrisoned in that year, or shortly after. It seems probable that these coins were specially imported into Britain to allow the army to implement the soldier's pay raise which occurred sometime in the reign of the Emperor Domitian. Inchtuthil was modified, even before it was completed, by the addition of a stone face to the turf rampart. Outside the fortress lie labour camps used by the troops engaged in the building operations and these exhibit two phases of use. It is possible therefore that if Inchtuthil was, on the coin evidence, being built in 86 (or after) work had not started before 85, the year following the retirement of Agricola. All three lines of argument, although unsatisfactory or uncertain in themselves, point to the same conclusion: building operations commenced at Inchtuthil no earlier than 85 and were abandoned in 86, or shortly afterwards, when *legio II Adiutrix* was withdrawn for service on the continent.

It seems perfectly possible that a legionary fortress, or rather most of it, could be constructed in two years. It is clear from Caesar and Josephus, for example, that complex siege works could be constructed with speed in a matter of a few weeks and modern experiments in fort building support the testimony of ancient authorities. Presumably the legion which was to occupy the fortress was mainly engaged on its construction while gangs from other legions were occupied building the auxiliary forts.

The fact that the network of forts north of the Forth was probably not completed renders the definition of the role of some of the forts difficult. This is an acute problem in relation to the glen forts. They have usually been interpreted as 'glen-blocking forts', guarding the mouths of the glens and preventing access to the province by the Caledonians to the north and west. This is possible and was certainly a device used on other frontiers of the empire, in particular in north Africa, though in later years. This argument presumes that the Romans considered that the occupation of the Highlands of Scotland was beyond their capabilities. To assume this is to ignore the more hostile terrain – and tribes – overcome in other parts of the empire such as Asia Minor, north-west Spain and the Alps. It is in fact possible that the construction of the glen forts formed the first step towards the occupation of the Highlands: they were the springboard for an advance up the glens, an advance which never materialised because the plan was abandoned uncompleted.

There is one other important piece of evidence: the position of the legionary fortress at Inchtuthil. Two factors generally influenced the position of legionary fortresses: they could either be springboards for an advance or supports for the frontier system, though at times and in certain places the two are difficult to distinguish. The early fortresses in the Empire seem to fall into the former category and as the province was being extended in Britain at this time it might be expected that Inchtuthil would also. This assumption might be considered to be supported by the position of the fortress, which lies on the very edge of the province in front of a river. The tactical position of the fortress suggests that defence was not a prime consideration, otherwise its relationship to the river would presumably have been reversed; while its isolation suggests that strategically it was to be the base for a major extension of the province north and westwards.

It seems best therefore to regard the glen forts as the springboards for advances up the glens: indeed forts may have been built up some of the glens and still await discovery. The glens would have been convenient lines of advance for an army intending to penetrate the Highland massif: in the not dissimilar mountainous terrain of Wales the valleys had been used in such a manner by the Roman army. No evidence survives relating to the use of the glens by the Caledonians. Montrose in the seventeenth century frequently moved along the glens but on occasions he led his army over the mountain ridges and there is no reason to believe that the Caledonians could not have done likewise and that the Romans would have found this unexpected. In such circumstances the Roman army may have found the position of the glen forts cramped their movements. This would, however, be of no account if the forts were part of an offensive forward movement up the glens. Certainly the glen forts, including Inchtuthil, do not form a defensible frontier and it is noteworthy that in the second century when outpost forts north of the Antonine Wall were occupied no forts were placed at the mouths of the glens.

Agricola clearly felt that having defeated the Caledonians he had completed the conquest of the island, and this view was shared by Domitian for he was duly rewarded. It would have been natural for this victory to have been followed by the establishment of a network of roads and forts in the area of the conquered tribes, the Highlands. The forts along the edge of the Highlands, in the mouths of the glens, would thus be best seen as the basis for advances up those glens in order to establish a pattern no doubt similar to that created by the Hanoverians 1700 years later. As it happened, Roman defeats on the Rhine and Danube led to the withdrawal of troops from Britain and the abandonment of Roman plans for the occupation of the Highlands of Scotland.

Roman and Native

While the province lay at its furthest extent we shall pause to consider the effect of the Roman advance upon the natives. Twelve hill forts in Scotland, in the Borders and in north-east Scotland, are known to have been abandoned uncompleted and it has been suggested that this was connected with the Roman advance. Some forts were abandoned in early stages of construction while others were abandoned as their original defences were being extended or improved. This work, it has been proposed, was being carried out as the Roman army advanced north, the Scottish tribes belatedly realising the danger that they were in. However, none of the unfinished hill forts are dated. Some, possibly many, could date to several years, even centuries, before the Roman advance and a variety of reasons could account for their unfinished state. Tribal or factional warfare could have ended work, financial or other difficulties on the part of the builder could have led his workforce to disperse. However, it is not impossible that some were constructed in the face of the Roman advance. Even if this was the case none of these forts, nor any others, was strong enough to force the Roman army to pause and construct the siege works in which they excelled.

The Roman advance through the territories of the Lowland tribes was swift and apparently uneventful: Tacitus remarks that the Roman army was not attacked. It is even possible that the Lowland tribes submitted voluntarily to Rome. Trajan's Column vividly portrays their fate if they had resisted the Roman advance. Scenes on the Column show the burning of enemy villages, the flight of their inhabitants, fighting between Roman and barbarian, the defeat and death of the barbarians or their imprisonment in stockades, and on surrender the separation of husbands from their families; on defeat the Dacian king, Decabalus, committed suicide. Following their defeat, or peaceful submission, the tribes would be incorporated into the province. No doubt Agricola commenced this operation in his third and fourth seasons when he paused on the Forth-Clyde isthmus. Those who had opposed the Roman advance will have become *dediticii*, conquered peoples without rights. Some may have been sold into slavery, others drafted into the army, though this, if it took place at all, was probably limited in scale. All the new provincials will have been subject to the census, so that their liability for taxation could be assessed, to the requisition of supplies such as corn and hides, though at set prices, and to forced labour on the roads. All will have fallen under military jurisdiction and there is no evidence either now or later that the Roman administration attempted to organise the northern tribes into *civitates*, self-governing tribal units.

Local law was probably allowed to operate as before, so long as it was not in direct contravention of Roman law. One difference is that the new provincials would now have the dubious advantage of appeal from their tribal court to the governor: in practice no doubt usually the local army commander. The army would, when necessary, have kept the peace as there was no separate police force in the Roman world. Many surviving documents from Egypt bear witness to the extra-military duties of soldiers. They were asked to investigate many crimes: theft, assault, arson, malicious damage, trespass, and even the settlement of disputes over wills and the search for missing persons.

It is difficult to determine the attitude of the Lowland tribes to the Roman advance. It is frequently stated that the Selgovae, Damnonii and Novantae opposed the Roman army, but not the Votadini. Suppositions concerning the attitude of the Votadini to Rome and their subsequent history depend mainly upon the history of Traprain Law. This hill fort had a long life from the Bronze Age into at least the fifth century AD. Unlike any other known hill fort within the province it continued in occupation through the Roman period. Indeed it reached its greatest extent at this time, the defences being extended in the late first or early second century so that the area within them grew from 12 to 16 hectares. The size of the fort, its continuing occupation and the range of important finds from the site combine to suggest that this was the capital of the Votadini. It seems possible therefore that this tribe voluntarily submitted to Rome, possibly even before the army entered her territory, and as a result a treaty was negotiated between the two. It is even possible, as Traprain Law continued in occupation, that the tribe became a client state and that the status continued through several generations. Such a position would not be unusual on Roman frontiers.

It is interesting to compare the situation at Traprain Law with that at Eildon Hill North, by Newstead, for a timber signal-station or watch-tower was planted in the centre of this hill fort. The exact date of the construction of the tower is not known: it could have been erected in either the first or second centuries. It might be expected that the construction of a Roman watch-tower would have led to the abandonment of the hill fort, and this might indeed have been the case, but the presence of second century coins and pottery of the second, third and fourth centuries points to renewed, if not continuing, native occupation.

The abandonment of many other native forts can be demonstrated for in the second century open settlements sprang up often spreading over the ramparts of former forts (fig. 32): it seems probable that such sites were abandoned as a result of the Agricolan rather than the Antonine advance. At Camelon, a defended homestead, and possibly other houses, was abandoned either now or in the mid-second century when the army constructed a large fort a few metres away. However, the site appears to have been re-occupied when the army withdrew.

The distribution of Roman forts may also hint at the attitude of the tribes to their conquerer. Forts were planted in the territory of the Selgovae and the Damnonii, but they are rarer in the area attributed to the Votadini and Novantae (fig. 4). However, the situation is not straightforward. Firstly, it is probable that the known distribution of Roman forts is incomplete. Few military sites have been discovered in Galloway, the land of the Novantae. This may be not so much because there were no forts, but as a result of the underlying geology which renders parts of this corner of Scotland unresponsive to aerial photography. In the east only one fort has been located east of Dere Street – at Low Learchild – but again more may have existed. Another factor is that Roman forts were situated with strategic as well as tactical considerations in mind. Thus forts would be placed on Dere Street in order to provide support for troops on the frontier as well as with the intention of controlling the local population: there was no need to establish garrisons throughout the territory of a tribe which had submitted, it could be controlled by units beyond its boundaries. A further difficulty lies in the fact that the boundaries of the tribes are not known. Finally, Rome's attitude to the tribes, friendly or otherwise, must be considered. Rome regarded even client states as part of the empire even though technically they were independent. In Britain this is demonstrated by the disarming of the Iceni in 47 by the governor Ostorius Scapula in spite of their client status. If the Votadini had been a client state, or at least been philo-Roman, it is possible that garrisons were still planted in their territory, for their protection if not to control them. If the army had wished to place a watch-tower or signal-station within the hill fort of a friendly tribe there is no doubt that it would have gone ahead and constructed the observation post: the appearance of such a watch-tower on the summit of Eildon Hill North is therefore not a secure indication of the status of the occupants of the site. The distribution of forts is accordingly of little help in determining the attitude of the tribes to their new lords.

With the move across the Forth-Clyde isthmus in Agricola's sixth year of office the Roman army met a new enemy. It is clear from the account of Tacitus that the Caledonians and the other northern tribes attempted to sink their differences in the face of the common threat. Treaties were negotiated between the various tribes in order to solve areas of disagreement and field as large an army as possible. From the available tribal leaders one was chosen to be the leader of the army, Calgacus. This was the first step in a process of amalgamation of tribes beyond the empire forced on them by the presence of Rome. In the event, the joint action of the northern tribes was to no avail for they were defeated at Mons Graupius. The process of assimilation of these tribes into the province would be repeated, though again nothing is known of this.

The sudden arrival of a monetary economy and of well-paid Roman soldiers requiring food, clothing, leather and other goods, might have been expected to bring about changes in the northern economy and society. Farmers no doubt turned to producing agricultural commodities for the army rather than for their old masters while traders and merchants would have been attracted north to sell goods and services to the troops. However, neither changes in the agricultural landscape in Scotland nor civil settlements outside forts have been certainly recognised at this time.

If such changes are difficult to recognise archaeologically it is certain that artefacts – brooches, glass vessels, pottery as well as coins – found their way into the hands of the new provincials, though these objects cannot speak of the method of their transmission – trade, stealing, plunder? Few objects have been found beyond the province (fig. 6). No more than 10 coins, brooches, or sherds of pottery, of first-century date, have come to light in the highlands and islands of Scotland; and some of these of course could have been lost several years after they were manufactured. This would seem to imply that there was little contact, certainly little friendly contact, as indeed might be expected, between Roman and barbarian: the contact between those who had fled before the Roman advance and the tribesmen to the north has already been discussed.

The Roman army imposed peace. And with peace came other 'benefits': taxation, slavery, forced labour, and so on. If hill forts were abandoned no new settlements of this period have yet been identified. Nor can any other results of the imposition of Roman rule on the north British tribes be identified archaeologically, though the flowering of metalwork among the tribes beyond the province in the late first century and beyond almost certainly arose from the presence of Rome.

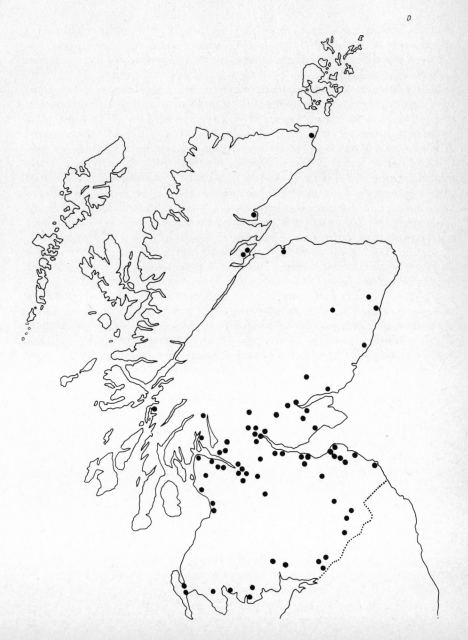

6 The distribution of Roman finds on non-military sites in
Scotland in the first century (after Robertson)

4

The retreat from total conquest

We have seen that the Romans probably saw Mons Graupius as the completion of the conquest of the island. Thereafter Agricola's unknown successor, no doubt acting on the orders of Domitian, commenced the construction of forts and roads north of the Forth-Clyde isthmus in the newly conquered territory. A legionary fortress was placed at Inchtuthil a little east of the Dunkeld Gorge and auxiliary forts were positioned at the mouths of the main Highland glens. To the south and east of these lay more forts on the road leading north through Strathearn and Strathmore as far as Stracathro, north-west of the Montrose Basin: the occupation of at least some of these forts seems to have been contemporary with the glen forts. It seems probable that the forts built at this time reflect the first stage in the implementation of Roman plans for the occupation of the Highlands. Forts were placed in the mouths of the glens, not to block Caledonian raiding, which they could not have done, but to act as springboards for the advance of Roman forces up the glens and the construction of forts within the Highlands. This would account for the position of the legion so far north: when the plans were fully implemented the legion would be far to the rear of the most northerly forts. A major disaster elsewhere within the empire was to lead to the abandonment of Domitian's plans for northern Scotland before even the first stage was fully completed.

In 85 an army of Dacians, from the area of modern Romania, crossed the Danube and in the ensuing fighting the governor of the province of Moesia was killed. Domitian took command of the Roman defence, but in a retaliatory attack on the Dacians the prefect of the praetorian guard, Cornelius Fuscus, was killed and *legio V Alaudae* annihilated. the Roman forces withdrew and regrouped and as a result of a second invasion in 89 the Dacians accepted terms, becoming a client state of Rome and in return receiving a subsidy and other assistance. Peace was, however, not permanently established for in 92 tribes living west of Dacia, the Marcomanni, Quadi, Jazyges and Sarmatians, invaded the empire destroying another legion, *XXI Rapax*, before they were driven out. To aid the Danubian armies troops were brought in from other frontiers: Britain supplied *legio II Adiutrix*. This legion was certainly on the Danube by 93, but other slight evidence suggests that it may have been withdrawn as early as the winter of 85/86 or 86, at the very beginning of the crisis.

The withdrawal of *legio II Adiutrix* marked a decisive change in the balance of Roman forces in Britain. The legion was not to return to the province, nor was another sent to replace it. The garrison of Britain was permanently reduced to three legions and this reduced the capacity of the army to take offensive action beyond the frontier: the withdrawal of the legion was thus an important factor in determining that the rest of the island would never be conquered by Rome.

As a result of the movement of *II Adiutrix* to the continent the legionary fortress at Inchtuthil was abandoned even before it was completed. All the barracks had been constructed, most of the granaries, several of the officers' houses and the principal buildings, with the exception of the commanding officer's palace. So far as is known the auxiliary forts, where building had commenced, had been completed, but it is possible that other forts in this line along the edge of the Highlands were planned but had not been started. The legion destined for Inchtuthil, probably *XX Valeria Victrix*, was instead moved to Chester to take the place of *II Adiutrix*. The abandonment of Inchtuthil was almost certainly accompanied by the withdrawal of the garrisons from the glen forts. It is not known where the units in these forts moved to but it is possible that they, or others, accompanied *II Adiutrix* to the continent. The abandonment of Inchtuthil, and the glen forts, must also have led to the relinquishing of whatever plans Rome had for the occupation of the Highlands.

The Gask frontier

Although the abandonment of Inchtuthil presumably carried with it the withdrawal of garrisons from the glen forts to the south-west, it is possible that no other forts were abandoned at this time. Several of the forts on the road north from the Forth had a more complicated history than the glen forts. Two first-century forts have been recognised at Ardoch while excavation has revealed two phases in at least part of the fort at Strageath. Nothing is known of the next fort to the north, Bertha at the crossing of the Tay, but the situation at Cargill, at the crossing of the Isla, is now complex. The fort, first century in date, lies only 3 kilometres south-east of the legionary fortress at Inchtuthil. Furthermore, an undated fortlet lies beside the fort. It is not possible to do more than speculate about the sequence of events. The fort may have been occupied at the same time as the fortress for the two served different functions, yet on the other hand their proximity may argue that they were not contemporary, one, presumably the fort, succeeding the other: the fortlet is an altogether unknown quantity. The continuing occupation of these 'road' forts after the abandonment of Inchtuthil may carry with it the two forts to the north, Cardean and Stracathro. The rebuilding of the more southerly forts in this line was probably occasioned by the abandonment of Inchtuthil: these forts were presumably initially built either at the same time as the glen forts, or perhaps in Agricola's third season, possibly, in view of the closeness of the two lines, being abandoned briefly when the glen forts were occupied.

Along the road north are a number of timber watch-towers and these are probably best dated to this time (figs 4 and 7, pl. 3). Each consisted of a timber tower, 3–4m square, based on four main timber posts, and surrounded by an earthen bank and one or two ditches. The towers fall into two sectors. From Ardoch northwards along the road to Strageath four have been found. The distance between Ardoch and the first tower, between each of the three towers and between the third tower and the fortlet at Kaims Castle, is in each case just under 1,000m. The fourth tower at present stands by itself, some distance to the north of Kaims Castle, and presumably more remain to be discovered in this stretch.

The distances between the eleven towers known along the Gask Ridge running eastwards from Strageath vary considerably from 760m to 1520m, though it is possible that some long gaps were broken by as yet undiscovered towers. The only indentifiable difference in planning between the regularly spaced towers from Ardoch to Kaims Castle and those on the Gask Ridge is that the former are surrounded by two ditches and the latter by only one.

The watch-towers are too close together to have been signal-stations: many

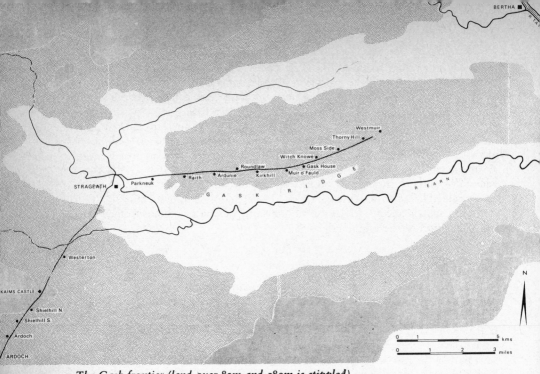

Westmuir
Thorny Hill
Moss Side
Witch Knowe
Roundlaw   Gask House
Raith   Ardunie   Kirkhill   Muir o' Fauld
STRAGEATH   Parkneuk

G A S K   R I D G E

R E A R N

Westerton

KAIMS CASTLE
Shielhill N
Shielhill S
Ardoch
ARDOCH

N

0   1   5 kms
0   1   2   3 miles

7 The Gask frontier (land over 80m and 180m is stippled)

would have been superfluous as they could have been by-passed by fire or smoke signals (pl. 8 for towers and bonfires along the Danube). The purpose of the posts was presumably to keep watch on the cleared strip of ground on either side of the road beside which they lay (fig. 9). The watch-towers, and the forts along the same line, therefore formed a frontier, or at least a line of control, a device to help the army monitor the movement of people into and out of the province. The garrison of the towers by itself was insufficient to prevent infiltration by the barbarians and bandits outside the province, but the system would enable the army to see what was happening and take appropriate retaliatory measures.

Regulations governed the movement of people into and out of the empire. No such regulations survive for Britain, but almost contemporary incidents concerning frontier regulations are recorded by classical writers. In 70 the Tencteri, a tribe living on the east bank of the Rhine, complained that they could only have access to the *Colonia Agrippina* – Cologne – unarmed and practically naked, under guard and after paying a fee. At the end of the first century Tacitus recorded how the Hermanduri from across the Danube had the privilege, unique among the Germans, of trading not just on the bank of the river but deep inside a Roman colony and could enter and leave without guards. These accounts, from two separate areas of the empire, would suggest that similar regulations were in operation on the northern frontier in Britain. The watch-towers can accordingly be seen as an attempt to operate such regulations, to ensure that tribesmen from beyond the province entered the province unarmed, were escorted to agreed markets, and charged a fee for the privilege.

This frontier system – the 'Gask frontier' (see note at end of this chapter) – is not closely dated. It is not mentioned in the documentary sources for Roman Britain and there are only two surviving sherds of pottery from the eight watch-towers investigated to date: both date to the late first century. By itself this is little evidence to date a whole frontier complex, but there are two other considerations: firstly the

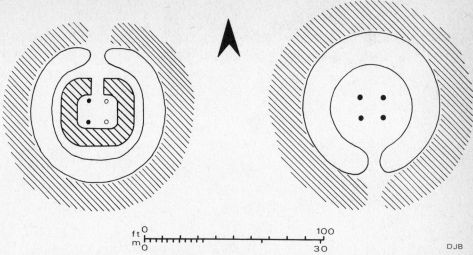

8 Plans of towers on the Gask Ridge: Parkneuk (after Robertson) and Witch Knowe (after Christieson)

relationship of the watch-towers to the history of the northern frontier and secondly the relationship of the British watch-towers to those in Germany.

There are a number of occasions when the watch-towers could have been constructed: during Agricola's move north in his third season, during the campaigns north of the Forth in his sixth and seventh seasons, as support for the glen forts, or during the years following the abandonment of those forts.

A frontier such as that under consideration is not compatible with the fluid military situation that existed during the years of Agricola's governorship. We have already seen that the first mention of a possible frontier in Britain was in Agricola's fourth campaigning season. It seems unlikely that a frontier would have been constructed 30 kilometres to the north in the preceding year. In the sixth and seventh seasons, on the other hand, Agricola was fighting the Caledonians and concerned neither to build forts nor frontiers. In the following years when Inchtuthil and the glen forts were being constructed it seems unlikely that a second line of defence should have been built to their rear, leaving, in particular, the legion beyond the line of watch-towers. The best time for the construction of the watch-towers therefore would seem to be in the years following the abandonment of Inchtuthil and the glen forts. As such they would represent the line to which the army fell back on the abandonment of the more northerly and westerly forts. Finally, it may be considered that the watch-towers served as extra protection in front of the Antonine Wall in the mid-second century, but this would seem to be out of character with the frontiers of the period and unparalleled on any other of the empire's frontiers at that time.

If the Gask watch-towers have been correctly dated they were exactly contemporary with similar structures in Germany. In the 80s the Emperor Domitian waged war against the Chatti east of the Rhine. The war probably started in the spring of 83 and at first the Roman army achieved victories: Domitian celebrated his triumph in the summer of 83. However, the war dragged on for at least another year and when it ended, probably as a result of the outbreak of more

9 *The Gask Ridge, view from the west. Reconstruction showing two of the fortified towers. (Drawn by M. Moore)*

serious trouble on the Danube, it led to the acquisition of very little territory by Rome. Nevertheless two most important events followed. The first was the creation of two new provinces, Upper Germany and Lower Germany. Hitherto there had been two army groups based on the Rhine, ostensibly waiting for orders to move forward and conquer the rest of Germany. On the completion of this operation the army groups would become the garrison of the new provinces. Now it was tacitly recognised that this move forward was unlikely to materialise. Secondly, a new frontier was laid out encompassing those areas brought into the empire as a result of the Chattan war. New forts were established through the Wetterau and Taunus from the junction of the Rhine and the Mosel to the Neckar. Still within the period of the Chattan war, it appears that these forts were supplemented by the construction of timber watch-towers, which were placed beside the path linking the forts. These towers were normally 500–600m apart, though under certain circumstances – on level ground and given good visibility – the distance might be as much as 1,000m. It seems probable that this new frontier should be associated with a statement by Julius Frontinus, a former governor of Britain and a member of Domitian's staff during the Chattan war, in his book, *Stratagems*. Here he states (1,3,10) that following raiding by the Germans Domitian advanced the frontier of the empire along a stretch of 120 miles (200km): the total north-south length of the new frontier is 120 miles. The construction of this type of frontier, for the first time anywhere in the empire, together with the establishment of the two new provinces marks a fundamental change in Roman attitudes towards frontiers, though of course this was not recognised at that time: a few years later Tacitus remarked in the *Germania* that the conquest of Germany was taking a long time, not apparently realising that Roman pretentions in Free Germany had been abandoned, at least temporarily, and the fact recognised by the establishment of the provinces and the frontier.

The creation of a similar frontier in Britain came a few years after that in Germany. Essentially the two were the same. Forts and towers connected by a road marked the frontier which was probably defined by a cleared strip of ground. This would allow for the observation of people coming into and out of the province, though of course it would not prevent it: the addition of the towers was merely to allow the Roman army better powers of observation and control.

The watch-towers in Scotland are at present known only for a distance of about 18km through Strathearn, along the line of the road leading north into Strathmore. It is possible that if they are part of a frontier system, as argued above, they started further south, possibly at Camelon, and continued further north. They presumably continued – that is if the construction of the frontier was ever completed – at least as far as Bertha on the Tay. No watch-towers have been recognised beyond the Tay, but it is possible that some had been built there, or had intended to be built, but were not constructed owing to abandonment of the project.

The Gask frontier would appear to have had a short life. It cannot have been constructed until after 86, if the preceding arguments are accepted, yet pottery evidence suggests that all sites north of the Forth Clyde isthmus were abandoned by about 90. At this time the forts and watch-towers were dismantled and burnt. The Gask frontier therefore, occupied for perhaps no more than three years, marks a brief pause before another major withdrawal south. Rome presumably considered that if intentions to occupy the Highlands were abandoned she could still maintain control over the peoples south of the Highland Line. But that was not to be. Whether the abandonment of all pretensions north of the Forth was the result of more troop withdrawals from Britain or simply a more realistic reappraisal of resources is not known.

The abandonment of Scotland

The forts abandoned at this time included all those north of the Forth and several to the south. The most northerly line of forts now lay on or, just to the north of, the Cheviots. They included Newstead, probably Oakwood, Milton, Dalswinton and Glenlochar (fig. 10). The evidence for the continuing occupation of these forts is ceramic and structural. At Newstead, Oakwood and Glenlochar two structural phases have been recorded in excavations, at Milton two or possibly three first-century phases are known, while Dalswinton had as many as four. In addition Newstead and Dalswinton have produced late first-century samian pottery. Two other sites must be mentioned: Castlecary on the Forth-Clyde isthmus has produced late first-century samian ware though the first-century site here has not been discovered, while as many as four first-century phases have been recorded at the small fort at Loudoun Hill in Ayrshire.

Four of the forts in the Scottish Lowlands at this time, Newstead, Milton, Dalswinton and Glenlochar, all on the same axis, were larger than usual. Newstead was rebuilt, probably at this time, and was both larger and more massively defended than its predecessor. It is possible that these large forts were the bases of garrisons charged with long-range patrolling and the maintenance of surveillance over those lands recently abandoned. Such an explanation might account for the occupation of stations further to the north and west: Castlecary and Loudoun Hill. Forts to the rear, on the roads north in the east and at Broomholm in the west, also continued in occupation.

These forts were not to be occupied for long before there was yet another

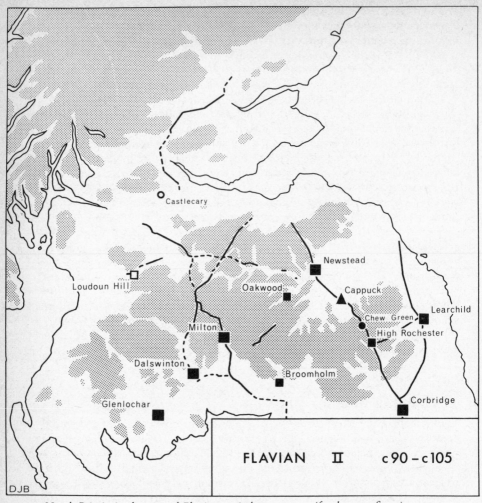

10 North Britain in the second Flavian period, c.90–c.105 (for key see fig. 4)

withdrawal, this time south to the Tyne-Solway isthmus. There are two pieces of evidence which combine to suggest a date in the first decade of the second century for this withdrawal. Firstly, the samian pottery from the sites north of the isthmus carry their occupation down to the last years of the first century or the first years of the second. Secondly, in 1973 a coin of 103 was found in a construction trench of the Trajanic fort at Corbridge on the Tyne. This must date the building of this fort to 103 or later. Again the abandonment of forts in southern Scotland and Northumberland may have been because troops were withdrawn from Britain for in 105 Trajan commenced his second war against the Dacians and this may have led to empire wide troop movement, though we can point to no positive evidence for this in relation to Britain.

There is a further possible occasion for the withdrawal of army units from southern Scotland. *Legio IX Hispana* was still at York in 107/8 when it was recorded on a building inscription but it had almost certainly left by 122 when *legio*

VI Victrix was sent to Britain from Lower Germany, presumably to replace it and provide more men to help in the construction of Hadrian's Wall. Its departure may have been sooner rather than later after 108. Archaeological evidence from York suggests that there was a reduction in the density of occupation of the legionary fortress from *c.*110–*c.*125/30. It seems likely that the legion was not at York during these years, and of course *VI Victrix* when it arrived went straight off to build Hadrian's Wall which accounts for the continuing lack of pottery on the site.

There were two significant events in Trajan's reign (98–117) which might have led to major troop movements in the empire: the Dacian wars of 101–106 and the invasion of Parthia 114–117. The earlier was before the building work by *legio IX Hispana* at York – unless the consequence of the incorporation of Dacia into the empire continued to be felt in the form of troop movements for some time after 106 – but the latter may be relevant. A tile stamp and a *mortarium* stamp found at the legionary fortress at Nijmegen on the Lower Rhine would fit this date and allow *IX Hispana* to be transferred to the continent as part of widespread troop movements connected with the Parthian war and thence east to be destroyed either in the Jewish revolt of Hadrian's reign or in the Parthian invasion of 161. The legion was certainly not destroyed before the end of the 120s, as the careers of certain officers of the legion demonstrate. If *IX Hispana* was withdrawn from Britain about 114 it might have been accompanied by auxiliary units and even if this was not the case the departure might have been the occasion for a rearrangement of the frontier garrisons in order to compensate for the loss of this force.

A date of about 114 for this reorganisation would be rather later than the pottery and structural evidence suggests for the establishment of the Tyne-Solway isthmus as a frontier. There is also, as is often the case, a complication. Tiles of *legio IX* have been found at Scalesceugh, about 4.5km south-east of Carlisle. These may date to the late first or early second century, though this is far from certain. It has been suggested that at this time *legio IX* was engaged in the construction of a new legionary fortress in the neighbourhood of Carlisle preparatory to evacuating York. Building work would take some time and presumably require the presence of a large part of the legion. This might account for the lack of pottery at York in these years, while the continuing, though small, army presence might explain why the fortress was not given over to civilian use, which would surely have happened if it had been abandoned completely. But this is speculation. The reason for the presence of tiles of *IX Hispana* at Scalesceugh is not known. The legion has left no record in Britain after 108 and it does not appear on the many building stones from Hadrian's Wall. All, perhaps, that can be said is that the movements of *legio IX Hispana* in these years are unclear and as a result none of the above possibilities can be ignored.

Many of the forts abandoned in the early second century were burnt and it is not impossible that this was the result of hostile action. Destruction material from the burning of timber buildings has been found to cover the whole area of the fort at Corbridge, but the most evocative evidence is from Newstead on the Tweed. Here, in pits, have been discovered burnt wattle and daub from timber buildings, damaged military equipment and human skulls. It has been argued that this all results from the destruction of the fort by the northern tribes, buried by the Romans after they had retrieved the situation. Yet a peaceful scenario is equally possible. The burnt wattle and daub could have resulted from the destruction of the buildings by the Roman army itself on abandonment of the site: this was the usual procedure. The buildings were demolished, usually it would appear in a methodical way, and the wattle and daub panels and the main timbers burnt. Sometimes the main timbers were not removed but were burnt *in situ*. Sometimes the fort's rampart was slighted, at other times not. The damaged equipment at Newstead could have been that in the workshops awaiting repair when word came that the fort was to be evacuated, and abandoned as surplus to requirements, or to transport capabilities. The skulls appear alone, without associated long bones. Human heads are shown on the almost contemporary Trajan's Column as trophies held by Roman soldiers. Heads, presumably Dacians', appear on poles placed in front of a Roman fort, while in another scene Roman soldiers themselves carry heads as they fight, held by the hair from their teeth. The skulls at Newstead therefore could be the remains of such heads buried when the fort was abandoned. The evidence for the cause of the evacuation of these forts north of the Tyne-Solway isthmus in the early second century is not clear, nor is the date certain. However, the action is definite enough and it led to the construction of a new frontier across this southern isthmus. This frontier, often called the Stanegate frontier, is as yet imperfectly understood. It will probably always be imperfectly understood because it was in part an addition to an existing screen of forts, while it was, it would appear, modified during its lifetime. Further, by its very nature, composed as it was of a number of disparate and separate elements, it is more difficult to understand and appreciate its growth and function.

The Stanegate 'frontier'

When the forts north of the Tyne-Solway isthmus were abandoned in the early years of the second century the handful of forts across the isthmus became the most northerly line of military stations in Britain (fig. 11). Occupation at three forts at this time has been proved by archaeology and it is possible on other grounds that a further one or two forts should be added to this group. In the east lay Corbridge, strategically placed beside the lowest crossing of the Tyne, just below the confluence of the North and South Tynes and where Dere Street passed northwards into *barbaricum*. A road, the Stanegate, crossed the isthmus from here to Carlisle where the western route north bridged the Eden. In between lay a fort at Chesterholm, 22km west of Corbridge, which was occupied at this time, and a second at Nether Denton, 18km from Chesterholm and 22km from Carlisle. This fort has not been excavated but is generally considered to date to this time. These forts, at a day's march apart, were probably all on sites chosen twenty years before even though they might have been rebuilt and moved slightly in the meantime. Their spacing is normal. Almost exactly halfway between Chesterholm and Nether Denton, however, lies another fort at Carvoran. Again the date of this fort is not known, but aerial reconnaissance here, as at Nether Denton, has revealed a large, 3.2 hectare, military enclosure below the known fort, which may be an Agricolan foundation at the north end of the Maiden Way. This road branches off the Stainmore road at Kirby Thore to pass northwards through Whitley Castle and connect with the Stanegate. Certainly there would appear to have been first century occupation here for the site had produced the famous Carvoran *modius* which dates to the reign of Domitian.

These five forts therefore would appear to have been the late first-century bases across the isthmus. They did not form a frontier at that time but lay within the province and their spacing and strength was no different from those of sites on, for example, the Stainmore road leading across the Pennines from Catterick to

Brougham. Now, the gradual withdrawal stopped and this line was strengthened, in time by the construction of Hadrian's Wall. The existence of the Tyne-Solway isthmus no doubt led to the halt here, but it may not be entirely coincidental that this marked the northern boundary of the Brigantes, a tribe undoubtedly regarded as part of the empire since it had accepted client status fifty years before.

The reign of Trajan saw major modifications to the line of forts across the isthmus, and this work may have continued into the early days of Hadrian's reign. Firstly, some of the existing forts may have been rebuilt. The fort at Corbridge was burnt down and reconstructed after, probably shortly after, 103, and indeed this work is one of the main pointers to the date of the withdrawal from the more northerly forts and the strengthening of the installations on the isthmus. At Chesterholm too one of the three pre-Hadrianic rebuildings may date to this time. Aerial photographs reveal that the fort at Nether Denton was remodelled at least once during its life and this may date to these years. At Carlisle the position is not known. Secondly, new forts were built across the isthmus. In the east, beyond Corbridge, a fort, apparently of two periods, has been discovered from the air at Washing Well, Whickham. The site is not excavated, but ought to be earlier than Hadrian's Wall, and therefore may well fit into Trajan's reign. In the west, beyond Carlisle, two forts are now known, at Burgh-by-Sands, a little south of the Hadrianic fort, and at Kirkbride, south of Bowness at the end of the Wall. The spacing is interesting, and indicative of what is to come, 8km and 9.5km. On the Stanegate a new fort was built at Old Church Brampton, between Carlisle and Nether Denton to break the gap of 22km, but no fort can positively be identified between Corbridge and Chesterholm, though fourth-century Newbrough, roughly halfway between, may have had a second-century predecessor. The spacing between most of the forts had now been reduced from about 22km to 9–11km, though the east, where the Tyne formed a clear line of demarcation, may have been more sparsely covered. Moreover the line was now extended both east of Corbridge and west of Carlisle.

To these forts a new element was added, the small fort. Only two such sites have been securely identified, Haltwhistle Burn between Chesterholm and Carvoran and Throp between Carvoran and Nether Denton, and only at the former site are the internal buildings known. It is clear from these buildings that Haltwhistle Burn is not a fortlet, but a small fort, a generic term indicating that the station was the base for the parent body of a military unit most, or many, of whose men were outposted elsewhere. Haltwhistle Burn contained a small building in the centre, possibly serving the purpose of a headquarters, a granary and a barrack-block, leaving space for several small buildings, but not another barrack-block: the plan is reminiscent of a *numerus* fort in Germany. The fort seems to have had a life of some years and pottery suggests occupation in the early years of the second century. It seems possible that the fort was constructed on, or shortly after, the move south to form part of a new system of frontier control.

The men from this, and other small forts, might have been sent to man the watch-towers which were erected in the years preceding the construction of Hadrian's Wall. Two of these towers lay on the high ground to the north of the Stanegate, as if providing extra eyes for the garrisons of the forts. That at Walltown, later to be incorporated into the Wall as turret 45a, produced, on excavation, no pottery earlier than the opening years of Hadrian's reign. At Pike Hill and Mains Rigg no pottery at all was found. It is possible, therefore, on the basis of the findings at Walltown, that these towers did not form part of the basic Trajanic plan, but were later additions to it.

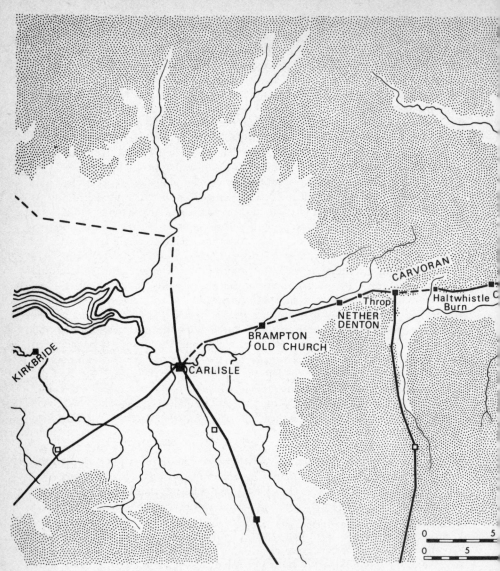

11 The Stanegate 'frontier' (land over 180m is stippled)

In spite of the uncertainties the main outlines of the new system of frontier control are now clear. Existing forts were renewed, probably with garrison changes, new forts built on the lower Tyne, west of Carlisle, and between certain of the existing forts. The main purpose of this greater troop concentration would be in order to help defend the province from attack. The close spacing of certain forts, however, and the addition of small forts, draws attention to the new concern with frontier control. Some soldiers were clearly as much involved with frontier police duties as with general defence. Finally, perhaps some years after the first moves to strengthen the Stanegate forts, watch-towers were built on the north rim of Tynedale. There appears, however, to have been no attempt to recreate the line of

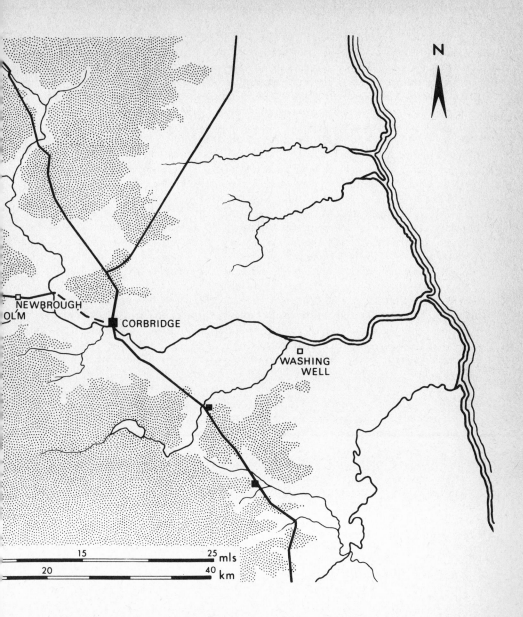

N

NEWBROUGH
OL'M
CORBRIDGE
□
WASHING
WELL

15   25 mls
20   40 km

timber watch-towers such as had previously existed along the road from Ardoch to Bertha.

One recently discovered feature which has been connected with the Stanegate remains to be noted. Beneath the 'Stanegate' fort at Burgh-by-Sands Professor Barri Jones has located from the air and subsequently examined through excavation a circular ditch and rampart containing a four post watch-tower or gate-tower. Pottery from one of the post-holes included black-burnished ware, which only entered this area about 120. The timber tower was succeeded after a short interval by the fort, again associated with early second-century pottery. It would appear that modifications were being made to the frontier arrangements in this sector in the very early years of Hadrian's reign.

Also at Burgh-by-Sands Professor Jones found a ditch and palisade underlying the north gate of the fort, and these features were later recognised at Finland 4.5km to the west, again, it would appear, associated with a watch-tower. As a result of these discoveries Professor Jones has suggested that between Carlisle and the sea at Kirkbride there was a palisade and ditch, perhaps not continuous but only filling the gaps between the mosses, with a patrolling garrison housed in the watch-towers. It is too early to be certain of the nature of the military works in this area or their history, not least because Professor Jones' work remains unpublished. Nevertheless it is clear that the military works in this area are much more complicated than hitherto realised and no doubt further discoveries can be expected.

No forts are known to have been occupied north of the Tyne-Solway isthmus during Trajan's reign following the withdrawal south in the first decade of the second century. Little too is known of the relationship between the province and the tribes to the north. Traprain Law continued in occupation but few Roman objects specifically of this time have been found north of the isthmus. It is possible, however, that some of the objects of first-century manufacture found in Scotland were not lost until some years later, in the second century. It is certainly unlikely that the Roman army abandoned all surveillance over the tribes north of the province. Through the reign of Trajan – and Hadrian – Roman army patrols will no doubt have continued to keep watch on the areas beyond the frontiers in order to try to ensure that nothing happened against Roman interests. In pursuit of this end they do not appear to have been altogether successful.

There is only one hint at warfare on the northern frontier during Trajan's reign. *Cohors I Cugernorum*, stationed in Britain, was awarded the title *Ulpia Traiana* in return for meritorious conduct sometime between 103 and 122. The occasion and scene of this event remains unknown, but the most likely place for it is on the northern frontier. Also at the beginning of Hadrian's reign his biographer records that the Britons could hardly be kept under control. Again the most likely place for the event which gave rise to this comment is the northern frontier. However, in spite of these disturbances it was possible, it would appear, to reduce the garrison of the province by moving *legio IX Hispana* to the continent. As so often is the case the main evidence of contact between Roman and native lies in the realms of war and not peace.

Note: The Gask frontier

The frontier formed by the line of watch-towers through Strathearn has no formally recognised name. Most of the known sites lie on the Gask Ridge, but Gask Ridge Frontier would be an inadequate title. Similarly Strathearn Frontier might be rendered too restricted by further discoveries. A title based on the date of the frontier is clumsy and again might be affected by later discoveries. A name based on the geographical location seems most appropriate and as the watch-towers were first noted on the Gask Ridge the Gask frontier is here suggested as the best description of the line.

5
Hadrian's Wall

It seems likely that the additions and modifications to the military establishment on the Tyne-Solway isthmus during the reign of Trajan, and possibly the early years of his successor, were in order to try to control more effectively movement into and out of the province. However, the construction of Hadrian's Wall in the 120s would appear to suggest that these measures did not meet with complete success. Hadrian's Wall provided the only effective method of frontier control by the provision of a new element, the linear barrier. As first planned Hadrian's Wall was intended to be a fairly simple and straightforward modification to the existing chain of forts. The barrier was to consist of a curtain of stone or turf to run across the isthmus from a new bridge to be constructed on the Tyne at Newcastle to Bowness on the Solway, with provision for military and civilian passage through this barrier in the form of gateways defended by small fortlets or milecastles and with observation towers placed at one third of a mile intervals (fig. 13). Nothing is known of the garrison of the milecastles or the turrets, but as it is clear that the pre-existing forts behind the Wall were to continue in existence it may be presumed that the units stationed there would provide the troops for the new establishments. The Wall was placed in the most sensible geographical position. In the east it ran along the north rim of Tynedale, linking up in the centre with the Whin Sill (pl. 5). In the west it came off the Whin Sill onto the escarpment above the River Irthing, following the north side of that river's valley until reaching the Solway Estuary. From Carlisle, where the Wall crossed the Eden, the Wall lay on the southern shore of the estuary until a convenient point was found to stop at Bowness.

The purpose of Hadrian's Wall was given by Hadrian's biographer who stated that the Wall was constructed for 80 miles (120km) from sea to sea to divide the barbarians from the Romans. This is manifestly correct for the barbarians beyond the province were separated from the empire by the most obvious and clear method: a wall.

Movement was provided for and allowed, but it was to be controlled. The addition of a curtain wall, a linear barrier, to the earlier forms of control – forts, small forts and watch-towers – was Hadrian's contribution to the development of Roman frontiers, and it is therefore appropriate that Hadrian's Wall is the best preserved and best known of all Roman frontier defences.

It may be considered that there was a special reason for the construction of a Wall in Britain at this time. When Hadrian succeeded his great-uncle Trajan in 117 his biographer remarks that Britain could hardly be kept under control. It is not known whether this refers to an internal revolt or a disturbance on the northern frontier, though the latter seems to be the most probable. There may also have been trouble in Britain during Trajan's reign as discussed above. Yet at the same time it seems that the garrison of the province was reduced by the transfer of *legio IX Hispana* from Britain to the continent during the years between 108, when it is last attested at York, and probably 122 when *legio VI Victrix* arrived. It seems that this

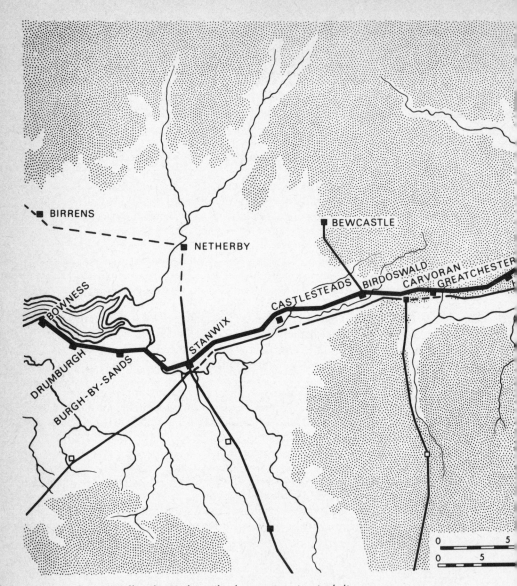

12 Hadrian's Wall under Hadrian (land over 180m is stippled)

move occurred between earlier warfare in Trajan's reign and the disturbance at the
end of it, unless the warfare arose out of the reduction of the provincial garrison.

The disturbance in Britain at the beginning of Hadrian's reign appears to have
been serious. Forty years later Cornelius Fronto wrote to the Emperor Marcus
Aurelius (161–80), his former pupil, to console the emperor for the heavy losses of
his army in the Parthian war, by recalling the serious losses incurred by Hadrian in
Judaea in the mid 130s and in Britain. There is no reason to doubt that the losses
occured in Britain during the disturbance recorded by Hadrian's biographer: there
is certainly no knowledge of a later war in Britain in this reign.

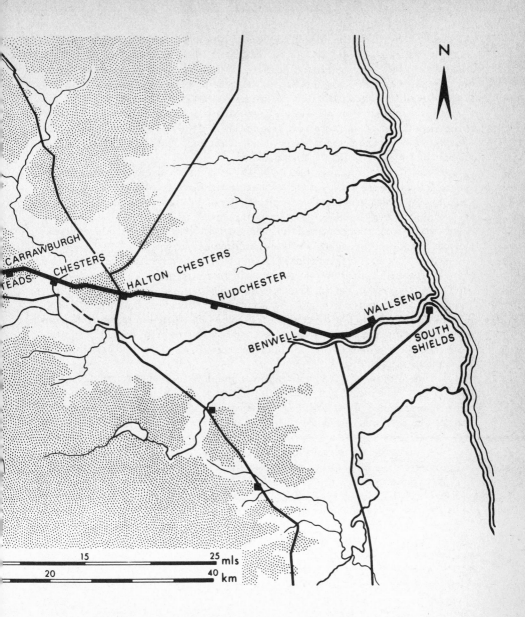

N

CARRAWBURGH

EADS- CHESTERS

HALTON CHESTERS

RUDCHESTER

BENWELL

WALLSEND

SOUTH
SHIELDS

15   25 mls
20   40 km

However, such warfare almost certainly had little to do with the construction of Hadrian's Wall, for two reasons. Firstly, Hadrian's Wall was concerned, not with the major attacks on the province, the only ones which might earn a unit military honours, and achieve mention in imperial records, but with the more small-scale, day-to-day problems of frontier control. If there had been a serious threat to the province at this time it would have been dealt with by the army units based in northern England, including those on the Tyne-Solway isthmus, and possibly with help from the legions, but the construction of a Wall would not have helped to deter or prevent such attacks. The defeat – and prevention – of such attacks could only be achieved by the strengthening of the army units in the area. Secondly, almost certainly Hadrian's Wall was not the first artificial frontier of this type to be constructed in the empire. Hadrian came to Britain in 122 from Germany and in both Upper Germany and in Britain he was responsible, according to his biographer, for the construction of artificial frontiers. The discussion of the frontiers in the biography is so closely related to the account of the visits as to lead to the natural, and no doubt correct, assumption that the frontiers were initiated by Hadrian while in the respective provinces. Hadrian's Wall was therefore not a unique solution to a unique British problem.

Nor were all the elements in Hadrian's Wall new. Thirty-five years before closely spaced watch-towers had been established on the Gask frontier in Strathearn in order to keep observation along the line of control. Fortlets, in use in Britain since the conquest, provided linear ancestors for the smaller milecastles. In both cases the towers and fortlets supplemented the main garrisons based in forts. The only new element introduced in the 120s was the continuous barrier.

The most remarkable fact about Hadrian's Wall is its very size. The curtain was planned, it would appear, in two sectors. The first was to run from Newcastle on the Tyne to the crossing of the River Irthing, a distance of 45 Roman miles (73km), and the second from the Irthing to Bowness on the Solway, a shorter length of 31 Roman miles (50km). The longer part was to be constructed in stone, 10 Roman feet (3m) thick and up to perhaps 15 Roman feet (4.5m) high, while the shorter, western sector was to be of turf 20 Roman feet (6m) thick at base and perhaps up to 14 Roman feet (4.3m) high.

The stone wall was placed on a shallow foundation formed of rough flags set in puddled clay. The facing stones were of roughly dressed blocks of sandstone, the finished appearance of the wall being defined in modern terminology as coursed rubble. The core was formed of rough stones usually bonded by mortar, though clay was occasionally used as a bonding material. In most areas the facing stones were of manageable size measuring about 15cm high by 22cm long, tailing back up to 40cm into the core, but in certain areas large blocks up to 40cm long and 30cm high were used.

There was an offset on both sides of the wall after either the first or the third or fourth course. It is not known how the top was finished off. On other frontiers, especially where the barrier was formed by a fence, there was patently no provision for a patrol along the top of the barrier. The width of Hadrian's Wall has led to the unsubstantiated conclusion that there was a sentry walk along the top. It is possible that provision was made for such a walkway, but this cannot be proved. No stones have been found which shed any clear light on the nature of the top of the wall, though two unusual L-shaped stones found at Cawfields may derive from the upper part of the wall. Most reconstructions complete the wall top as crenellated, on the model of the later city walls of Rome and the provinces: in view of the lack of contemporary parallels such reconstructions can only be accepted with reservation. However, the near contemporary Rudge Cup (pl. 7) and Amiens Skillet do suggest that the wall top was crenellated.

Earth Wall should be a better description than Turf Wall for the western sector of Hadrian's Wall for turf was not the only material used. In some places beaten clay was the material of construction, and in one area 'clods' dug out of a marsh or pond were used. Such differences probably reflect changes in the local vegetation cover, which in turn was largely dependent upon the underlying geology. Roman military manuals laid down the regulation size for turves: 18 by 12 by 6 inches, but actual Roman turves revealed by excavation can rarely be shown to approach that size. The wall was placed on a bed of coursed turf, three or four layers thick. Above this both faces rose steeply. The highest archaeological section dug through the wall revealed that the front was at first near vertical, while the back rose at an angle of 1 in 4. The top is as much a mystery as that of the stone wall. If there was a sentry walk there must have been wooden duck-boarding along the top, such as appears on Trajan's Column. There may also have been a breastwork, perhaps of brush-wood rather than split logs.

The reason for the different use of materials in the construction of Hadrian's Wall is not known. It has been suggested that good building stone is lacking in Cumberland, or that a scarcity of limestone in this area led to construction in turf, but as the Turf Wall was later rebuilt in stone neither explanation seems to contain the whole truth. A further element has therefore been added and that is that external considerations required the speedy construction of the Wall in the west. Such considerations can only have included a threat to the Roman forces or the province by dissident tribesmen to the north and this in turn has been linked with the placing of three forts beyond the Wall at Bewcastle, Netherby and Birrens. However, there seems to be no special military reason for outpost forts here: advance patrolling and scouting would have no doubt been carried out to the north of the Wall as a matter of course all along its length by the troops in the forts behind the Wall, while in event of a major attack these army units would advance beyond the Wall and combine to protect the province: in some ways with the Wall in existence isolated outpost forts may have been more of a liability than an asset, though this may not have been understood at the time. The discovery of an inscription to Brigantia at Birrens may provide the answer for the outpost forts, for this may suggest that part of this tribe extended beyond the Wall into modern Dumfriesshire and that therefore the outpost forts were constructed to protect these people, still part of the province, but left beyond the military boundary by the erection of the Wall. It might be expected that the Wall was built on the most convenient geographical line and that this did not coincide with the political boundary of the province, or for that matter the most convenient line for military forces operating in order to defend the province from attack. Finally, it may be remarked that if there was a threat to the security of this area during building operations it would have been dealt with by the army independently of building work: it is a totally false picture to imagine Hadrian's Wall being constructed by troops on the defensive and possibly even fighting off attacks while building. Such trouble as there may have been, and the evidence for this is uncertain, would have been seen to by the army before building work was allowed to commence.

The reason for the building of part of the Wall in turf is therefore unknown. It may be that with all the other building operations on the Wall proceeding the army may have decided that it was wiser to build part of the Wall in turf initially and then rebuild it as and when necessary in stone at leisure rather than allow carting and supply difficulties to drag the building works out even longer. The existence of outpost forts to the north may have been felt to affect in some way the requirements of the Wall to the rear. It must, however, be noted that when compared to other frontiers it is not the turf sector of the Wall that is unusual, but the stone.

Hadrian's stone wall is indeed unusual. The contemporary frontier in Germany was merely a timber fence, while the linear barrier in north Africa, the *Fossatum Africae*, parts of which could be contemporary with Hadrian's Wall, was of dry stone walling or earth. Other, later, frontiers were also of timber, earth or turf, with the single exception of the frontier in Raetia (modern Bavaria) which consisted of a stone wall, though only 1.3m wide. The narrowness of this wall, removed in time and space from Hadrian's Wall, emphasises the unique nature of the English frontier. It has been suggested that the massive nature of Hadrian's Wall could be a compensation for the abandonment of territorial pretensions to the north, an alternative memorial to Hadrian, as indeed it is. Further, Hadrian was a great builder – the Pantheon, his villa at Tivoli, cities and another frontier were all his inspiration – and the wall which still bears his name may be a further reflection of this facet of his character: great builders seldom seem to require justification for their actions! It may be that the stone wall was built so massively because the Roman engineers were not sure that a narrower wall could stand without buttresses – this was, after all, the first such linear barrier – and decided that it was as easy to construct a broad wall as a narrower wall with buttresses. This would allow for the later narrowing of the curtain when it was discovered that a narrower wall would stand without support, and the even narrower wall in Raetia. The Romans were used to constructing large buildings and understood stresses and such problems, but this was the first such engineering project they had tackled and they might well have leant on the side of caution. In truth, however, the reason for the scale of the stone wall is not known and almost certainly never can be: further all suggestions fail satisfactorily to explain the use of turf in one sector rather than stone throughout.

In front of the wall, and separated from it by an open space or berm, lay a wide and deep ditch. This varied considerably in size, from 8 to 12m wide and from 3 to 4m deep, though the smaller figures seem to have been the more normal. Its profile appears to have been the normal V-shape. The material from the ditch was spread out on the north side to form a broad mound or glacis. The berm too varied in width. On the stone wall it was usually 20 Roman feet (6m) wide and on the turf wall 6 Roman feet (1.8m), but a width of 40 feet (12m) has been recorded at one place on the turf wall and here and elsewhere it appears that the berm was widened to take account of unstable geological conditions. A number of places are known where the ditch was not completed, nor the glacis smoothed off. Along the front of the crags, purposely, no ditch at all was dug, while in certain areas along the Solway shore no ditch was dug for the sea was considered sufficient barrier.

At several places the Wall crossed a stream or river. Streams would no doubt have been channelled through the wall, a straightforward operation on the stone wall, but more difficult in the turf sector, while the rivers were bridged. The two main river crossings were at Chesters where the North Tyne afforded a formidable obstacle, and at Willowford where the Irthing lay at the foot of a steep bank, Harrow's Scar. There was to be no attempt to carry the wall itself over the rivers, merely a walkway. At Chesters, where more is known of the earlier, and presumably Hadrianic, bridge, at least four piers, with cutwaters up and down stream, made provision for a walkway 3m wide. The ditch may have simply run out at the rivers, but at Willowford the end of the berm was protected by part of the abutment of the bridge.

The wall, of either turf or stone, and the ditch formed the linear barrier. The two main types of structures placed on this barrier were the milecastles and turrets. The milecastle, the linear descendant of the earlier fortlet, was attached to the rear of the wall (fig. 13). On the stone wall it generally measured about 60 by 50 Roman feet (18 by 15m) internally, being constructed of stone, while the turf and timber milecastle on the turf wall appears to have been usually about 10 feet (3m) larger in

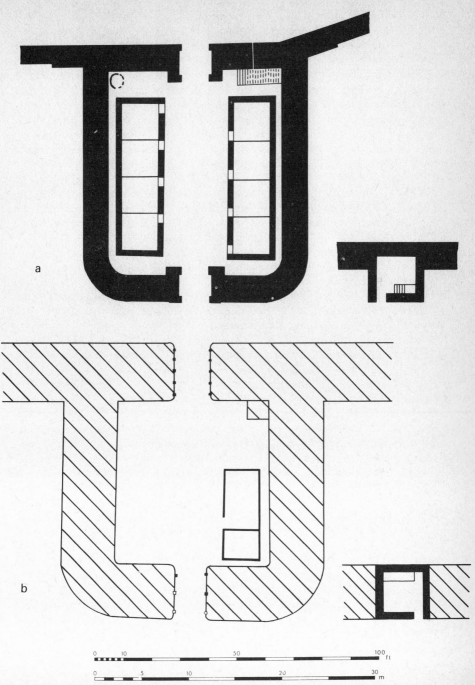

13 Milecastles and turrets on Hadrian's Wall: (a) MC 48 (Poltross Burn) and T 18a (Wallhouses East); (b) MC 50 TW (High House) and T 52a (Banks East)

both directions. In the north wall of the milecastle a gate led through Hadrian's Wall, while a second entrance led into the milecastle from the south. It is probable that both gates were surmounted by towers, the northern one forming part of the chain of towers or turrets along the Wall. Inside each milecastle there generally appears to have been a small barrack-block, sometimes an extra storehouse, an oven and also a flight of steps. These steps will probably have led to the tower, they may also have led to the wall top. They survive best at MC 48 Poltross Burn and by calculation it is possible to suggest that the wall top was 3.7m high at the rear and, because of the slope of the ground, 4.3m at the front. At MC 37 Housesteads so much survives of the north gate that it is possible to calculate that the height of the arch was 3.6m, the voussoirs adding another 60cm to give a minimum height for the wall of nearly 4.3m.

Milecastles were not generally protected by ditches, though in four cases the provision of a single ditch has been noted (MCs 23, 25, 29 and 51). In one case the ditch was unfinished, but it is difficult to argue that an original proposal to provide all milecastles with ditches was dropped before full implementation, for the milecastles with ditches were constructed at different times in the building programme. Finally, it is remarkable that there is evidence for a causeway across the Wall ditch in front of the north gate of only two milecastles (MCs 50 and 54, both on the turf sector). It is not known how the Wall ditch was crossed at the other milecastles: it is conceivable that a bridge was used, but if that was the case, why were these two milecastles treated differently?

Two towers or turrets lay between each milecastle (fig. 13). These were constructed of stone on both the stone and turf walls. On the former they were built with wing walls in order to aid bonding, while on the turf wall they were built as free-standing towers. The turrets were about 4.3m square internally and were recessed into the thickness of the Wall. The doorway was placed in the south wall. Turrets often contained a hearth and a stone platform, which in most stone wall turrets appears to have been the base for a stair or ladder to an upper floor. The height of the turret is unknown, but a minimum height of 7 to 9m for the roof, which presumably served as an elevated observation platform might be expected (cf. pl. 8 for towers on the Danube bank). The Rudge Cup (pl. 7) and the Amiens Skillet, which appear to have been souvenirs of the Wall, suggest that the towers had a flat top with crenellations and stood about twice the height of the wall. There was probably an intermediate floor at the same level as the wall top. This would allow continuous passage along a wall walk, if such movement was required; the building-up of the recesses when turrets were demolished may suggest that such access was desired, though it is also possible that this work was to protect an otherwise weak point in the curtain.

Little is known of the garrisons of the milecastles and turrets. Artefacts found at the sites have been used to argue that the troops were similar in status and type to those in the adjacent forts, and that they were not. Certainly there is no evidence for a separate force on the Wall and it is probably best to assume that the soldiers who manned the milecastles and turrets were sent out from the forts on the Stanegate, and possibly further south, in the manner attested on many Roman military documents. It is not known how long these soldiers might be expected to serve on the Wall, but documentary evidence from another unit based on the Eastern frontier demonstrates that 100 years later soldiers could be away from their base on detached duty for periods of three years and more, while contemporary documents furnish ample evidence for the practice of troops serving away from the colours.

Above: *The hill fort on Eildon Hill North. The ramparts of the fort are visible, while within the hut circles show up as 'pock marks'*

Below: *Burnswark Hill looking north. The ramparts of the hill fort are clearly visible. To the near side lies the south camp with the Antonine fortlet in the north-east corner*

3 Above: *The Gask Ridge looking west. The circular earthworks of the watch-tower at Gask House lies a few metres to the south of the road*
4 Below: *The fort at Ardoch looking south-east. The complicated ditch system to the east and north of the fort represents several periods of occupation*

5 Above: *Hadrian's Wall at Cawfields looking east. MC42, Cawfields, lies in the foreground, while the Wall snakes along the crags and the Vallum crosses the lower ground to the right*
6 Below: *The fort at Housesteads on Hadrian's Wall looking west. The headquarters building, commanding officer's house, granaries and, in the right foreground, fourth-century barracks, are all visible*

7 Above: *The Rudge Cup, probably made in the mid-second century, appears to be representation of the Wall with turrets. Presumably one of a pair, this contains the names of the seven western forts on the Wall:* A MAIS ABALLAVA UXELLODUM CAMBOGLANS BANNA

9 Right: *The Antonine Wall on Croy Hill looking east. In the foreground the rampart lies on the top of the crags and the ditch at the bottom. Further east an area of 'dead' ground lies in front of the Wall*

8 Below: *Two towers and two bonfires on Trajan's Column. There is a balcony at first-floor level on each tower, while a torch projects from a window. The towers seem to be of stone, the balcony and palisade of wood*

10 Below right: *The fort at Rough Castle on the Antonine Wall looking north. The Antonine Wall crosses diagonally and to the south two ditches defining the fort are visible. The annexe, with one south ditch and three east ditches, lies to the east*

11 Above: *A model of the Romano-British native farmstead at Riding Wood in Northumberland*

12 Below: *The fort at Chesterholm looking south with the civil settlement to the west: the military bathhouse lies in the right foreground*

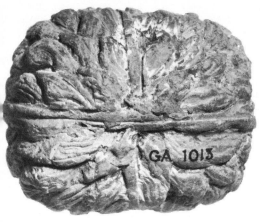

13 Above: *A terra cotta model of a bail of hides or fleeces found at Dun Fiadhairt, Skye. It is probably a votive offering made by a merchant from the Roman empire*

14 Right: *A glass jug, probably manufactured in the second century* AD *and found in a sandy hillock at Turiff in Aberdeenshire*

15 Right above: *This stone, found at Traprain Law, has inscribed on it the letters, A, B, C and part of D. It is possible that when complete the stone contained the whole alphabet*

16 Below: *Five objects from the late fourth–early fifth-century Traprain Treasure. The treasure was probably either booty, almost certainly from the continent, or part of a subsidy paid by Rome to the Votadini*

17 Above: *The Bridgeness Distance Slab recording the construction of about 4⅔ miles of the Antonine Wall by soldiers of legion II Augusta. To the left a Roman soldier rides down a group of four barbarians, while to the right a sacrifice is celebrated*

18 Above: *The Glamis Pictish symbol stone, dating to the seventh century. Inscribed on the stone are a serpent, fish and mirror, all common symbols: there is possibly a second fish at the top*

19 Right: *The Aberlemno churchyard cross, dating to the eighth century. The rear face has a Z-rod and disc at the top, while below is a scene including both cavalry and infantry, armed with spears and protected by helmets and round shields. There appear to be two groups of warriors, those on the right turning to flee: a dead warrior lies in the right-hand lower corner*

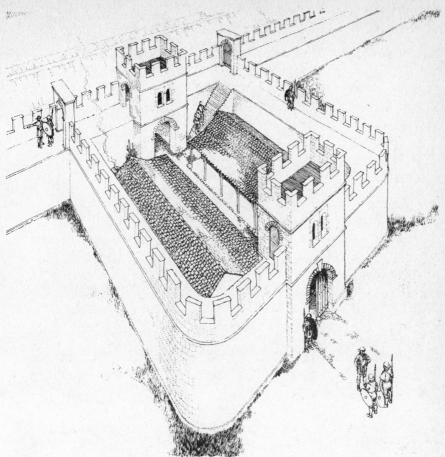

14 A stone milecastle on Hadrian's Wall, view from the south east. Reconstruction showing a barrack-block, storehouse, oven and steps. (Drawn by M. Moore)

The size of the garrison of the milecastles and turrets is another problem. The full complement of barrack-blocks is only known for six milecastles. In four cases the barrack was a small two-roomed block, while in the other two examples two blocks provided approximately four times as much accommodation. The smaller two-roomed unit was roughly equal in size to a double room in the barrack-block of a normal fort and may therefore have contained the same number of men, eight. The two larger milecastles may accordingly have provided accommodation for four times that number, 32 men.

There is no evidence to determine whether the soldiers on duty at the turrets normally lived there, or went out each day from the milecastles. The hearths within turrets, and the quantities of pottery found at all, point to the preparation of food, but not necessarily sleeping. The space available in a turret was not inconsiderable. The lower floor was little smaller in area than a small barrack-room and there was presumably an upper floor available in addition. If soldiers went out to the turrets from the milecastle each day, then the total garrison for the Wall line might have been about 650 men. If, as perhaps seems more likely, some soldiers lived at the

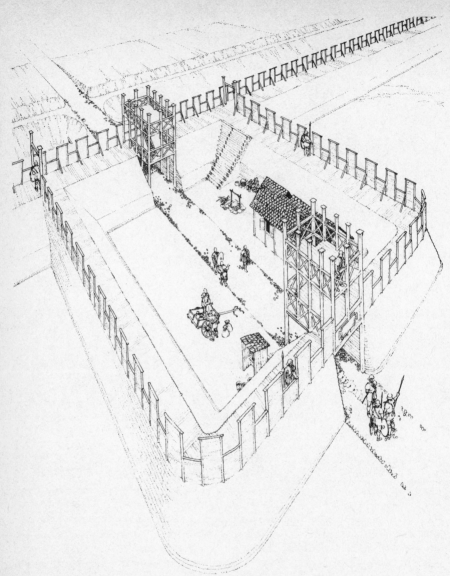

15 *A turf and timber milecastle on Hadrian's Wall, view from the south-east. Reconstruction of MC 50 TW. (Drawn by M. Moore)*

turrets then the strength of milecastle and turret garrisons combined might have been between 1700 and 1900.

It is possible to suggest the size of the garrison of the milecastles and turrets in a different way. It seems probable that each turret and each milecastle north tower will have required two soldiers on duty at any one time. The milecastle gates might be expected to have had an additional guard of two men. If the soldiers worked in eight-hour shifts then 24 men will have been required to man a milecastle and the turrets on either side, a total of nearly 2,000 men for the whole Wall line, which is close to the putative combined garrison of the milecastles and turrets based on the available accommodation. This figure seems more likely to be close to the correct total, for quartering both milecastle and turret guards at the milecastles each night might be thought to place intolerable burdens on the accommodation available there.

The planning – and construction – of the Wall, with its attendant milecastles and turrets, seems to have been accompanied by activity in the forts on the Stanegate. The fort at Corbridge was probably rebuilt at this time and its garrison changed, while one of the several pre-Wall phases at Chesterholm may be contemporary. To the east one of the two phases recognised on the aerial photographs of the unexcavated fort at Washing Well may date to these years. Beyond Carlisle both the newly discovered forts at Burgh-by-Sands and Fingland may be contemporary with this initial scheme for the Wall. It thus appears that work on the construction of the linear barrier was accompanied by the reorganisation of the army units immediately behind the Wall, presumably in order to allow these units to relate better to the changed frontier conditions.

The Cumbrian coast

Although the Wall stopped at Bowness the system of milecastles and turrets continued down the Cumbrian coast, though there they are termed milefortlets and towers. The spacing was the same, and also the materials of construction: stone for the towers, turf and timber for the milefortlets. It has been considered that milefortlets were only provided with one entrance, placed either front or rear, but recent work suggests that there may usually have been two. The system of milefortlets and towers has been traced for nearly 40km down the Cumbrian Coast to just beyond Maryport, by modern Workington. It is possible that it continued for a further 22km to St Bee's Head, which was a convenient stopping point, though no structures have been noted in this area. A further 32km on at Ravenglass a fortlet, of the same size as the milefortlets to the north, has been found under the later fort, and there is the possibility that another may lie 1.5km (a mile) to the south. This may suggest that the system, or at least part of it, continued for nearly 100km beyond the end of the Wall at Bowness, though at present the regular series of milefortlets and towers can only be traced as far south as Tower 26b.

The provision of the cordon so far along the coast may reflect concern at a threat from beyond the Solway. Certainly the Galloway coast looms very close, even at Maryport, 37km beyond Bowness, but there is no evidence that the tribes of this region were ever troublesome to Rome. It may well be that the Cumbrian Coast chain was simply a product of the rigid mind so clearly at work elsewhere on the Wall. The spacing of milecastles, and milefortlets, turrets and towers, with scant regard for topography, points to the planning of the frontier far away from the area through which it was built: the Cumbrian Coast may be no more than a reflection of this.

A word must be said about the latest discoveries on the more northerly sector of the Cumbrian Coast. Professor Barri Jones has located from the air parallel ditches in various places between Bowness and Silloth. The milefortlets and towers lie between the ditches, and although no obvious breaks for access can be seen on the aerial photograph, excavation has revealed that one milefortlet had both front and rear entrances thus allowing movement across the ditches. Ditch is the most obvious term to describe these features but in fact they are little more than trenches. Generally they are no more than 40cm wide and deep, and some appear to have held a thorn hedge. In some areas the trenches were recut, elsewhere the double line of trenches was replaced by a single palisade. This palisade consisted of twin stakes set about 40cm apart, presumably supporting a wattle fence. It has also been suggested that in an early phase in the sequence there may have been timber towers on the Cumbrian Coast, but the evidence for this consists of one platform of clay on the site of the later Tower 4b. The major difficulties in interpreting these recent discoveries lie in their incompleteness and in the fact that they have not yet been definitively published. It is to be hoped that Professor Jones' camera and pen will help to remedy both deficiencies.

The function of Hadrian's Wall

How was Hadrian's Wall to operate? The barrier certainly separated the barbarians from the Romans, in the phrase of Hadrian's biographer. The wall would hold up both small-scale raiding and major attacks, but would not prevent either: this could only be done by the army. Certainly raiding parties would now find it most difficult to operate with a barrier blocking their access to the peaceful, undefended settlements of the province, and, more importantly, hindering their swift return north. It may have been possible to enter the province quietly, but much more difficult to escape laden with booty, especially as that booty would have probably included flocks and herds. Thus the Wall will have aided the peaceful economic exploitation of the province to the south, protecting the inhabitants of the province, and their goods, from the tribes to the north who presumably still continued with their ancient and traditional warlike activities.

These activities occasionally erupted in full-scale warfare. The late second and the late fourth centuries were particularly disturbed times in the north when the tribes beyond the province gave the Roman army serious cause for concern. At such times the Wall would be – and was – largely irrelevant to both sides. It would be a hindrance to movement, but that was all. The tribal army would be a sizeable force no doubt able to overpower the smaller garrison present at whichever point on the Wall it chose to cross. The Roman army would be concerned to seek a successful conclusion to the invasion in the field, where the Romans knew they were predominant. To the Romans the Wall merely got in the way. Scouts would have maintained surveillance over the territory north of the Wall and, in the original plan, would have communicated with the units behind the Wall on the Stanegate. If warning of an attack was received the army units strung out in forts along the Stanegate and further south would assemble to attempt to intercept the enemy, reports presumably being sent back to York to inform the legionary commander of the local situation. The Wall would not aid such an army and it is instructive to note that no provision was made for the establishment of units on the Wall line at this time.

The very massiveness of Hadrian's Wall invites comparison with a medieval castle or town wall, but in reality the comparison is false. Medieval battles were generally between two forces roughly equally armed and from similar political and social backgrounds. The armies were capable of fighting set-piece battles and undertaking or sustaining sieges. The battles of Roman Britain, on the other hand, were not fought between equally armed or equally disciplined forces. Furthermore, one army was paid to fight while the other fought to defend its territory. In this unequal struggle might was on the side of the Romans. Indeed they had become so used to success that their army was not armed with defensive weapons such as

16 Hadrian's Wall, view from the east. Reconstruction showing a turret and, in the distance, a milecastle. (Drawn by M. Moore)

would be required during a siege. The Roman army was an offensive army, and would seek to decide the issue in the field and this was so much part of the military traditions and practice that it found itself at a disadvantage when besieged in its own camps or forts. In one famous siege the Roman soldiers were reduced to throwing turves at their attackers because they had not appropriate weapons to fight with. Although, according to the second-century writer Arrian and the fourth-century commentator Vegetius, Roman soldiers should be trained in the use of the bow there is no evidence that this was treated as a serious form of defence, while documentary and archaeological sources both imply that soldiers were not normally supplied with this weapon: generally bows and arrows were restricted to the specialist units of archers, such as the Hamians stationed at Carvoran in the second century nor was this deficiency rectified by the provision of alternative weapons such as spears. The normal issue for each soldier was two javelins and, so far as can be determined, no extra quantities were kept in case of siege.

The Wall itself was also a serious obstacle to its use as a fighting platform. The top must have been fairly narrow, perhaps 2–2.5m wide on the broad wall, but as little as 1.3m wide on the later narrow wall and about 1.3–1.6m wide on the turf wall. Access too was restricted, there being steps up to the Wall top only at milecastles and turrets one-third of a Roman mile apart. There was no provision for enfilading fire on the Wall, and none for artillery, which in any case was not usually available to auxiliary troops at this time.

All arguments combine to reinforce the conclusion that the Wall was not a fighting platform, merely a barrier to free movement, a means by which the army could control the movement of people across the frontier and channel it through certain guarded points.

The Wall, although probably not the actual boundary of the province for all or even part of its length, may well have become the customs boundary: it was after all the most convenient place for the examination of merchants and the exaction of tolls. Foreign trade, at least across the Eastern frontier, was charged a duty of $12\frac{1}{2}$ percent, which was relatively high in relation to the tolls of $2-2\frac{1}{2}$ percent levied on internal trade and collected at internal boundaries or towns. It was also strictly controlled, at least in the later Roman empire. In the east foreign trade was only allowed at a few licensed places. The export of certain articles, such as iron, bronze, arms and armour, was banned, no doubt for security reasons and customs officials were posted at these trading posts to control the trade and tax both incoming and outgoing goods. The taxing of imports and exports demonstrates that this was not a protective tariff, merely a means of raising revenue. The customs officers at the time of Hadrian were private individuals to whom the imperial government farmed the collection of taxes and over whom they maintained a close scrutiny. From the later second century, however, these *conductores* were replaced by a system of direct collection under imperial procurators.

Surviving documents demonstrate that customs officers had the right of search, and undeclared goods were forfeit. However, if they chose to search and found nothing the customs collector had to reimburse the merchant for the expense of unloading and provide written confirmation that all goods had been declared. Some tax officers exceeded their authority and an edict issued in the late second century ordered such unscrupulous officers to desist from demanding extra charges and from blackmailing merchants into paying for quicker treatment.

It may be presumed that the movement of people across Hadrian's Wall would be governed by regulations such as have been discussed in relationship to the Gask frontier. Access was only allowed at certain points, meeting places were stipulated, traders had to be unarmed but were nevertheless guarded, and finally these relations were taxed. It is possible that members of any client state which might have existed to the north might have had the regulations relaxed for them, as they were relaxed for the Hermanduri. Finally, it may be noted that there may have been two types of officials involved, the tax collectors and the army – though this is not certain, for soldiers in some parts of the empire acted as customs officers, collecting tolls on the frontier. Later, in the late second and third centuries, special army officers, *beneficiarii consularis* appear in the north of England. Elsewhere in the empire these were appointed to special frontier stations where they served as customs officials, frontier guards, intelligence agents and police officials. These soldiers are attested at Housesteads, Chesterholm and Risingham and in the hinterland at Lanchester, Binchester, Greta Bridge, Catterick and Lancaster. Although none are attested as early as Hadrian's reign, it is possible that their predecessors had some responsibility for customs and frontier control on the Wall.

It is not clear how and where the frontier regulations were enforced. There were two types of gates through the Wall, the regularly spaced milecastle gateways and those at roads. Only two of the latter may be presumed. Nothing is known of the gate by Stanwix where the road led north to Netherby, Birrens and beyond, but on Dere Street a special gate has been found on the top of Stagshaw Bank at the Portgate, though only its mere existence has been attested by archaeology: other special gates may have existed. It seems probable that these gates may have been customs stations where taxes were levied on goods in transit and *bona fide* travellers allowed into the province. Whether soldiers then escorted such travellers to villages, such as those which sprang up outside forts, or at Corbridge or Carlisle, is a matter for speculation.

The milecastle gateway can be seen in another light. While each milecastle on the Wall was provided with a gate through the barrier the provision of milefortlets down the Cumbrian Coast demonstrates that the guarding of such gates was only part of their function. Milecastles were probably more important as bases for the surveillance garrison of the Wall, with the gate provided almost as a matter of chance. In view of the regulations operating on other frontiers it seems probable that if travellers did try to cross the Wall at a milecastle they would be escorted to a customs post. The major restriction on the use of the milecastle gateways would appear to be the lack of a causeway across the ditch in front of the gate. While this might have been of little consequence for civilian traffic, it would have been a serious matter for the army for whose use, it might otherwise have been argued, the gates were provided. Clearly much has yet to be learnt about the function of the milecastles.

The building of the Wall

Inscriptions demonstrate that the Wall was constructed by soldiers from the three legions of Britain: *II Augusta* from Caerleon in South Wales, *XX Valeria Victrix* from Chester and *VI Victrix*, newly arrived in Britain from Lower Germany and the new occupant of the legionary fortress at York. There is no evidence that native levies played any part in the building operations, though it is possible that they helped with the fetching and carrying.

Constructional differences in the milecastles, turrets and curtain wall suggest that three different groups took part in the building operations and inscriptions confirm that these groups can be identified with the legions: differences have been noted between the milefortlets and the towers on the Cumbrian Coast but it is not possible to relate these to legions.

On both the stone and turf walls there are areas where only one particular type of milecastle, turret and wall base is found, with no other type intervening. In these sectors it is reasonable to assume that one legion was responsible for the discrete block of work which contains only these types. It appears that inscriptions, recording the name of the emperor, legionary builder and occasionally governor, were erected over both the north and south gates of the milecastles. Only one inscription survives from the turf wall for these were of timber, but four inscriptions from three milecastles on the stone wall firmly establish the type of milecastle built by *legio II Augusta*, and by extension its type of turret and curtain wall. There is still an element of doubt concerning the attribution of the other milecastle, turret and curtain types to the other two legions. The recent discovery of an inscription at T 33b Coesike suggests that the traditional allocation of milecastle, turret and curtain types to legions *VI* and *XX* should be reversed. Be that as it may, the evidence accumulated to date allows a picture to be built up of the order and progress of work on the Wall.

It is clear that building on the stone wall started at the east: there is no evidence for the turf wall. On both stone and turf sectors the constructional work was divided into lengths of 5–6 Roman miles (8–9.6km), each the responsibility of a single legion. Within that block the milecastles and turrets were generally constructed first, with work probably proceeding on the foundations of the wall at the same time. One legion at least also commenced the construction of the curtain wall before it had completed all the milecastles and turrets in its sector. Where bridges fell within a block of work priority appears to have been allotted to these as well as to the milecastles and turrets. The relationship of the excavation of the ditch to these operations is not known: apart from where solid rock approached close to the surface this was a straightforward operation and presumably could be completed quicker than the building work. The speed of work on the stone and turf walls and the attendant structures would have varied considerably in relation to the proximity of supplies of turf, stone, limestone for mortar, timber and water as well as the nature of the terrain. The discovery of military building inscriptions – centurial stones – on the stone curtain implies that an attempt was made to supervise the work and ensure that standards were kept broadly similar. Each legion marked the end of its length of wall with an inscription, and within that each cohort marked both ends of its allocation and finally each century similarly denoted its workload. In some areas these centurial stones have been found in sufficient number to suggest that the length of the stretch allotted to each century was about 40m. The stones were generally placed on the south side of the wall, but some have been found on the north face.

The figures of 5–6 Roman miles for the length of a legionary block can be recognised on both the turf and stone walls. The turf wall divides neatly into six such lengths, presumably representing two three-legion blocks, though only one such legionary block can be identified as a result of excavation. On the stone wall, about which much more is known, the situation is more complicated. There is a short length of 3 Roman miles (5km) at the east end which does not appear to fit into any pattern, then follows a 15-mile (24km) sector divided into three legionary lengths. Thereafter, however, the legions seem to have been split, one legion continuing working westwards towards the North Tyne, while the other two moved further west and commenced building in the 20km running eastwards from the Irthing leaving a 14km gap to be completed later. These sectors, and probably some of the previous allocation, were not completed to the original specifications for before the work was finished the wall was reduced in thickness from its original 10 Roman feet (3m) to either 8 or 6 Roman feet (2.35 and 1.80m). This decision appears to have followed another, the transfer of many troops from constructing the wall to building new forts. It was presumably in order to speed the work of the remaining gangs that the wall was narrowed. When this order was given all the milecastles between the North Tyne and the Irthing had been erected, at least so far as can be determined, and most of the turrets, but work on the curtain was not so well advanced: in fact on the crags the foundation of the wall was not laid in many areas, partly owing to the difficulties of transporting water, stone and mortar in this hill country, partly because it was not everywhere necessary as the bedrock was so close to the surface.

In the meantime most of the soldiers hitherto working on the wall had started to implement a major policy change which had far-reaching consequences. Previously there had been no forts on the Wall itself, but it was now decided to abandon those behind the Wall on the Stanegate and construct new forts on the line of the Wall itself. This decision was not undertaken lightly, for it involved the abandonment of at least eight forts, the demolition of several turrets, one milecastle and several yards of curtain, the infilling of lengths of the Wall ditch, and the construction of 12 new forts (pl. 6). The decision to move the forts up onto the Wall, presumably grew out of the realisation that once the Wall was constructed it would create a barrier to the free movement of the army. In order to get to grips with an enemy north of the Wall the army would have had to move up from their forts on the Stanegate and pass through small milecastle gateways. A desire to deal with this problem would appear to have lain behind the construction of the new forts astride the Wall, wherever the terrain allowed, even though in some instances this resulted in the demolition of more curtain and the infilling of more ditch than would otherwise have been necessary. The forts were constructed with a third of their area and three of their four gates north of the Wall (fig. 18). Communication with the province to the south was improved by the unique addition of two side gates, at either end of the *via quintana*. The result of this unparalleled arrangement was that the equivalent of six single-portal milecastle gateways now lay in the northern part of the fort, north of the Wall, while four portals opened to the south. Thus movement was considerably facilitated.

The position of the forts astride the Wall emphasises the nature of the problem that the army authorities were trying to combat. There were three possible positions for forts in relation to the linear barrier: behind, in front or on the Wall line. Patently the position of forts behind the Wall was unsatisfactory. Presumably forts in front of the Wall would have suffered in a similar way, for the Wall would again have got in the way of the free movement of the army; while in the event of a serious attack the divorce of an army unit from colleagues to the south by the Wall itself might have been embarrassing. As a result the solution adopted was to place the forts astride the barrier, thus enabling troops stationed in each enclosure the freest possible movement both north and south. There is no reason to assume that this major change was brought about as a result of native opposition to the construction of the Wall. It would have been obvious to the Roman commanders that the River Tyne and the Irthing Gorge, lying between the forts and the new Wall, would have been a serious hindrance to communication: it may be no coincidence that the earliest forts to be built on the Wall were apparently Benwell and Halton Chesters in the east, precisely those whose predecessors would have experienced the most difficulty of communication with the Wall. Without a Wall the Stanegate was a sensible enough line for the frontier troops, but as soon as the Wall was built it became a nonsense to leave the troops there.

The new forts, with one probable exception, were each designed for a single auxiliary unit (fig. 17). In view of the rigidity of planning displayed on Hadrian's Wall, this is not surprising, but it was a relatively new concept at the time. Up to the end of the first century many forts were built either for detachments or for composite garrisons. The forts on Hadrian's Wall may have been the first group of forts to be built for one single, complete auxiliary unit. They were also perhaps the last for most of the forts on the Antonine Wall were designed for detachments not whole units. The average distance between each of the new forts was about 11.5km, that is about half a normal day's march. The distances varied a little for account was taken of the major rivers on the Wall line when positioning the forts. Chesters, for example, was moved a little to the east so that it lay beside the North Tyne, while Stanwix was moved about 1.5km to the west so that it could lie beside

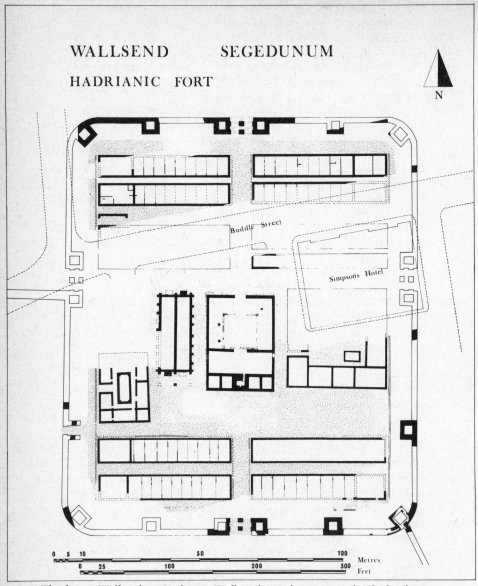

WALLSEND   SEGEDUNUM

HADRIANIC FORT

N

Buddle Street

Simpsons Hotel

0	5	10		50		100	

0   25   100   200   300   Feet

Metres

17 *The fort at Wallsend on Hadrian's Wall in the Hadrianic period. The headquarters in the centre is flanked, left by a granary and hospital, right by the commanding officer's house. To the north and south lie barrack-blocks and ?stables. (Drawn by C.M. Daniels)*

Carlisle and the main road north. It was also decided at this time to extend the Wall 4 Roman miles down the Tyne to Wallsend where the most easterly fort on the Wall was now built.

The new forts, in their materials of construction, closely followed the Wall. On the stone wall the fort walls and apparently all the principal building were of stone.

The barrack-blocks, stables and storehouses, however, appear in most cases to have been completely of timber or at least timber on stone sill walls. On the turf wall all the forts seem to have been constructed with turf ramparts and timber buildings, with the exception of Birdoswald, at the eastern end of the turf wall, which was constructed of stone.

The forts on the Wall were strengthened by the addition of new forts on the flanks, built, or at least planned, now. In the east lay South Shields at the mouth of the Tyne, but on the southern side of the estuary. In the west two forts appear to have been added to the Cumbrian Coast at Beckfoot and at Moresby, while further south Ravenglass was built later in Hadrian's reign and may have been planned at this time; the fort at Maryport appears to have been built at an earlier date, though still within Hadrian's reign.

Inscriptions demonstrate that both legions VI and XX took part, no doubt over several years, in the construction of these forts, while the similarity between the masonry in the *legio II* milecastle gateways and certain fort gateways suggests that this legion was also involved in this task. As in the milecastles and turrets there was a certain amount of standardisation in fort planning. Four forts, for example, were 177m long or wide, Benwell, Chesters, Birdoswald and Stanwix, while the opposing measurement at Stanwix, 213m, is close to the length of Bowness on Solway, 216m. It is interesting to note, too that the only five Hadrianic bath-houses known on the frontier – Benwell, Chesters, Carrawburgh, Netherby and Bewcastle – were clearly all built to the same blue-print even though the forts to which they were attached fall into three different groups: Benwell and Chesters were primary forts, Carrawburgh secondary, while the other two were outpost forts.

The new forts on the Wall, and possibly also on the Cumbrian Coast, took the place of existing forts to the rear yet the units in the Stanegate forts were not apparently moved up into the nearest fort on the Wall. Certainly the *cohors milliaria equitata* which abandoned Corbridge did not move to Halton Chesters 5km up Dere Street. It seems probable that the disposition of forces on the Wall line was carefully planned. The senior officer on the Wall was stationed at Stanwix for here was placed the senior auxiliary unit in the provincial army, the *ala milliaria*. There were only 10–11 of these units in the empire and never more than one in each province. The commanding officer was in the final stage of his career in the auxilia and would expect to pass on to other commands, notably procuratorships, including the governorship of minor provinces. But his rank did not accord him any special position, any authority over his colleagues commanding other units on the Wall: the nearest officer with authority over the auxiliary commanding officers was the legionary legate at York. The *ala milliaria* was presumably placed at Stanwix because of the central position of this fort and because it lay beside one of the two major roads north: there is no need to assume that there was a special threat to the province from the west which led to the placing of the unit here.

Only one other cavalry unit is definitely known to have been stationed on the Wall, the *ala Augusta ob virtutem appellata*, the unit named *Augusta* for valour, at Chesters by the North Tyne, though the plan of the fort at Benwell suggests that a cavalry unit may also have been stationed there. Most of the units on the Wall seem to have been either infantry or the mixed infantry and cavalry type. It may not be coincidental that the infantry units all appear to have been placed in the centre of the Wall in the forts furthest from the roads north and facing inhospitable country.

The additional units required to garrison the extra four forts on the isthmus, and also the three outpost forts, appear to have been drawn from the Pennines and Wales where archaeological evidence suggests that a number of sites were abandoned at this time.

The construction of the forts did not proceed without change. Although most of the forts were constructed astride the wall, some were not. These include Greatchesters, among the last of the forts to be constructed, and Carrawburgh, an addition to the Wall. It seems that, once the forts were on the Wall line, it was realised that it was not necessary for them to project to the north. Thus in addition to this modification the gates at some forts seem to have early fallen into disuse, as if there was overprovision of entrances. Finally, it may be noted that none of the forts on the Antonine Wall were built astride the rampart.

One fort, it should be noted, does not fall into the neat categories discussed above. Asymmetrically between Burgh-by-Sands and Bowness-on-Solway a small fort was placed on a convenient knoll at Drumburgh. The original fort was of turf and timber and was incapable of holding a complete unit. The relationship of the fort to the turf wall is not known, though they are probably broadly contemporary, and both were replaced in stone later. It seems probable that the difficult terrain of the Solway estuary had here compelled a different arrangement of the forts.

The placing of the forts on the Wall itself confused and muddled two distinct functions – that of the control of movement across the frontier and the protection of the province from attack. That distinction had been clear in the earlier plan for the Wall, but it was now no longer so obvious.

One further addition to the Wall remains to be considered, the Vallum. This earthwork extends along the whole length of the Wall from Bowness to Newcastle, with the exception of the short extension to Wallsend (pl. 5). It consists of a ditch with a mound set back on either side. The Vallum is essentially incorrectly titled for the main feature is the ditch, the *fossa*, not the mounds, the *valla*, but it was so named by the Venerable Bede over a 1,000 years ago and the name has been retained, hallowed by tradition. The Vallum, 120 Roman feet (35m) across, offered no advantage to either side, but it served to mark the rear of the military zone which was now clearly defined by the ditch to the north and the Vallum to the south: it was the Roman equivalent of barbed wire. The importance of the Vallum is emphasised by the care taken to ensure that its ditch was completed, unlike the Wall ditch. Thus at Limestone Corner the Vallum ditch was dug through solid rock and finished while the gangs digging the Wall ditch failed in their appointed task.

Passage through the Vallum was only possible at a fort or presumably where one of the two main roads to the north crossed the Wall. The Vallum often diverged from its straight line to avoid a fort, and here gaps were left through the mounds and a causeway provided over the ditch. The causeway was protected by a gate, closed from the north. Civil settlement in the area between the Vallum and the Wall was forbidden and when civilians came to build their houses outside forts these had to be constructed south of the Vallum. At Housesteads, where there is the only known Hadrianic civil settlement on the Wall, the buildings were erected well beyond the Vallum on a low hill some 200m south of the fort. The effect of the Vallum was to reduce the ease with which the Wall could be crossed. Hitherto it had been necessary to walk no more than half a Roman mile in order to cross the Wall, but it was now necessary to walk up to 4 miles (7km) in order to gain passage through the Wall.

It seems probable that the construction of the Vallum was designed to increase Roman control over the movement of people across the frontier. The regulations

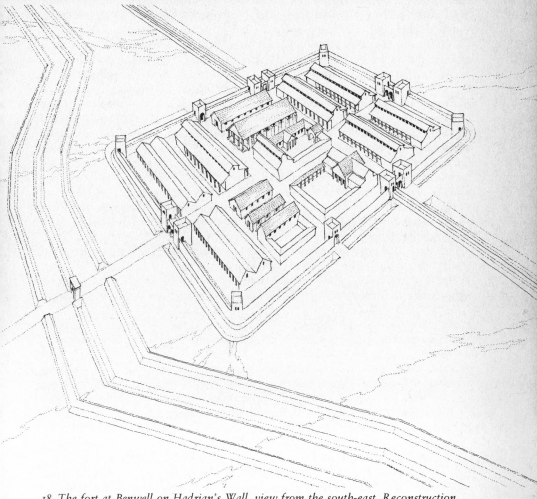

18 *The fort at Benwell on Hadrian's Wall, view from the south-east. Reconstruction showing the fort, stone wall, ditch and glacis, Vallum and the crossing south of the fort. (Drawn by M. Moore)*

had, up until now, presumably been enforced by the soldiers in the milecastles, but now they were to be enforced by the officers at the forts: possibly it was felt that the soldiers had been – or were likely to be – too slack in carrying out their duties. It has been suggested that the Vallum demonstrated that the local inhabitants of the area had showed their opposition to the construction of the Wall, possibly because it cut across their traditional pasturage routes. The construction of the Wall will obviously have affected the free movement of people, possibly affected their farming practices, but there is only one instance where the Wall appears to have had a visual impact on the local inhabitants of the Wall. Between the Wall and the

Vallum at Milking Gap, 3.5km west of Housesteads, a farm or settlement of five huts appears to have been swept away by the army because it lay within the military zone. But there is no evidence that there was any military opposition to the construction of the Wall or any attacks on the army during building operations. It seems possible that the Vallum was merely an attempt to increase the bureaucratic control of the army over the passage of civilians across the frontier.

One feature not constructed on Hadrian's Wall was a road to link the forts. Hitherto the Stanegate had formed the line of communication between the forts across the isthmus from Corbridge to Carlisle, where the two main roads led north. After the forts moved up onto the Wall the disadvantage of not having a road along the Wall line may not have become immediately obvious. Light road-metalling has been discovered on the south berm of the Vallum at three places and in one place on the north berm. Thus it seems possible that the Vallum was used as a line of communication. But there were hindrances to this. The only gaps in the south mound of the Vallum and causeways across the ditch, with the exception of one certain and a second possible example, were at forts. There were, on the other hand, apparently original gaps in the north mound of the Vallum. Thus the way would be open for traffic to cross the Vallum ditch at a fort and proceed along the north berm to a milecastle where access was possible through a gap in the north mound.

Hadrian's Wall took many years to build. It seems probable that it started during or soon after Hadrian's visit to Britain in 122. In that year, in July, a new governor Aulus Platorius Nepos, arrived in the island. He came from Lower Germany, and it seems probable that he accompanied the emperor, who also came to Britain from there. A third arrival from that province was *legio VI Victrix*. The date of the arrival of the legion is not known, but it certainly had arrived before the close of Nepos' governorship and it is tempting to assume that it came with the governor – and the emperor. If that was the case it is possible that Hadrian had already decided to build a Wall in Britain before he arrived, presumably in the wake of a similar decision in Upper Germany. However, it is equally possible that he only took the decision after seeing for himself the position of the northern frontier in Britain and then sent for the legion, and perhaps also the governor.

Aulus Platorius Nepos was an old friend of Hadrian, though they were later to fall out, and it seems probable that he was specially chosen by the emperor to carry out this undertaking. Since military glory was not possible under Hadrian, Nepos was being allowed the nearest equivalent: only his name appears on building stones in addition to Hadrian's. Before building work commenced the line to be taken by the Wall would have to be surveyed, troops informed and marshalled and a start made collecting materials. New bridges were required, across the Tyne at Newcastle, where the bridge was named Pons Aelius in honour of the emperor, across the North Tyne at Chesters, and over the Irthing at Birdoswald. It would be logical to commence the construction of these first, in order to aid communication, and there is some evidence to suggest that the bridge at Newcastle came early in the building sequence.

It is not known how long it was expected the Wall would take to construct. The division of work into legionary blocks might suggest that each block was planned to take a year to complete. In this case the original estimate was three years. However, the addition of the forts, and to a lesser extent the Vallum, will have lengthened the programme considerably.

It seems probable that originally the legions were divided into gangs working simultaneously on the stone and turf walls and possibly also on the Cumbrian Coast. Once soldiers were taken off the construction of the Wall itself in order to build forts, work must have proceeded in an apparently haphazard fashion to anyone trying to follow the proceedings. The construction of the Wall in the crags sector had already been held up by the difficulties of the terrain. Now there were many milecastles and turrets unconnected by the curtain wall, short lengths of curtain completed, possibly to full height, longer lengths of foundation, all being linked together slowly by one legion, while other soldiers built forts and yet more dug the Vallum. Work on the Vallum in some areas proceeded quicker than the erection of the Wall and it seems that in the area of Carrawburgh the Vallum was dug before the Wall, planned years earlier, was built.

Other changes took place during the building operations. Greatchesters was built wholly behind the Wall, unlike most other forts, but it is possible that when this decision was taken work had already commenced on the site for the fort sits uncomfortably within its ditches. Further, when the curtain was constructed in that area the new builders ignored the foundation which had already been laid and placed their wall in front of the overgrown remains. Twenty-three kilometres to the east a new fort was added at Carrawburgh, which necessitated the obliteration of the Vallum dug shortly before. Modifications continued to be made to the Wall throughout Hadrian's reign. The fort at Carvoran had been specifically excluded from the Wall zone by the construction of the Vallum which diverged to the north to avoid the fort, which was therefore presumably abandoned, or at least intended to be abandoned. In 136 or 137 work was proceeding on the building or rebuilding of Carvoran in stone. It is not clear whether the intention was to rebuild the whole of the turf wall, but by the time Hadrian died only the eastern 8 km had been replaced.

Hadrian's Wall must have caused its designers some headaches. The rigidity in the spacing of milecastles and turrets in the original scheme suggests that the Wall was not planned by someone locally. It suggests a designer working at some distance from the north of England, possibly the governor in London, perhaps even the emperor. The forts showed more concern for the terrain and topography, but even they were regularly spaced. Nevertheless many aspects of Hadrian's Wall reveal flexibility in the minds of the planners and builders. In the first place the Wall was unique. Not only had no such frontier ever been built before in the Roman empire, but its only predecessor, the Upper German frontier, was itself almost certainly still being built when Hadrian's Wall was being planned. Furthermore Hadrian's Wall bore little resemblance to the German frontier. That barrier was of timber, not stone or even turf and did not have the same provision of fortlets, or, it would appear, the same rigidity of planning. Once building was well advanced two other unique elements were introduced, the position of the forts astride the Wall, and the Vallum. And then, when it was discovered that it was not necessary to place the forts astride the Wall once they were on the frontier itself, the positions of the later forts were modified and they were built attached to the rear of the barrier. All these changes, several of them unique experiments in an attempt to deal with a unique situation, more than many others during the long life of the empire, demonstrate in a tangible form the flexibility of the Romans, the flexibility even of the military mind. It is unfortunate that more is not known of the response of the locals to the construction of this monumental frontier.

The construction of Hadrian's Wall appears to cut off contact between provincial and barbarian, but that was not necessarily the case. The purpose of the

Wall was to regulate such contact, not prevent it. Few artefacts of the first forty years of the second century have been found north of the Wall, and what finds there have been could equally well have been lost in the middle rather than the early years of the century. That, however, is not to say that there was no contact either between civilian or between soldier and civilian. The construction of the Wall would not automatically have resulted in the loss of interest by the army in the events to the north. Army units would no doubt continue to patrol the lands to the north. It is possible that relations with the tribes of the Scottish Lowlands were governed by treaty, as was the case on other frontiers. Certainly it is to be expected that the Votadini would have been party to a treaty with Rome: there is no definable break in the flow of Roman goods to their capital on Traprain Law in these years. However, as always the activities and attitudes of the barbarians remain obscure.

6

The Antonine Wall

The move north

The Emperor Hadrian died on 10 July 138. By the following year Britain had a new
governor, Quintus Lollius Urbicus, and the building projects initiated by this
governor in that year demonstrate unequivocally that a new policy for the northern
British frontier had been promulgated. An inscription from Corbridge recording
the construction of a granary in 139 is the first indication of this new policy, which
is recorded in the *Life of Antoninus Pius*, Hadrian's successor: 'for he conquered the
Britons through the governor Lollius Urbicus and after driving back the barbarians
built a new wall of turf'. The activity of Urbicus is recorded not just at Corbridge,
but at High Rochester in Northumberland and at Balmuildy on the Antonine Wall.
There is no doubt what was initiated at this time, but the reasons are another
matter.

There are two schools of thought on the reason for the abandonment of
Hadrian's Wall and the construction of a new Wall, the Antonine Wall: they might
be termed the insular and the empire solutions. The first emphasises that trouble on
the northern frontier led to a reappraisal of the Roman position, while the second
suggests that the advance in Britain was merely a political move, a foreign
adventure, by an emperor who needed to strengthen his position in Rome.

The phrase 'drive back the barbarians' in the passage in the biography of
Antoninus Pius certainly seems to imply that forcible action was necessary on the
part of Lollius Urbicus and this receives some support from an enigmatic aside by
Pausanias in his *Description of Greece:* 'Antoninus deprived the Brigantes in Britain
of most of their territory because they too had taken up arms and invaded the
Genunian district, the people of which are subject to Rome'. This passage as it
stands makes little sense. The Brigantes were already within the province and could
therefore hardly be deprived of their lands, while the Genunian district is not
known. Various interpretations of the passage have been offered: 'Brigantes'
simply means Britons rather in the same way that English is used as a synonym for
British; the Brigantes were those members of the tribe in modern Dumfriesshire left
outside the province by the construction of the Wall; Genunia is a corruption of
Novantae, the tribe of Dumfries and Galloway; Pausanias, perhaps relying on
memory, transferred to Britain events which really happened in Raetia (modern
Bavaria) where a tribe of similar name, Brigantii, and the Genauni, are attested. In
view of the uncertainty surrounding this passage it is hardly possible to use it to
support the theory that warfare on the northern frontier caused Antoninus Pius to
move the frontier forward 160km: the trouble, if it had existed, could have been
dealt with more straightforwardly by military intervention.

It has also been suggested that although Hadrian's Wall was a tactical success it
was a strategic failure because it was built in the wrong position: on the Tyne-
Solway isthmus it was out of contact with the main centres of opposition to Rome,
the tribes of the Highlands of Scotland. It is certainly true that there is no evidence

that the Lowland tribes ever gave the Romans any serious cause for concern. Opposition to Rome, in the first century, the late second and early third centuries and in the fourth century, always came from the Highland tribes. But there is no evidence that these tribes were creating a disturbance on the northern frontier in the early years of the Emperor Antoninus Pius, or the last years of the reign of his predecessor. If they had, it might be expected that such warfare would be mentioned in the biography of Antoninus Pius, in the spirit of the justification of military action prevalent at the time. As it is, Pius' biographer contents himself with a colourless reference to driving back the barbarians, which may be no more than a literary allusion to Tacitus' comment in the *Agricola* that after the construction of a chain of garrisons across the Forth-Clyde isthmus the enemy had been pushed, as it were, into another island. The passage may have been intended to mean simply that: the construction of the new Wall had pushed back the boundaries of barbary. Unlike the references in the *Lives* of Hadrian and Marcus Aurelius to serious disturbances in Britain at the beginning of their reigns, the biographer of Antoninus Pius is curiously reticent about the events, real or otherwise, in the late 130s. It may be fair to conclude that there was no warfare on the north British frontier at this time that required military intervention by Rome and the construction of a new frontier.

The alternative explanation for the advance into Scotland in the early 140s rests on an appreciation of power politics in Rome. Antoninus Pius was not Hadrian's first choice as successor. The old emperor had no children but both his sister and his sister-in-law had descendants. However, while seriously ill in 136 Hadrian had become suspicious of his sister's husband, the 90-year-old L. Julius Servianus, and his grandson, Cnaeus Pedanius Fuscus Salinator, and, although he had already hinted that Servianus might succeed him, on his recovery he forced both to commit suicide. Hadrian now chose as his successor L. Ceionius Commodus, who took the names L. Aelius Caesar. The reason for the choice is unclear, but it is possible that Commodus was chosen as a placeholder until his real successor Marcus Aurelius, then only 15, was old enough to reign: Marcus was the grandson of Hadrian's wife's half-sister, Rupilia Faustina. However, Hadrian's careful plans were upset by the death of Commodus on 1 January 138. Two months later Hadrian named his new successor, T. Aurelius Antoninus, the maternal uncle of Marcus Aurelius. Less than five months later Hadrian was dead and Antoninus succeeded him without opposition.

The new emperor had played a small part in public service, sufficient only to fulfil his honourable obligations to the state, but he had never served in the army and had only held one appointment outside Italy, the proconsulship of Asia, probably in 134–35. This was the only time he had ventured out of Italy. His qualifications for office seem to have been that he was an honourable man, without ambition, and a close relative of Marcus. However, Marcus had other relatives, in particular L. Catilius Severus his step-grandfather and prefect of Rome in 138 until removed from office by Hadrian, apparently when he allowed his ambition to show. Severus had been one of Trajan's marshals, indeed the only governor of the short-lived province of Armenia abandoned by Hadrian in 117. He had considerable experience of civilian and military affairs and was also, having held the consulship twice, senior in status to Antoninus.

Although Antoninus' succession was peaceful there were therefore tensions beneath the surface. The new emperor had been designated Caesar less than five months before, apparently mainly because of his relationship to the young Marcus

Aurelius, while another relative of this young man had revealed his ambition for the purple. The adoption of Antoninus in February 138 had caused ill-feeling, according to contemporary sources, and no doubt many in the leading circles of government felt they had an equal claim to be emperor. Finally, Antoninus was the nominee of a man cordially disliked by the senatorial aristocracy. In those early months he may well have cast round for a means of strengthening his position. The most straightforward way to gain popularity, and the support of the army, was through a successful military venture. Tacitus remarks how important military prestige was to an emperor and it worth noting that from Augustus to Septimius Severus no emperor, apart from during the civil wars of 68/9 and 193, was removed by the army. Britain may well have seemed a good place to gain military prestige, as Claudius had realised almost 100 years before. Any military expedition there could be limited by geography, and also no doubt presented as a reclamation of former provincial territory. At the same time it was so far away that the successful general would not be in a position to get too ambitious himself.

There are two aspects of the war which lend support to this interpretation. Firstly, this was the only war for which Antoninus Pius accepted the imperial acclamation. During his reign there was a serious revolt in Mauretania in the 140s, while at the beginning of the reign a disturbance in Dacia led to the appointment of a special commanding officer. Later the frontier in Upper Germany and Raetia was advanced a short distance. Yet Pius accepted no salutation for the successful conclusion of these wars, most notably for the advance in Germany. This would suggest that the British war held a particular significance in his eyes. The second point concerns Fronto again. The orator wrote that 'although the emperor committed the conduct of the operations to others while remaining in the Palace at Rome, yet like the helmsman at the tiller of a warship, the glory of the whole navigation and voyage belongs to him'. While this passage is no doubt largely flattery it again appears to emphasise the close relationship between the emperor and the British war.

While the reason for the advance north in Britain is uncertain we do not move onto much firmer ground in discussing the events themselves. Building work commenced at Corbridge in 139, so it would appear that Antoninus decided on his new policy within months of his accession. Pius accepted his imperial salutation in 142 and in that year or early in the following a new coin issue commemorated the victory. Building work in Scotland commenced under Lollius Urbicus, but as his name does not appear on most of the building inscriptions from the Antonine Wall it seems probable that the bulk of the construction work was carried out under his successor.

Nothing is known of the fighting itself, but it is unlikely that the tribes which had given Agricola no trouble sixty years before, and which had presumably been under surveillance since then, would provide serious cause for concern to the Roman army at this time. In fact it seems possible that the Roman 'invasion' was little more than a formality. Preparations will have taken some time. They included the rebuilding of the fort at Corbridge which was required now that Dere Street would be utilised as one of the two main routes into Scotland. In addition to the reconstruction of this and other forts supplies would need to be gathered. This activity, if carried out thoroughly might take at least a season to complete: certainly building was going on at Corbridge in 139 and 140. In that case the army may not have moved until 141 to complete the re-occupation of the land up to the Tay in a single season, prior to Antoninus' acceptance of the title of Imperator in 142.

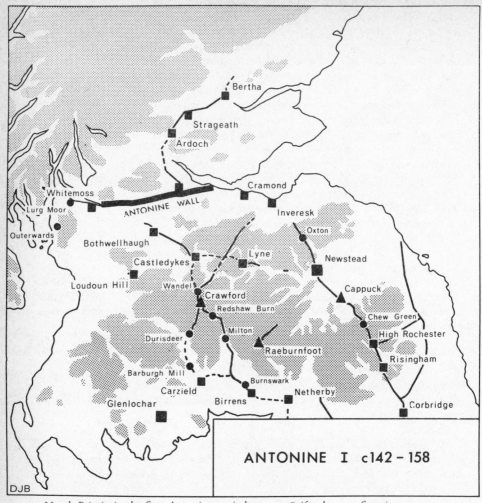

19 North Britain in the first Antonine period, c.142–58 (for key see fig. 4)

Once the tribes had been formally incorporated into the empire the army turned to the task of controlling and protecting them (fig. 19). The Lowlands of Scotland were covered by a network of forts and fortlets connected by roads: a milestone from Ingliston near Cramond, dated to between 139 and 144, was presumably erected when the road thereabouts was repaired. Many of the forts were placed on or near their Agricolan predecessors. The pattern of forts was in fact very similar to that of sixty years before, though generally the garrisons were rather smaller. There was, however, one distinctive difference. Much greater use was made in the second century of the fortlet. Such sites cluster especially thickly in the valleys of south-west Scotland, Annandale, Nithsdale and Clydesdale. Eight or nine of these fortlets are known, each capable of holding a garrison of between 40 and 80 men. The most

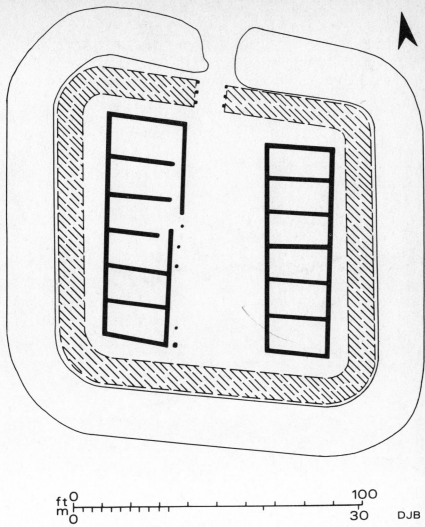

ft 0   100
m 0   30   DJB

20 *The fortlet at Barburgh Mill in Dumfriesshire*

extensively excavated site at Barburgh Mill in the Nith valley contained two timber barrack-blocks suitable for an infantry century 80 strong (fig. 20). In between certain of these fortlets have been found timber watch-towers or signal-stations presumably forming links in the communications between forts and fortlets.

The organisation of the Scottish Lowlands was carefully planned. The garrisons of the fortlets were outposted from certain forts where no provision was made for their accommodation. It would thus appear that these detachments were expected to remain permanently outposted, though the individual soldiers might interchange. Elsewhere complete units might be kept together. Carzield in the lower Nith valley, for example, appears to have been garrisoned by an *ala* which had no men outstationed.

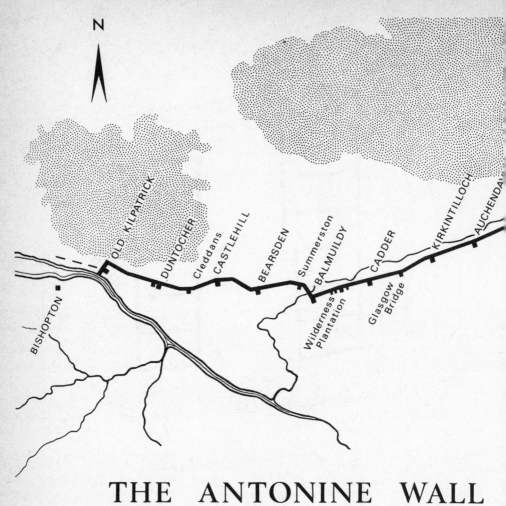

N

BISHOPTON

OLD KILPATRICK

DUNTOCHER

Cleddans

CASTLEHILL

BEARSDEN

Summerston

BALMUILDY

Wilderness Plantation

Glasgow Bridge

CADDER

KIRKINTILLOCH

AUCHENDA

THE ANTONINE WALL

21 The Antonine Wall (land over 180m is stippled)

The Antonine Wall

To the north of these forts lay the Antonine Wall. This new Wall was exactly half the length of its predecessor, 40 Roman miles. It ran from modern Bo'ness on the Forth to Old Kilpatrick on the Clyde, ending beside the Erskine Bridge. For the first 6–8km from the east the Wall ran along the raised beach overlooking the Carse of the Forth. Thereafter until 11km short of the western termination the Wall utilised the Central Valley of Scotland, the valley formed by the River Carron in the east and the River Kelvin in the west. The Wall lay on the southern slopes of this valley overlooking the Campsie Fells to the north and the flat, marshy ground between (pl. 9). For the western 11km, however, where there was no such convenient geographical feature to follow the Wall jumped from high point to high point before reaching the Clyde low enough downstream to guard most of the fording points. Although the tactical position of the Antonine Wall was often stronger than

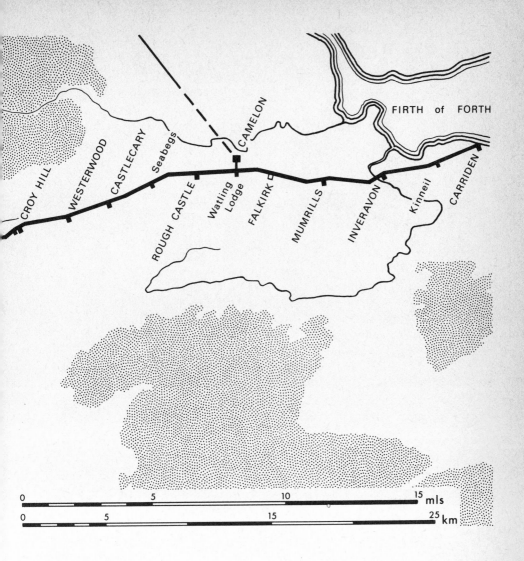

that of Hadrian's Wall it did not slavishly follow the best ground. Thus on Croy Hill there was a wide area of 'dead' ground in front of the Wall while for the most western 3km the lie of the land lay against the Romans.

The new wall, as Pius' biographer recorded, was of turf. Excavation has confirmed this, but also demonstrated that where good turf was not available blocks of clay were used. The turves – or clay blocks – were placed on a base of stone. Formed of rough boulders, bordered by dressed kerbs, this base was generally about 15 Roman feet (4.35m) wide. The height of the rampart is not known. In the 1890s experiments with the turf lying round a section through the rampart demonstrated that it could be restored to a height of nearly 3m. This is, of course, a minimum figure for the rampart. On its solid base it is possible that it rose as high as the turf sector of Hadrian's Wall. The excavators of the 1890s pointed

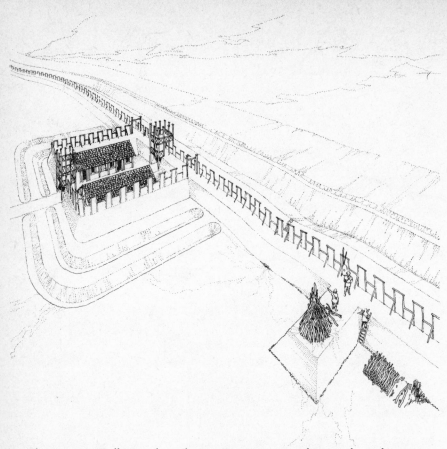

22 *The Antonine Wall, view from the east. Reconstruction showing the turf rampart, ditch and glacis, milefortlet in the background and beacon-platform (expansion) in the foreground. (Drawn by M. Moore)*

out that if a batter of 1 in 3 was allowed on both sides of the rampart, and a walk 2m wide on the top, then the wall may have been as high as 3.6m; if the width of the wall top walk was reduced then the rampart could have been built higher. There is even less evidence from the Antonine Wall to suggest how the wall top was completed, for no Rudge Cup or Amiens Skillet survives from the Scottish Wall. However, if it is assumed that provision was made for passage along the wall top then some protection would have had to be provided. This probably took the form of a wattle breastwork rather than, say, a fence of split logs: analysis of burnt debris found in front of the east rampart of the fort at Bearsden, debris probably deriving from a timber breastwork, included branches of willow and ash three to five years old and some 1–1.5cm in diameter, entirely appropriate for such a fence.

In front of the rampart, and separated from it by a berm, lay a ditch. This varied in width from nearly 6m to 12m and in depth from 2m to 4m. The larger measurements only pertain in the central sector of the Wall from Falkirk to Bar Hill; both east and west of these points the ditch usually conformed to the narrower figures. The width of the berm generally varied in relation to the width of the ditch. Where this was 12m wide, then the berm was 6m in width, but when the ditch narrowed then the berm widened to about 9m. It would thus appear that the main marking out lines were the front of the rampart and the centre of the ditch, the intention being to keep the two lines the same distance apart even though the ditch might narrow. In some areas this was not possible. Croy Hill provided the most difficult terrain for the army to cross, yet even here where crags rendered it superfluous the ditch was always dug, except for two points where the hardness of the bedrock defeated the Roman navvies. In order to provide a ditch the berm had to be allowed to widen, and in some places it not only achieved widths of up to 30m, but it also lay 14m and more below the level of the rampart on the top of the crags.

As on Hadrian's Wall the earth excavated from the ditch was not required for the construction of the wall and it was therefore tipped out onto the north side to form a wide, low outer mound or glacis. Where the rampart has long since been destroyed this upcast mound often survives. Strangely the turf from below this mound does not appear to have been stripped for use in the rampart before being buried. In some areas at least the northern edge of the upcast mound was marked by a low bank before dumping commenced.

At regular intervals along the Wall forts were constructed. Some forts were planned or built before the rampart, others added later. Recent work has suggested that these belong to two quite separate schemes: like Hadrian's Wall the Antonine Wall was subjected to changes in plan during its construction. The first plan appears to have been for six forts on the Wall, about 13km apart, and each capable of holding a single auxiliary unit. Between each fort, at approximately one Roman mile intervals, were to be fortlets, similar in size, and no doubt function, to those on Hadrian's Wall. At present only nine such fortlets are known, out of a possible original total of 29, or thereabouts, but in each instance the fortlet was contemporary with the rampart, or even preceded it, demonstrating that they were part of the original plan. The Antonine Wall in fact was planned to be similar to its predecessor as completed: forts at half a day's march apart with fortlets in between. The only element lacking was the turret. No turrets or towers have been found on the Antonine Wall, but if they were of timber and placed within the thickness of the rampart they would be difficult to find. A slightly different structure has, however, been discovered. Aerial photographs have revealed the existence of small enclosures attached to the rear of the rampart. Three such enclosures are known in the Wilderness Plantation-Balmuildy sector. They measure about 12m within a single ditch and, together with the fortlet at Wilderness Plantation, they form a sequence of four sites at roughly regular intervals of 250m: one-sixth of a Roman mile. This spacing, half the distance between turrets on Hadrian's Wall, may not be coincidental. Excavation of one enclosure in 1980, however, failed to reveal any structure in the interior so in the meantime their precise function must remain uncertain. It is not even definite that they formed part of the original plan for the Antonine Wall, nor that they continued along the whole length of the barrier.

One totally new element was added to the Antonine Wall: a road. With the Stanegate in existence behind much of Hadrian's Wall the need for a road on the Wall line itself may not have been strongly felt. But on the Antonine Wall there was no pre-existing road and the need will have been obvious from the first: there is some evidence to suggest that the road, the Military Way, was part of the original plan for the Wall. This road presumably ran along the whole length of the Wall, though it has not been found east of Watling Lodge, and it continued beyond the west end of the Wall, perhaps heading for a Roman harbour in the vicinity of modern Dumbuck or Dumbarton.

This plan for the Antonine Wall was modified, probably before it was completed. The modification took the form of the addition of a further 10 or 11 forts, possibly even 13, to the Wall. Excavation has revealed that several of these forts were simply attached to the rear of the existing rampart, and presumably all followed a similar pattern. The new forts were all smaller than the primary forts and many were incapable of holding even the smallest auxiliary unit in the Roman army. Some forts replaced earlier fortlets. At Duntocher the fortlet was incorporated within the new enclosure, but at Croy considerations of topography led to the construction of the fort some 50m to the east of the fortlet (fig. 25). Elsewhere it seems probable that some forts were placed in entirely new positions, for different reasons governed the siting of fortlets and forts. Thus at Bearsden, in spite of extensive investigations, no fortlet has been discovered in the immediate vicinity of the fort, which is presumed to be secondary.

The forts, both primary and secondary, were similar in materials of construction to those on Hadrian's Wall. The ramparts were of turf, sometimes on a stone base, with the exception of two of the primary forts, Balmuildy and Castlecary, which had stone walls. The reason for this is quite uncertain. Balmuildy in fact was provided with stone wing walls as if the builders were expecting to bond in with a stone wall rather than a turf rampart. The fort was one of the earliest to be built on the Wall, perhaps the earliest, for it is the only site which has produced an inscription of Lollius Urbicus, and the provision of the stone wing walls may hint that at one time the Roman commanders were considering building the Antonine Wall in stone.

Within the fort ramparts lay both stone and timber buildings. Stone was generally used for the principal buildings such as the headquarters, commanding officer's house and granaries, while the barrack-blocks, storehouses, stables and workshops were of timber (fig. 23 and pl. 10). Most of the forts were provided with an annexe, an enclosure commonly found attached to forts in Britain, though not on the continent. Annexes are not found on Hadrian's Wall, presumably because they were not necessary: the Vallum formed a sort of elongated annexe along the whole length of the Wall. As there was no Vallum on the Antonine Wall recourse was had to the annexe. This enclosure was provided in order to protect the military buildings which could not be accommodated within the fort. Thus the bath-house often lay within the annexe, though sometimes it was built within the fort and in at least one instance in neither: at Camelon the annexe contained furnaces and smithing hearths. The annexe was not for the use of civilians: the exclusion of civilians from the space between the Vallum and the wall on Hadrian's Wall emphasises this. No protection was provided for civilians by the army.

In one important particular the forts on the Antonine Wall differed from those on Hadrian's Wall and that is in the direction of their main axis. On Hadrian's Wall the forts were separate entities, clearly on the Wall line for convenience only. The headquarters building faced along the long axis even though this might result in the fort facing east rather than north. On the Antonine Wall, however, with the single exception of Cadder all the forts faced north even though this might result in the headquarters building facing along the short axis. The impression is therefore given of forts more closely tied to the frontier line than before.

The forts varied considerably in size from Duntocher, less than 0.2 hectares in internal area, to Mumrills containing 2.6 hectares and holding the only cavalry unit attested on the Wall. Most other forts were garrisoned by auxiliary units or detachments of such units, but in some cases it appears that legionaries were used to

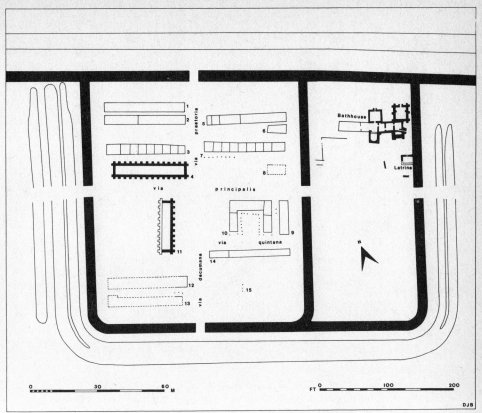

23 *The fort at Bearsden. 3, 7 and ? 13 barrack blocks; 1, 2, 5, 6 and ? 12 stables; 4 and 11 granaries; 9 storehouse; 10 workshop; 15 works area ?; 8 and 14 unknown*

supplement the Wall garrison. The weight of this garrison lay towards the western end of the Wall. Here the Campsie Fells and the Kilpatrick Hills loom especially close to the Wall, but it is unlikely that this would have caused the Romans any special concern. Perhaps the reason for the lack of troops in the eastern sector of the Wall is to be found in the presence of outpost forts to the north here, in Strathearn and Strathallan. As on Hadrian's Wall so on the Antonine Wall the barrier itself was not the provincial boundary, which presumably followed tribal borders rather than geographical features or military structures.

The fortlets also were constructed of the same materials as their predecessors on the turf section of Hadrian's Wall. Their ramparts were of turf, though on a stone base, and the internal barrack-block was of timber. It has only been possible in one case, Duntocher, to demonstrate the size of the barrack-block and there it measured 11m by 5m, rather larger than the smaller barrack-block found in certain milecastles on Hadrian's Wall. Fortlets were provided with a ditch, in some cases two, but, as on Hadrian's Wall, no provision seems to have been made for a causeway across the Wall ditch in front of the north gate. Causeways appear to have been provided at the primary forts – though not across all the three ditches at Old Kilpatrick – but not at all the secondary forts, where it may be presumed the Wall ditch had already been dug. There was a causeway outside the north gate at

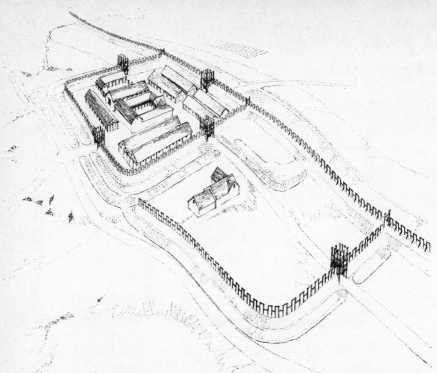

24 *The fort at Rough Castle on the Antonine Wall, view from the south-east. Reconstruction showing the turf rampart, ditch and glacis, fort, annexe containing the bath-house, and the military way passing through the fort and by-passing it to the south. (Drawn by M. Moore)*

Cadder and at Rough Castle while at Croy Hill the section of unexcavated ditch a few metres east of the fort appears to have been used as a causeway. But there was no causeway outside the forts at Westerwood, Duntocher and, it appears, Bearsden.

One final feature remains to be noted on the Antonine Wall, the 'expansion'. This is literally a rearward expansion of the Antonine Wall rampart. Excavation has demonstrated that the expansion is a turf platform placed on a stone base about 5m square and resting against the rear of the rampart. These platforms always appear in pairs. Two pairs are known on either side of Rough Castle and a third pair on the west brow of Croy Hill. It is presumed that the platforms were associated with signalling, the eastern four being concerned with signalling to the outpost forts to the north, while those on Croy Hill formed a connection with the garrison at Bothwellhaugh in the Clyde Valley. However, an element of doubt still surrounds these structures, not least because it is not clear how far fires lit on them might be seen and how messages might be sent using two fires.

The Antonine Wall, like Hadrian's Wall, was built by soldiers from the three legions of Britain. This is demonstrated by inscriptions, which also show that while *legio II Augusta* was present in full strength the other two legions only provided detachments. The size of these detachments is not known, but some of the camps occupied by them during construction work have been recognised through aerial photography. Many of the highly decorated inscriptions erected by these soldiers to record their labours have also been found. These reveal the distances constructed by each legionary gang and hence have been termed 'distance slabs' (pl. 17).

Together the distance slabs and the temporary camps show that all the Wall, with the exception of the four most westerly miles, were divided into major blocks of work, each subdivided in turn into three legionary blocks of 3, 3⅔ or 4⅔ Roman miles (4.3, 5.3, or 6.6km). Within each block, in at least two sectors, the legions were divided into four groups working from the ends towards the middle. This is perhaps clearest in the most easterly length, 4⅔ miles long from Bridgeness, where a distance slab found in 1869 revealed that this was the length of *II Augusta*, to the River Avon at Inveravon where there was almost certainly a fortlet. Two temporary camps have been found at each end of this stretch. It is not known, of course, how the work was divided between the camps, though the fact that the turf does not appear to have been normally stripped from below the upcast mound for use in the rampart may point to separate rampart and ditch gangs. The provision of equal blocks of work for each legion suggests that part of *II Augusta* was engaged in other activities. Inscriptions from Balmuildy, a primary fort, demonstrate that it was working here and it is possible that all the primary forts, and possibly all the fortlets, were constructed by this legion.

That part of the Wall under discussion, all but the western four miles, was measured in paces on the distance slabs. Remarkably the unit of measurement was different on the slabs from the western four mile stretch; these legionary lengths were measured in feet. This may have been to allow apparent symmetry between the new and the old measurements. There were five feet to the pace and the new, smaller, distances measured in feet would appear, on superficial examination of the inscriptions, to be the same as the distances recorded on the easterly stones. There may, however, be further complications. It seems possible that the change in the unit of measurement on Castlehill was connected with the decision to build more forts on the Wall line. Castlehill lay within the area where the legions were working when they moved off to build the new forts, and it is tempting to assume that this was the very point they had reached when they left for their new task. When they returned to complete the western end of the Wall – after the construction of a fort at Duntocher – they were organised differently and took the opportunity to record their labours differently in order not to minimise their achievements.

The reason for the addition of the new forts to the Wall line is not known; nevertheless this action is consonant with other aspects of the occupation of Scotland at this time. On the Wall itself the close spacing of forts – on average about 3.5km – and the large garrison – proportionately almost twice as large as the garrison of Hadrian's Wall – reflects the close spacing of the small one-sixth mile enclosures. Behind the Wall is a similar pattern. The network of forts and fortlets is more dense now than either before or later in Scotland or in any other part of Britain. It seems unlikely that the Roman army was preoccupied with the local tribesmen, fearing attack from them at any time and therefore going out of their way to control them. A case might be made out for special defence from the Caledonians to the north. But again this threat would be met by moving the army out into the field, not by sheltering behind fort walls: the closer attachment of the forts to the Wall only gives a superficial impression of immobility. It seems better to connect this emphasis upon control, either of the people behind the Wall or of movement across it, with the reason for the advance into Scotland. If the advance had been merely in order to gain for Pius military prestige, prestige necessary to secure his position on the throne, it would be expected that his legate in Britain, Lollius Urbicus, and his successors, would do everything in their power to ensure that nothing soured that victory. This might account for the special measures taken at this time, not only on the Wall but also behind it in the territory of the Lowland tribes.

In spite of this apparent concern for control, the flanks of the Antonine Wall do not appear to have been protected in the same way as those on Hadrian's Wall. 17.5km to the east of Carriden, the easternmost fort on the Wall, lay a normal fort at Cramond and 14.5km on was Inveresk. Both these forts were placed beside river mouths and both estuaries may have been used as harbours. The west flank of the Wall was also protected by a fort, Whitemoss at Old Bishopton, on the south side of the Clyde with a wide panoramic view of the western end of the Wall. Further on two fortlets, Lurg Moor and Outerwards, both placed on the high ground overlooking the Clyde estuary, had wide views over the river and the land beyond. While the picture at present is of isolated flanking stations this picture could easily change. All three of the sites on the west flank of the Antonine Wall, and a fourth, first-century, site, have been found in the last thirty-five years: further sites, radically altering the above pattern, could be discovered at any time.

The Antonine Wall will have taken some years to complete. Most governors had a tenure of about three years so it is possible that Lollius Urbicus left Britain in 142. However, in view of the task allotted to him it is possible that he was given a slightly extended governorship, perhaps an extra year. Certainly work on the Wall had commenced before he left Britain for two inscriptions from Balmuildy record building under Urbicus, and as Pius does not appear to have been acclaimed as imperator until 142 this seems to be the earliest date for the commencement of building. Unlike on Hadrian's Wall there are no other dated inscriptions to help provide a chronological framework for the building activity. The chronology and time scale have to be estimated from the archaeological data.

Most of the Wall appears to have been divided into three-legion blocks of work. The relationship of the forts to the Wall suggests that building started in the east, for although Mumrills was planned and probably nearly completed before the rampart builders arrived on the site, Balmuildy and Old Kilpatrick further west, and also the fortlet at Duntocher, were completed before the arrival of the rampart, while the fact that both the fort and fortlet were constructed at Duntocher before the rampart suggests that some time had elapsed between the various building operations. The most easterly legionary length was $4\frac{2}{3}$ Roman miles long, close to the 5 miles generally apparently allotted to each legion on Hadrian's Wall, and this may not be coincidental. It may be therefore that it was expected that each three-legion length of Wall would take a year to complete.

If the above argument is accepted it would appear that the original proposal was to complete the construction of the whole of the Antonine Wall in three seasons, a similar period of time as initially planned for Hadrian's Wall. It seems unlikely that the Wall would be divided into three three-legion blocks if it was intended to complete all within one season, while various factors combine to suggest that it would not have been possible to work on all three sectors simultaneously. A start in 142 or 143 should have led to completion in 145 or 146. The distance of $4\frac{2}{3}$ miles constructed by *legio II Augusta* hints that the original intention may have been to divide the Wall into three three-legion blocks of 13 miles each. If so the proposal was altered after the first season, perhaps in view of the more difficult country in the centre of the Wall, which indeed was to give trouble, perhaps because work had been slower in the first season than expected. A reduction in the amount of work allotted to each legion in the second and third seasons – though it was increased slightly in the latter year – would have led to the gap of 4 miles at the west end of the Wall. However, before that could be completed it appears that many, perhaps all, the soldiers moved to the task of building new forts on the Wall line. This will have lengthened the building programme by an indeterminate period, at least another three years, if experience on Hadrian's Wall is a sound parallel. In that case the Antonine Wall may not have been completed until 147 or 148 at the earliest. Although several forts have produced legionary building inscriptions three have furnished auxiliary building stones, Rough Castle, Castlecary and Bar Hill: at the latter two sites both legionary and auxiliary building inscriptions have been found. The auxiliary stones are not dated within the reign of Antoninus Pius: they may date to either the original building of the Wall or a later phase. It may be, however, that auxiliary units were brought in to help construct some forts as the building operation was taking so long, just as auxiliaries had been brought in to help dig the Vallum on Hadrian's Wall and build the fort at Carvoran. It must be remembered too that the Wall was only one item that required to be constructed in these years. Forts and fortlets in the Scottish Lowlands were also built at this time.

The Antonine Wall in its final state was very different, superficially at least, from its predecessor. The main difference, and the reason why the Antonine Wall has not weathered the years as well as its southern neighbour, is that it was built of turf and not primarily of stone. In this, the Antonine Wall was the more usual, conforming to the norms established on other frontiers. The Antonine turf rampart was improved by the addition of a stone base not found on Hadrian's turf wall. A second, obvious, distinction to be drawn between the two Walls is that the forts were much closer together on the Antonine Wall and these forts were more closely related to the linear barrier. The original proposal for the Antonine Wall seems to have been for a frontier similar to the second scheme on Hadrian's Wall with forts at about half a day's march apart and fortlets at about Roman mile intervals between. While the fortlets seem to have been very similar to those on Hadrian's Wall the forts, all placed behind the rampart, give the impression of being more closely related to that rampart. The addition of more forts to the Antonine Wall brought more men to the frontier so that the number of troops based in the forts along the barrier was doubled from about 3,000 men to perhaps between 6,000 and 7,000 men, a high number in comparison to the 8,000 to 9,000 troops probably based in the forts on Hadrian's Wall. But it must not be assumed that the troops on the Antonine Wall were becoming frontier police. The linear barrier still served primarily as a base for these troops: if the province was threatened with invasion the army would move out into the field to deal with the invaders in the open, where it knew that its superior discipline, training and weapons gave it a better chance of victory.

Cavalrymen seem to have been even less common on the Antonine Wall than Hadrian's Wall. An *ala* was based at Mumrills and a mixed unit of infantry and cavalry at Castlehill, some cavalrymen from here possibly being outposted at Bearsden where cavalry-type barrack-blocks have been found. This lack of cavalry may be due to the terrain. The Campsie Fells and Kilpatrick Hills north of the Wall may not have been good cavalry country while between those hills and the Wall lay the marshy ground of the Kelvin and Carron valleys, also unattractive to cavalry.

Another, slightly less obvious, distinction between the two Walls is the greater flexibility and freedom displayed on the Antonine Wall. On Hadrian's Wall milecastles, turrets, bath-houses and to some extent forts, were built to set blue-prints, but on the Antonine Wall no such regularity can be traced. Little can yet be said about the fortlets, but all the forts and their bath-houses seem to have been built to different plans with considerable variety in their dimensions, internal buildings and defences: even where it seems that two forts were built by the same legion this variety occurs.

In spite of these differences the two Walls hold several problems in common. How were the troops divided between forts and fortlets? How was the ditch crossed where no causeway appears to have been provided and no trace of bridges found? How did the command structure operate and the local commanding officers relate to the legionary legate at York and the provincial governor at London? These and many other problems remain to be solved.

The abandonment of Hadrian's Wall

The construction of a new Wall and of all the forts in the newly conquered territory led to the abandonment of Hadrian's Wall. The Wall itself does not appear to have been deliberately destroyed, but all the milecastles and turrets seem to have been abandoned and the gates of milecastles were forcibly removed from their sockets thus rendering them open to unimpeded traffic. An attempt was also made to slight the Vallum. In some areas the north and south mounds were backfilled into the ditch at regular intervals. However, this operation was not carried out along the whole length of the barrier. The position at the forts appears to have been different, at least in some cases. Although the Wall served no useful purpose once the frontier lay 160km to the north and a new Wall was constructed, the forts could continue to have an independent life of their own: they were, after all, only on the Wall for convenience. At Chesters two stones indicate building activity by *legio VI Victrix* during the reign of Antoninus Pius, while a legionary centurion dedicated an altar at Benwell. However, none need necessarily indicate a legionary garrison at this time. An auxiliary diploma dating to 146 has also been found at Chesters, which may imply that there was an auxiliary unit in garrison at that time. So many units are attested at Chesters as to make it more than likely that the fort was garrisoned during the years the Antonine Wall was occupied.

The actual date of the abandonment of Hadrian's Wall is not known, though it was probably late in the building programme for the Antonine Wall. Until their new buildings were ready to receive them the auxiliary soldiers presumably remained in residence in their old forts, at least in the winter when they were not out building or soldiering themselves. As their new forts became ready for occupation they will have marched north abandoning most of the forts in the Pennines and no doubt many on the Wall itself. It seems unlikely that caretaker garrisons were left in the forts, but on the other hand they do not appear to have been handed over to civilian use for many were reoccupied some years later when the Antonine Wall was abandoned. Some forts were still maintained in the Pennines and in certain areas arrangements were made to allow military operations to continue in spite of reduced strength. Thus the abandoned forts at Binchester and Ebchester appear to have been replaced now by a new site at Lanchester about half-way between them.

Antonine Scotland

The only known effects of the Roman advance of the 140s on the inhabitants of the

Scottish Lowlands are seen through the medium of archaeology. Excavation and field work have revealed a growth in native settlements at this time, the establishment of settlements outside forts and a drift of Roman goods northwards into barbary. It has been argued that the passage in the *Life of Antoninus Pius* recording the advance, that the barbarians were transported into another island, should be taken literally. The phrase was associated with the appearance of *numeri* (irregular army units) of *Brittones* on the Upper German frontier. Many of the ten or more of these low-grade units bore subsidiary titles taken from the river by which they were stationed. This is unusual and has been taken to imply that these were no ordinary military units but groups of soldiers accompanied by their wives and families. There is, however, no evidence for this and moreover it has now been discovered that the type of small fort occupied by these units had been in existence on the Upper German frontier for about forty years before the first appearance epigraphically of the units in 145–6.

It is still not impossible that men from the northern frontier region were drafted into the Roman army when southern Scotland was reoccupied in the 140s. Such recruitment may have taken place at any time, possibly as early as Agricola, and may have occurred even though the area from which the men were recruited was not part of the empire: the Roman army throughout its history attracted recruits from beyond the borders of the empire and there is no doubt that Britons from beyond the northern frontier would have joined the army even though they are not attested in any of our surviving sources. The early 140s would certainly have been an appropriate time for men from the newly reconquered tribes to join the army for they would have come more immediately under the attention of the recruiting officers and if any of the tribes had offered opposition to the Roman advance they would have lost their legal rights and thus been especially prone to the draft.

The tribes of southern Scotland would once more have been incorporated into the province, having their legal rights defined. There is no evidence that any of the tribes gained self governing powers either now or later, though presumably as before the Votadini held a special position. Authority over the tribes will have been the responsibility of the army, though special officers may have been appointed to help administer the civilians.

The returning Roman army will have brought in its wake taxation and other less welcome benefits. The army itself will have required servicing. Arms, armour, food, leather, clothing, pottery and horses, all were necessary to the proper working of the military machine. Many will have been imported from southern Britain or the continent. The Roman army in the fourth century had their own factories producing arms and armour: such factories may have existed in earlier years and some may have been located in Britain. Most goods, however, were purchased from civilians or were supplied as taxation.

The taxation was no doubt usually collected fairly, but Roman officials could be rapacious, harsh and cruel. The spark which ignited the rebellion of Boudica was the heavy-handedness of the Roman officials sent to the kingdom after the death of Prasutagus. Tacitus recorded that 'Agricola eased the levy of corn and the payment of tax by equalising the burden and abolished the devices invented by profiteers, which were more bitterly resented than the tax itself'. 'The provincials', Tacitus continues, 'had been compelled to wait outside locked granary doors and to buy back their own corn at farcical prices. They were forced to deliver it by devious routes and to distant locations even though there were permanent quarters for troops close by'. This passage should not be treated too seriously for Agricola's predecessor, Julius Frontinus, was a figure of great rectitude. Nevertheless, Tacitus would hardly invent a situation which did not exist somewhere and to some degree. He records a similar story elsewhere. The taxation of the Frisii, on the right bank of the Rhine, had been assessed by Drusus in ox-hides required for military purposes: the dimensions and quality of the individual hides were not specified. In AD 28 the officer in charge of the collection of the taxation interpreted the size of the hides as that of a wild ox, an auroch. Although these could be found in the forest, the size of domestic animals was small. The Frisians tried to meet the stipulation, in the process selling their cattle, lands and finally their wives and children into slavery. Eventually, their complaints having brought no relief, they rebelled and their revolt was only put down after considerable Roman loss. No such events are known in north Britain, but the two accounts do illustrate the type of burden placed on the native tribesmen as a result of their incorporation into the empire. And in addition to the perversion of the official system there was the private extortion of individual soldiers, the existence of which is amply testified by the edicts of various provincial governors banning such actions.

The main items required by the Roman army will have been corn and hides. Tents were not made of canvas, but leather and stocks would continually require to be replenished: a single tent for eight men would use the skins of about 38 calves. Leather would also be needed for clothing, shoes, bags, shields and shield covers and saddles, together creating an enormous requirement. Corn was the staple food, but the Roman soldier had a varied diet, including fish and shell fish, vegetables and fruit in addition to meat: cattle, sheep and pig bones are found at most Roman forts in some quantities as well as the bones of poultry and wild animals such as deer. Sour, or ordinary, wine was the common drink.

An important recent source of information on the Roman military diet has been the writing tablets found at Chesterholm-Vindolanda by Hadrian's Wall. One tablet is a list of food containing the following: spice, goat's milk, salt, young pig, ham, corn, venison and flour, all again pointing to a varied and sophisticated diet. Another list includes vintage wine, Celtic beer, ordinary wine, fish sauce and pork fat, while the site has yielded the physical remains of another variety of food, part of a cabbage. Another writing tablet from the site, incidentally, points to another requirement of the soldiers, clothing, for the letter mentions two pairs of sandals, woollen socks and two pairs of underpants.

The seasons will have affected the diet of the Roman soldier more than that of his modern counterpart. There will have been many times when meat, vegetables or fruit were unavailable. Recent excavations at Bearsden have emphasised that corn must at all times have been the basic item of food and also indicated that the soldiers' diet was more sophisticated than often realised. In a waterlogged deposit beside the latrine have been found the debris of both wheat and barley – the latter was fed to horses and used as punishment rations for soldiers – but in addition coriander and opium poppy, used to flavour bread. The seeds of figs, raspberry and wild strawberry survived in the deposit and also traces of hazel nuts and wild celery. Other remains, incidentally, suggest that peat may have been burnt in the fort, mosses may have been used instead of toilet paper, while foreign grain pest beetles indicate that the corn was not grown locally.

The remains indicate that soldiers would have eaten what was locally available as well as importing supplies. Some corn may have been acquired locally in addition to wild fruit, and presumably some animals were available from the immediate neighbourhood. Most cattle bones, for example, on Roman military sites in northern Britain were from adult and well-grown animals of the Celtic short-horn variety – the kind of beast that would have been found on the local farms. The soldiers made good use of these animals, often splitting or smashing the bones for marrow. The cattle bones from Newstead stand out in contrast for here many young animals were eaten and the marrow tended not to be extracted, while there were also indications of improved breeds: it seems probable that here cattle were in rather greater supply than in many areas, and also that local stocks had been improved.

The requirements of the Roman army in the staple item of food, wheat, were considerable. Each Roman soldier received about three pounds of corn a day. The units stationed north of Hadrian's Wall in the Antonine period will therefore have needed over 6,000 tons a year, the produce of at least 8,000 hectares. The impact of such requirements on the local population can scarcely be judged. In the western zone of the hinterland of Hadrian's Wall the construction of roads seems to have aided the growth of settlements in their vicinity, as if farmers were adapting themselves to supplying the military market: no such development can be detected in Scotland. Some of the Cumbrian farms, such as Ewe Close and Crosby Garret, grew to a considerable size, being surrounded by extensive field systems, and this can be paralleled in Scotland.

The Antonine advance appears to have heralded an era of peace and expansion in the frontier region. One tangible expression of the *pax Romana* appears to have been the change from timber to stone as the material used in domestic dwellings in large parts of the eastern half of the inter-mural zone (pl. 11). Stone had certainly been used before in houses, for over 3,000 years in some parts of northern Scotland, but it is only in the Roman period that this material became popular in the Borders. Datable artefacts from stone-built settlements range from the late first century to the mid-fourth century at least and the establishment of such a settlement at Milking Gap between the Wall and the Vallum, apparently before the construction of the Wall, emphasises that building in stone in this area had probably started early in the Roman period, if not before. However, the Roman era, and in particular the second century, appears to have witnessed a considerable growth in the number of these stone-built houses.

It is clear that on many sites the stone houses reflect continuing occupation of the settlement. However, in some instances the stone houses were built over the abandoned defences of earlier forts (fig. 32). Most houses had their own enclosures attached, though it is clear that these were essentially farmyards rather than defensive stockades. The average number of stone-built houses in each settlement was between four and five, though some contained only one house and others ten or more. The average size of the settlements in the coastal plain of Northumberland, where timber continued to be the material used in the construction of the houses, seems to have been the same. It is possible that all the huts in a settlement were not in occupation at the same time, and that some were used for animals rather than by humans. However, it has not been possible by excavation to demonstrate which, if any, were not used as dwellings, while the plans of many settlements argue for contemporaneity of occupation of all huts. Allowing five persons to each house, which may be on the low side, the average population of each average settlement may have been about 25 souls, though the full range in size of the social groups will have been from five to 50 persons.

Another phenomenon of these years appears to be the growth of both stone and timber settlements. It is immediately clear from the plans of many settlements that they grew from an original nucleus, with new houses being constructed both within the farm enclosure and outside it: in some cases the farmyard was extended to incorporate the latter houses. A small number of settlements grew into villages: that at Greaves Ash in Northumberland contained at least 30 houses with another ten less than 100m distant. It also seems probable, though this is as yet incapable of proof, that some folk left their ancestral homes to create new settlements for their families. It is certainly clear that this picture of growth and expansion in the Scottish Lowlands during the Roman period is at variance with the suggestion that families were transported wholesale to the continent.

Another form of settlement which grew during the Antonine period was the village outside the Roman fort. Merchants and traders will have accompanied the army into Scotland. Many will no doubt simply have moved with a unit on its way north from its old base in the Pennines or on Hadrian's Wall to its new fort in the Lowlands. A number of civilians are attested on inscriptions from the Antonine Wall but little is known about their dwellings. Recent excavations at Inveresk, however, have demonstrated that the civil settlement outside the fort there must have been extensive – it appears to have been larger than the fort – and contained both timber and stone houses which were rebuilt on at least one occasion. There seems to have been a main street leading from the east gate of the fort, and side streets branching off it. Analysis of the pottery from the site suggests that at least one potter moved north to Inveresk in order to improve his share of the lucrative northern market. Other discoveries point to the presence of at least four other potters working in Scotland at this time and selling their wares to the soldiers.

South-east of Inveresk a pattern of rectangular fields and enclosures have been revealed by aerial photographs and also in the vicinity at least five rectilinear settlements, possibly of the Roman period, are known: interestingly, and probably significantly, the only similar concentration of such sites lies around Traprain Law.

It is not possible to tell whether or not Inveresk was a typical civil settlement. Its position by the mouth of the River Esk, where there may have been a harbour, would give it a special importance. Cramond too, at the mouth of the Almond, appears to have been the site of an extensive settlement and one which continued in occupation, at least in part, beyond the withdrawal of its Roman garrison. Unfortunately recent excavations there have been unable to determine the layout of the settlement or even much about individual buildings, but they have demonstrated the presence of a variety of craftsmen at the site. Industrial activity appears to have taken place in open-ended timber sheds, and the trades practised included tanning, shoe-making, carpentry and iron working.

Practically nothing is known about the other settlements believed to exist outside forts on the Wall and in the Borders, with the exception of that at Carriden at the east end of the Antonine Wall. Here aerial photographs have revealed a complex pattern of boundaries and enclosures but these appear to relate more to agricultural activity than a town. However, this site has produced an inscription recording that the inhabitants of this town, called Velunia or Velunias, had gained self-governing rights. The acquisition of such powers suggests that the settlement was of some size, but its extent, even its position, is unknown. If one settlement on the Antonine Wall had achieved self-governing rights it might be expected that others also had.

Coincidentally the only civil settlement on the Antonine Wall extensively examined, that outside the fort on Croy Hill (fig. 25), has also kept its secret regarding its dwellings. Wide-ranging excavation has revealed traces of agricultural and small scale industrial activity, and a burial, but not the settlement

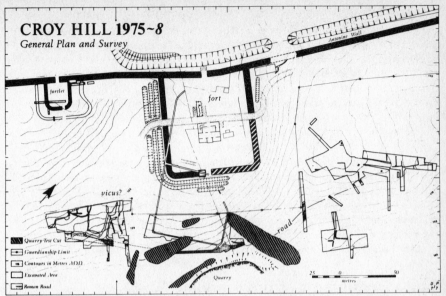

CROY HILL 1975~8
General Plan and Survey

Antonine Wall

fortlet

fort

vicus?

road

Quarry Test Cut
Guardianship Limit
Contours in Metres A.O.D.
Excavated Area
Roman Road

Quarry

25   0   50
          metres

25 *The fortlet and fort at Croy Hill on the Antonine Wall and the surrounding field boundaries. (Drawn by D. Powseland)*

itself. At other sites, Westerwood and Bearsden, also examined recently, even less traces have been found, though clay and cobble foundations to the west of the fort at Bearsden were presumably part of civilian buildings.

The presence of the army in Scotland and the influx of many civilians from the south must have had an impact on the local population. The demand for food, leather, clothing might be expected to have led to a boom in farming, and indeed would help to account for the growth of native settlements at this time. The number of Roman objects reaching these settlements increased dramatically, but the total number of such objects found during archaeological excavations, or by chance, is still very small. Excavated settlements rarely produce more than the odd fragment of pottery from one or two Roman vessels, part of a rotary quern, an iron object, such as a brooch, a spindle-whorl also attesting the wearing of woollen clothes, occasionally a bone weaving comb and very rarely a coin: coins are rare no doubt partly because the local economy would have been mainly dependant upon barter. The standard of living of the inhabitants of such settlements, measured in terms of material possessions, would thus seem to have been low. But it is of course quite possible that their wealth was measured in different terms, in, for example, cattle. Certainly the rearing of cattle and sheep continued to be the main activity of the Border farmer, though goats and pigs would also have been found in the farms. Along the coast fish and shell fish were gathered while all would have supplemented their diet by hunting and gathering. There is no evidence for increased crop cultivation in these years.

There is some evidence for mining and smithing in the north by the native peoples. The iron ore of Redesdale and North Tynedale was probably already being exploited in the Iron Age and smelted in small bowl-furnaces, smithing continuing into the Roman period. Further north a smelting furnace for iron has been discovered in Constantine's cave on the Fife coast together with Antonine pottery. Some of the products of this 'cottage industry' will probably have found their way into Roman workshops: a large ingot, made up of small blooms of iron hammered together, was discovered at Corbridge. Stone moulds for casting small bars of copper alloy hint at bronze working in some settlements. Coal was also won, from outcrops rather than mining. This appears to have been put to little use by the natives, but it was put to good use by the army: a coal store was found at Housesteads. It is possible that the soldiers helped to exploit this and other local minerals as they did in certain parts of Wales and England.

The find spots of Roman objects on native sites in the second century, or as casual discoveries away from Roman forts, is closely restricted to the new provincial territory (fig. 26). The line of the provincial boundary across the north-west shoulder of Strathmore can almost be drawn from a distribution map of these finds, though of course the line also marks the edge of the Highlands. Relatively few objects found their way beyond that border. There was a drift of artefacts along the east coast, into the Moray Plain and as far north as Caithness, but a mere handful of objects occur in the west of Scotland and the northern Isles. As in earlier years the contact between Roman and barbarian appears to have been limited.

The abandonment of the Antonine Wall

The date of the abandonment of the Antonine Wall is one of the most vexed questions of the northern frontier. Over the last 100 years the suggested dates have ranged from the 160s through the 180s to 197 and 207, and finally back to the 160s. There is no guarantee that the date of about 163, which is the one now accepted by most scholars, is correct: it is merely the most probable in the light of the evidence available at the present time. However, before turning to the abandonment of the Wall it is necessary to consider its history.

Life for the soldiers on the Antonine Wall was not altogether uneventful. This is demonstrated by numismatic, epigraphic and archaeological evidence. In 154–5 a commemorative coin issue bore a portrait of *Britannia*, the personification of the province. It is usually assumed that this coin issue commemorates a particular event in Britain, on the basis of similar issues, a victorious campaign, in this case presumably on the northern frontier. Some time must have elapsed between the disturbance and the coin issue so whatever happened probably took place in 154, even 153 or 152. There is no corroborative evidence for trouble at that time – unless the garbled passage in Pausanias' *Description of Greece* is relevant. It is just possible that this coin issue is a repeat of the earlier commemorative issue of 142/3–4, with changes, as happened under Hadrian, though this seems unlikely. These coins of 154/5 are very rarely found on the continent, though they are common site finds in Britain. This has led to the suggestion that the coins were specially minted in Britain, and this receives some support from the fact that some of the coins are less well struck than usual.

Epigraphic material points to building activity on the northern frontier in the late 150s. An inscription from Hadrian's Wall, now unfortunately lost, records rebuilding activity in 158. A second inscription from Birrens in Dumfriesshire attests building there in 158 under the governor Julius Verus, while a third found at Brough-on-Noe at the southern end of the Pennines reveals that the fort there was rebuilt under the same governor. It seems probable that so much building activity reflects the implementation of a new policy in north Britain. The construction work on Hadrian's Wall implies that it was the intention to reoccupy that Wall and

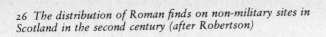

26 *The distribution of Roman finds on non-military sites in Scotland in the second century (after Robertson)*

rebuild its outpost and hinterland forts: presumably this carried with it the intention to abandon the Antonine Wall.

Archaeological evidence points to a break in the occupation of the Antonine Wall sometime before its final abandonment, and also demonstrates that the fort at Birrens was destroyed before its rebuilding in 158. However, while archaeology can demonstrate that a fort was rebuilt, abandoned for a time or even destroyed, it can rarely prove the reason for such an event. The damaged armour, tools, personal ornaments and skulls found in pits of this date at Newstead may suggest destruction of the fort by the northern tribesmen, but different interpretations have been offered. Some artefacts may have come from votive deposits, others may have been equipment left by the army when they abandoned the fort peacefully; the skulls may have been trophies. Recent excavations at Birrens have been unable to prove conclusively the reason for the destruction of that fort. Hostile action may have been the cause, but equally the Roman army may have destroyed the fort itself preparatory to a change in garrison: such a practice was quite usual. Evidence from one fort recently excavated on the Antonine Wall, Bearsden, demonstrated that the fort there was demolished by the Roman army, presumably in connection with the rebuilding further south. It is tempting to connect these events and suggest that the army abandoned the Antonine Wall in favour of a return to Hadrian's Wall in 158.

The reason for such an event is, however, another matter. In the past it has been connected with a putative revolt in northern England by the Brigantes. The evidence for this event is open to more than one interpretation. The reference to the Brigantes by Pausanias is enigmatic, the archaeological evidence unclear, while the coin issue discussed above, appears to refer to events before 154 and the inscriptions to rebuilding in 158. If there had been an internal revolt in 154 the Roman reaction – if it did not occur until 158 – would appear to have been rather belated. However, one other inscription must be considered. A stone from Newcastle records the arrival of legionary reinforcements for the three legions of Britain from the army of the two provinces of Germany. Such reinforcements may suggest that the army had suffered reverses in Britain, but on the other hand they may have been required in order to supplement the normal recruiting patterns of the British legions.

It is perfectly possible that the events commemorated by the coin issue are not connected with the rebuilding of 158. A disturbance on the northern frontier, shortly before 154, may have been put down successfully, though at some expense, thus requiring reinforcements for the army to be brought in from outside. The same governor who received these reinforcements, Julius Verus, may then have decided to withdraw the army units from Scotland, abandon the Antonine Wall and reoccupy Hadrian's Wall and the forts in the Pennines. This would account for the building inscriptions.

There is some evidence to suggest that the abandonment of the Antonine Wall and the forts in southern Scotland was of short duration. Two forts, Newstead and Crawford, seem to have been reoccupied after the briefest gap, while there is nothing from the other excavated sites to oppose the possibility that the gap there was equally short. It is surprising that the army withdrew from Scotland only to return shortly afterwards. It seems unlikely that there was sufficient local military pressure to force the army to move: if there had been a revolt it would surely have been dealt with by the army in its usual way and not by the abandonment and destruction of all its forts. If the reconquest of Scotland in the early 140s had been merely in order to gain military prestige for Antoninus Pius then the decision by Julius Verus to abandon the Antonine Wall, taken without reference to the emperor, may have resulted in a counter order from Rome bringing troops back into Scotland and the rebuilding of the Wall. Such may seem a far-fetched scenario, but we are used to such policy changes today and imperial motives are a perhaps more likely reason for such moves than minor frontier disturbances.

The break in the occupation of Scotland in the late 150s was followed by the rebuilding and reoccupation of most of the forts on, behind and in front of the Antonine Wall. On the Wall itself several of the garrisons appear to have changed, and in a few instances it appears that the new force was slightly smaller than that in occupation earlier, but only one fort, Bearsden, does not appear to have been rebuilt. The garrison of at least two of the outpost forts seems to have changed, and Ardoch now contained a smaller garrison. In southern Scotland several forts and fortlets were abandoned. This is most noticeable in south-west Scotland, where the net of forts and fortlets was drawn most closely in the earlier Antonine period. In Nithsdale no military station can be shown to have been rebuilt at this time, while in Annandale and Clydesdale other fortlets were also not reoccupied. Elsewhere the fort at Lyne seems to have been replaced by a fortlet. It is possible that this process of disengagement commenced before the end of the previous period of occupation. The fortlet at Wandel in Upper Clydesdale does not appear to have even been completed, while the excavator of the small fort at Raeburnfoot considered that the occupation of this site was brief. However, it is difficult from archaeological evidence alone to judge the length of occupation of a single site, while the network in Antonine I seems to have been so integrated that it seems unlikely that many forts or fortlets were abandoned piecemeal. More likely, opportunity was taken of the brief disengagement about 158 to reorganise the forces occupying the Lowlands.

The pattern of occupation in the second Antonine period marks a return to the normal network of forts and fortlets (fig. 27). The close density of military stations found in the earlier Antonine occupation was abandoned and the normal spacing between forts returned to a day's march. If the advance into Scotland in the early 140s had been in response to hostile moves north of the frontier it might be expected that the reorganisation reflects increasing Roman confidence in controlling the Lowland tribes. If, on the other hand, the move north was in order to help smooth the succession of Antoninus Pius then the change in occupying forces might reflect the fact that the heat was now off the local situation in Britain and matters could be allowed to return to normal.

The reoccupation of the Antonine Wall and its ancillary forts appears to have been of short duration. Ceramic experts suggest that the abandonment of the Antonine system came in the mid-160s. However, although the Wall and forts in south Scotland may have been occupied for no more than five or six years, there is no evidence to suggest that the reoccupation was intended to be brief. The army moved back in force after 158, rebuilding the Wall and the forts and fortlets as if they were to be occupied permanently, as no doubt was the intention. In the second century as in the twentieth, defence policy could change radically in a short time.

A number of pieces of evidence combine to suggest a date for the abandonment of the Antonine Wall. The ceramic material points to a general date, but documentary and epigraphic sources can narrow this down. The documentary material, however, does not state that the Antonine Wall was abandoned, or even mention it, and, as usual, the actual events have to be pieced together from several fragments of evidence of differing quality.

Antoninus Pius, emperor for 23 years, the longest since Augustus, died on 7 March 161. He was succeeded, peacefully, by the long chosen Marcus Aurelius.

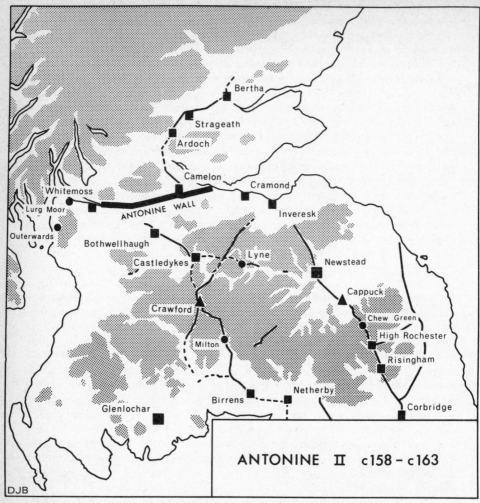

27 *North Britain in the second Antonine period, c.158–63 (for key see fig. 4)*

The first official action of the new emperor was to associate with him his adoptive brother Lucius Verus, and the senate agreed that the two would rule jointly. Ironically the reign of the stoic philosopher, Marcus Aurelius, began with invasions of the empire and was to continue in warfare through the nineteen years of his rule. In 161 the Parthians invaded the Roman protectorate of Armenia, while there was a threat of war in Britain and the Chatti invaded Germany and Raetia. Marcus' biographer goes on to record that Calpurnius Agricola was sent to deal with the Britons. Although this is a straightforward statement it is clear from other evidence that Agricola was not the first governor sent out to Britain by the new emperors to deal with the disturbing situation there. In the year of their accession they moved Statius Priscus from Upper Moesia on the Danube, where he had only recently been appointed governor, to Britain, only to send him to Cappadocia on the eastern frontier when a whole legion, just possibly *IX Hispana*, was massacred by the Parthians and the governor of Cappadocia committed suicide.

Sextus Calpurnius Agricola was their choice to replace Priscus. He probably arrived in 162. The nature of the trouble he had to deal with is unknown, though it may be presumed that it was on the northern frontier. Agricola may have campaigned against the northern tribes though there is no evidence for this. Building inscriptions from the Pennines, however, demonstrate that he was active there. Such records have been recovered from the forts at Carvoran, Chesterholm and Corbridge on the Stanegate, from Ribchester and possibly Ilkley. Although there are no inscriptions of his governorship from Hadrian's Wall it may be presumed that reoccupation of the forts further south would have carried with it reoccupation of the Wall. Building inscriptions dating to a few years following Agricola's governorship have been found at Stanwix and Greatchesters on the Wall and it may be that the task of recommissioning the forts and the Wall took several years to complete.

If warfare in Britain was imminent in 161 this might be considered an appropriate reason for the army to disengage from Scotland. On reflection, however, this is unlikely. Warfare on the northern frontier would be dealt with by the army in the field, or by diplomacy. It is improbable that in itself it would cause the army to abandon the Antonine Wall. As at the beginning of Pius' reign events in Britain cannot be examined in isolation. The serious situation on the eastern frontier led to major troop movements. Legionary detachments from the Danube and three entire legions from the Danube and Rhine provinces were sent to the east. As part of these arrangements it is possible that troops were withdrawn from Britain for service on the continent. As a result of these admittedly hypothetical withdrawals it may have been decided to abandon the recent conquests in Scotland and restore Hadrian's Wall as the frontier. A further possible reason can be found in political realms. If the advance in the 140s had been merely to allow Antoninus Pius to acquire military prestige it is possible that his adopted sons and successors, Marcus and Verus, decided to abandon his conquests, realising that they had served their purpose; if this would have released troops for service elsewhere, this might have helped their decision. It is interesting to note that 100 years before, after the death of Claudius, whose expedition to Britain had, according to Suetonius, merely been to obtain a triumph, his successor Nero toyed with the idea of abandoning Britain.

A totally different reason advanced for the abandonment of the Antonine Wall is that the holding of so many northerly forts caused serious problems of supply to the army. There is, in fact, little evidence that this was the case, though in the nature of the problem it would be difficult to prove the truth either way. Certainly the distribution of pottery vessels on the Antonine Wall demonstrates that it was possible to supply these goods to the troops in considerable quantities, and from all parts of the province, for pottery vessels have been found on the Wall from Colchester, Kent, Dorset, the west midlands, north-west England, south Yorkshire as well as southern Scotland. Nevertheless the apparent use of legionaries to garrison some of the forts on the Antonine Wall suggests that in one sphere the occupation of so much territory may have been causing difficulties. Whatever the reason it appears that the Wall was abandoned, the forts and fortlets destroyed by the withdrawing forces, and work started, yet again, on the repair of Hadrian's Wall and its outpost and hinterland forts.

The process of abandonment and rebuilding would take some time to complete and this may account for the discovery of coins later than 163, or thereabouts, on the Antonine Wall. Such coins have been found at Bar Hill and Mumrills and also possibly at Kirkintilloch. However, it is equally possible that although the new army bases were further south patrols continued to keep watch on the Lowland tribes and visit their former bases. Indeed some outposts may have continued to be held after the formal evacuation of the Antonine Wall. This might account for the erection of a temple at Castlecary, probably in the 170s or 180s. Certainly the army would not have lost all interest in the area to the north of Hadrian's Wall and would have maintained surveillance over the tribes beyond the province as they did on other frontiers. However, these new arrangements open up a new era on the northern frontier: from about 163 until well into the fourth century Rome was to control the northern frontier in a different way than during the previous forty years: now Walls were to become largely irrelevant.

7

War and Peace

The second century might in simplistic terms be called a century of war, the third century one of peace. This is certainly the impression provided by the contemporary sources. Through the second century references to warfare or disturbances on the northern frontier appear frequently, though usually as an aside, in the imperial biographies and other documents, but from 211 to 297 there is not a single such comment in the, admittedly sparse, literary sources. The difference between the two centuries may not merely reflect the different sources, or the change in imperial interest in Britain, but may accurately reflect the actual situation on the northern frontier for the picture which emerges from the literary sources is supported by the testimony of archaeology.

The unsettled state of the frontier in the first half of the second century continued into the early years of the third. The earlier years of the century had already seen remarkable vicissitudes. At the beginning of the century, it would appear, all or most forts north of the Tyne-Solway line were abandoned, though there is no mention of this in the literary sources. Epigraphy, however, suggests that there was warfare in Britain later in Trajan's reign, for an army unit based in the island was awarded decorations usually only given during warfare. At the opening of Hadrian's reign his biographer informs us that the Britons could not be kept under Roman control and, following the emperor's visit to the island, a Wall was built across the Tyne-Solway isthmus. Twenty years later this was abandoned for a return to Scotland, though Pius' biography makes no explicit mention of warfare at the time. Twenty years later, at the start of another reign, again war was threatening in Britain. The action initiated by the governor of the time, Calpurnius Agricola, presumably on imperial orders, was the abandonment of the Antonine system in Scotland and a return to Hadrian's Wall. Thereafter the units based on this Wall were to be the protectors of the province, and the literary sources demonstrate that this task was no sinecure.

There is a reference to Britain in a comment on the state of the empire in 169 following the death of the Emperor Lucius Verus. The biographer of his co-emperor Marcus Aurelius states that the Parthians and the Britons were on the verge of war. This bald statement is very similar to that made at the beginning of the reign and indeed may have been repeated in error. Such times – the death of an emperor and the succession of another – were often the occasion for a general resumé on the condition of the empire: they appear at the beginning of the reigns of Hadrian, Antoninus Pius, Marcus and Commodus, and at the death of Verus – and have consequently to be treated with care. It may be safer to ignore this particular comment.

The next reference to Britain is also rather enigmatic, though for very different reasons. In 175 Marcus Aurelius secured a temporary respite in his struggle on the Danube through making peace with the Sarmatian Iazyges. As a result of the alliance now concluded with this people, 100,000 Roman captives in their hands were surrendered and 8,000 cavalry was provided by the Iazyges for service in the Roman army, 5,500 being sent to Britain. It is possible that these cavalrymen were sent to Britain in order to help in warfare currently being fought there, or to strengthen the provincial army, but the fact that Britain was an island and far removed from the homeland of the Iazyges probably also played a part. It is not known where within Britain the Sarmatians were sent; the *ala Sarmatarum* later attested at Ribchester may or may not have been formed from the Sarmatian Iazyges.

It is probably to the reign of Marcus Aurelius that an inscription found at Kirksteads, three miles west of Carlisle, should be assigned. The altar was dedicated by Lucius Junius Victorinus Flav(ius) Caelianus, legate of *VI Victrix*, because of successful achievements beyond the Wall. This man may be identical with Junius Victorinus, governor of Upper Germany in the reign of Marcus. The brief statement on the altar does not allow the events in which the legate participated to be linked to any literary references to the northern frontier; indeed they may have no connection with any other known events.

This is certainly true of the event recorded on a late second or third century inscription from Corbridge. This records that Quintus Calpurnius Concessinius, prefect of cavalry, fulfilled his vow by dedicating an altar after slaughtering a band of Corionototae. This tribe, sect or group is otherwise unattested; nevertheless the inscription, and its fellow from Kirksteads, is eloquent testimony, of an unusual kind, of one type of activity which must have been fairly common on the northern frontier. A third inscription, also dated to the late second or third centuries, records the burial at Ambleside of two men, a retired centurion and an *actarius*, accounts clerk, probably father and son, the latter having been killed in the fort by the enemy. It is unfortunate that no further information is given about this enemy.

The beginning of the reign of the Emperor Commodus in 180 saw a more serious state of affairs. The main account survives in the *History of Rome* by the Greek Cassius Dio. He states that the greatest war of the reign was that in Britain and continues: 'the tribes in the island crossed the wall that separated them from the Roman forts, did a great deal of damage, and cut down a general and his troops, so Commodus in alarm sent against them Ulpius Marcellus, who inflicted a major defeat on the barbarians'. It was not until 184 that victory in Britain was celebrated by a commemorative coin issue and coins carrying the same message continued to be struck during the following two years. The date of the attack, however, is not known. There are three epigraphic reference to Ulpius Marcellus in Britain. Two are from Chesters on Hadrian's Wall, one clearly recording the construction of an aqueduct during his governorship, the other fragmentary. The third is also from Hadrian's Wall, in this case Benwell, a dedication in the governorship of Ulpius Marcellus by Tineius Longus who, while prefect of cavalry, had been adorned with the broad stripe of a senator and designated quaestor by the decree of the Emperors. The latter are not named, but they are certainly in the plural and therefore the inscription cannot refer to Commodus alone. It has been suggested that there was another, later Ulpius Marcellus governing Britain under Caracalla and Geta in the early third century under whom this inscription was erected.

It is perfectly possible that a governor is missing from the fragmentary provincial roll at this time and certainly the early third century was a period when extra facilities such as aqueducts appear to have been provided. However, it is also possible that Longus was designated as quaestor before the death of Marcus Aurelius, when he and Commodus were joint emperors, but did not make his dedication until some months later when a new governor had been appointed. Perhaps more likely is the possibility that the disaster on the British frontier occurred at the end of the joint reign of Marcus and Commodus and that Dio, in his summary of the state of the empire transferred to the beginning of the reign of Commodus events which had happened a few months before: such a transposition certainly can be demonstrated to have taken place in relation to another event of the time. The result of this plausible explanation would be to increase the length of the British war by about a year.

Much of the epitome of Dio's account of Ulpius Marcellus and his activities is concerned with anecdotes about his hero. It is thus doubly frustrating that he does not mention in his narrative the single most important fact to the present day historian: the precise Wall that was crossed. Archaeologists and historians have long argued about the identity of this Wall. The tortuous language employed has not helped: the wall which separated them from the Roman forts. In the past both Walls have been considered for this honour; it has even been suggested that the language employed by Dio could imply that it was the abandoned Antonine Wall, still somehow regarded as the frontier of the province, or at least separating the barbarians from the Roman forts, that was crossed. It seems, however, easier and simpler to assume that it was the Wall which was occupied at the time that was crossed and that Wall, at least on present theories, was Hadrian's Wall.

Archaeological evidence for the destruction of certain sites on Hadrian's Wall, dated on general archaeological grounds to the later second century, has been related to this disaster. In the past it has been considered that the Wall was destroyed wholesale during this invasion, but it now seems more probable that the effects were localised. At the forts at Halton Chesters and Rudchester destruction deposits have been assigned to this time and the burning of the military depot and town at Corbridge appears to be contemporary. However, investigations at other forts on the Wall line, and in particular at Carrawburgh, Housesteads, Wallsend and South Shields, have failed to furnish equivalent evidence. This seems to suggest that the barbarians moved south down Dere Street, using the Roman road against the Romans, and sacking the sites in their path, Halton Chesters, Corbridge and Rudchester. How far south they reached is, of course, unknown. The Roman officer killed was of senior rank and may have been the legate from York or even the provincial governor; the death of the latter might more easily account for the dispatch of a new governor to the province.

The measures taken by Ulpius Marcellus to protect the province are not known. There is but one hint: in 197 it is recorded that the Caledonians failed to honour their promises. This might suggest that the Caledonians had previously entered into a treaty with Rome and one suitable occasion for such an alliance might have been in the early 180s.

Although we hear of no more warfare on the northern frontier during the reign of Commodus the British army was in a ferment. The army tried to elevate two officers to the purple. At first they chose a legate, Priscus, but he refused. Then they sent a delegation of 1500 soldiers to Rome to protest against the praetorian prefect Perennis, an act which led directly to his downfall and death. The new governor of Britain, the later emperor Helvius Pertinax, was their next choice as usurper, but he also refused and although he managed to return most of the army to its loyalty to Commodus he did have to deal with a rebellion by one legion, during which he almost lost his life. His severity in putting down this mutiny caused resentment and as a result Pertinax asked to be relieved of his command. The reason for the turmoil in the army during these years is not known, though it may have partly resulted from the strict discipline of Ulpius Marcellus, a martinet of the old school, or possibly the sudden idleness of the army following years of activity.

The mutinous state of the British army in the late 180s is an interesting and unusual aside, an interlude, between the invasion of the first half of the decade and the civil war which began in 193 and which in Britain was followed by serious disturbances on the northern frontier culminating in the imperial expedition of 208–11. The position of the army on an island may have helped to create the conditions conducive for rebellion in the 180s; it certainly helped the governor in his bid for the throne in 193. On 31 December 192 the Emperor Commodus was assassinated. His successor, P. Helvius Pertinax, previously governor of Britain, did not enjoy his success for long before he too was murdered, as was his successor. In the ensuing struggle there were three main contenders for the empire, the governors commanding the main provincial armies. In the east Pescennius Niger was governor of Syria, in the west D. Clodius Albinus governed Britain, but in the centre, and commanding the only other three legion army, was L. Septimius Severus. Severus, the junior of the three governors and the least popular so far as the Senate was concerned, was well placed in Pannonia (modern Hungary) to reach Italy first. He won Rome in June 193 and on assuming the purple his first task was to deal with his rivals. Severus naturally chose to turn against Niger first: to move against Albinus was to risk being caught on an island while his other rival was still at large. Time was bought by recognising Albinus as consul for 194. The defeat of Niger in that year was followed by campaigns against the Parthians and other eastern nations while Severus' army was besieging the last stronghold of Niger's supporters, Byzantium. When that city fell at the end of 195 Severus returned to Rome and began preparations against Albinus. The decisive battle was fought at Lyons on 19 February 197 and after a hard fought engagement the forces of Severus were successful.

It seems probable that Clodius Albinus took measures to protect the province when he took the army to Gaul for the battle with Severus. It has been suggested that he made a treaty with the Caledonians, possibly implied by a statement by Dio that in 197 the Caledonians refused to honour their promises, and that he defended the towns of the province by the construction of walls. Neither suggestion can be proved. It may even be doubted that Albinus did much to protect the province: if he was successful he would have the full resources of the empire to repair any damage in Britain and if he failed such matters would no longer be his concern. At any rate the situation does not become clearer until after his defeat.

The new governor of Britain appointed by Severus was Virius Lupus. Dio records that Lupus found the northern frontier in an unsettled state: 'the Caledonians, instead of honouring their promises, prepared to assist the Maeatae. As Severus was at that time concentrating on the Parthian war, Lupus had to purchase peace from the Maeatae for a great sum, recovering a few prisoners'. Severus soon after the battle of Lyons had returned to Rome but the same summer set out for the east where he devoted himself to the Parthian war until 199. Although Lupus clearly had a difficult situation to deal with it would appear that it was not serious enough for it to interfere with the emperor's other plans.

The outline of the events on the northern frontier is straightforward and cannot be elaborated by reference to any other source. The Maeatae had been causing a disturbance, the nature of which is unknown but as it involved the capture of some Romans, possibly soldiers, it presumably included warfare. It would appear that

Lupus could keep this situation under control, but when the Caledonians, seemingly in treaty relationship with Rome, prepared to abandon their former position and help the Maeatae, Lupus changed his policy, and, preferring diplomacy to war, bribed the Maeatae in the time-honoured Roman tradition. The five coin hoards ending with Commodus and perhaps some of the four coin hoards ending with Severus found in central and eastern Scotland may reflect the payment of subsidies to these northern tribes. Thereafter no further trouble is recorded on the northern frontier for nearly ten years.

The Maeatae are an enigmatic people. They only appear in the record at this time and the precise location of their homeland is not known. Dio later states 'the two principal tribes of the [free] Britons are the Caledonians and the Maeatae, the names of the others having being merged in these two. The Maeatae live close to the wall which divides the island in two and the Caledonians beyond them.' Frustratingly again the name of the Wall is not stated as it would presumably have been obvious to the readers of the time. It seems almost certain that the Maeatae lived beyond the province: the names of the Lowland tribes continue through the Roman period with no hint of change while the names of the tribes beyond the frontier in eastern Scotland changed on at least two occasions.

Two place names appear to retain the name Maeatae: Dumyot Hill overlooking Stirling and Myot Hill south of the Forth at the east end of the Campsies. It seems probable that these places are so named because they lie on the edge of Maeatian territory and therefore that the tribe extended north from the Forth basin, presumably into Strathearn and Strathmore, possibly Fife as well (fig. 28). The apparent extension of this tribe south of the Forth is interesting. It seems probable that the Maeatae was an amalgamation of the tribes recorded by Ptolemy and reflects one of the regular impacts of Rome upon the barbarians: the coalescence of tribes beyond the frontier into ever larger units. Alternatively, this may be the 'lost' tribe of Ptolemy in Strathearn and Strathmore (cf. pages 29–31).

Dio's brief statement hints that the Romans treated the Maeatae and the Caledonians differently, though they were both presumably in treaty relationship with Rome. They were clearly two separate peoples and it might be that Rome, through her diplomacy, played one off against the other, losing this game in the late 190s when the tribes moved to combine against her.

The governorship of Virius Lupus saw the beginning of a long series of building inscriptions relating to forts on Hadrian's Wall and its hinterland. Over 30 inscriptions survive from the period 197–*c*.250. Several of the stones record the buildings erected or repaired: the gates and walls, granaries, headquarters building, armoury, exercise hall, bathhouse, aqueduct. It has been suggested that the earlier inscriptions at least relate to repairs carried out following an attack on the northern frontier while the army was away in Gaul with Albinus. Archaeological evidence from the forts, milecastles and turrets on Hadrian's Wall has been cited as support for the destruction of the frontier at this time. However, the destruction of those forts which more clearly suffered at the hand of the northern barbarians is now considered to date to the early 180s and not the late 190s, while the repair work at other sites may be better interpreted as part of a programme of rebuilding and improvement necessitated by the ravages of time rather than the ravages of an enemy.

The inscriptions seem to demonstrate that the intention of Severus was not to reconquer Scotland, but to repair Hadrian's Wall and its hinterland forts and maintain this Wall as the frontier. Thus Virius Lupus is recorded building at

28 *The tribes of north Britain in the early third century*

Brough under Stainmore, Bowes and Ilkley, his successor, Valerius Pudens, at Brough-by-Bainbridge and the next governor Alfenus Senecio at Bowes, Greta Bridge, Brough-by-Bainbridge, Corbridge, Chesters, Birdoswald and Risingham, the work extending over the ten years from 197. This work stopped at precisely the time that there was a major change in frontier policy in Britain and did not recommence until the 210s.

The events which led up to this change in frontier policy are tolerably well recorded by the contemporary historians Cassius Dio and Herodian. In 207 Dio recorded that Severus' generals were winning wars in Britain, yet in the following year he decided to come to the island to take command of the Roman forces himself. Herodian records that the governor of Britain wrote to the emperor informing him that the barbarians were overrunning the province, plundering and causing great destruction, and that for effective defence either more troops or the presence of the emperor was required. Severus was delighted with the chance of winning more victories and also, both Herodian and Dio assert, removing his sons from the decadent atmosphere of Rome. It has been pointed out that the Persian and German wars of Severus Alexander (222–35), Septimius Severus' great-nephew, were also prefaced, according to Herodian, by letters from governors reporting invasions and requesting the presence of the emperor. Although the invasions certainly took place, it seems possible in these cases that Herodian is just using stock phrases to elaborate an actual situation. It is therefore also possible that the British letter may have been engineered by Severus in order to give him an excuse to remove his sons from Rome and subject them to the discipline of military life as Dio and Herodian aver. Dio goes on to record that Severus' intention was to conquer the whole of the island.

The emperors – Severus and his elder son Caracalla – appear to have left Rome in 208, accompanied by members of their family, including Caracalla's younger brother Geta, and a large expeditionary force. The army included most, possibly all, of the praetorian guard and detachments from other legions: Dio states that a large sum of money was also taken. The expedition was marked by an issue of coins showing Severus and Caracalla on horseback accompanied by legionaries and by a coin with, on the reverse, a galley, in which are a flag and standards, indicating a military expedition by sea. Severus travelled quickly in spite of the fact that for most of the journey he was carried in a litter owing to his arthritis, the speed of his arrival together with the size of his army disconcerting the enemy who sued for peace. The envoys were, however, dismissed and Severus continued his preparations. Those put in hand now, or earlier, probably included the rebuilding of the granaries at Corbridge in order to aid with supply up Dere Street, which the evidence of temporary camps informs us was the main route taken by the army, and certainly included the construction of 20 new granaries within the fort at South Shields. This major undertaking at South Shields may in fact be more closely related to the planned occupation of Scotland rather than the campaigns, though the presence of detachments of the Rhine and Danube fleets in Britain at the time emphasises the concentration on transport by sea: this is reinforced by coins issued in 209 with Neptune and Oceanus on the reverse. Severus placed his younger son, Geta, supported by counsellors, in charge of affairs in the Roman part of the island while he and Caracalla took charge of the fighting.

Campaigning probably began in 209. Both surviving literary accounts concentrate more on the marshes, rivers, forests and hills which the Roman army had to cross, than furnish details of the route taken. Study of the surviving marching camps, however, suggests that the army marched up Dere Street and, after negotiating the Forth and the Tay, passed through Strathmore (fig. 29). Two series of camps have been assigned to the Severan period and the earlier camps, 25 hectares in size, appear to go no further than the northern end of Strathmore, the territory probably of the Maeatae. The later series – archaeological excavation has proved the relationship between the two series – are larger (44–52ha), and extend further north, passing round the Mounth and almost reaching the Moray Firth. It seems unlikely that the camps were built in the same season for at Ardoch one partially overlies the other; the two series presumably therefore reflect different campaigns or seasons. The smaller camps are almost exactly half the size of those in the other series. They march up Strathmore in two lines. This may indicate either two armies on the march, or simply a smaller force on a circuitous route.

The mention of the crossing of rivers by Dio and Herodian finds echo in coins. An *as* or small medallion of Caracalla dating to 209 shows a bridge of boats being crossed by soldiers. The location of this bridge is not known, but the Tay at Carpow, where there are defensive enclosures on both sides of the river, is generally the favourite choice for the stretch of water depicted on the coin. Other coins of this year show Caracalla galloping over a fallen barbarian and Caracalla accompanied by legionaries, indicating the campaigning.

The distribution of the few Severan coins found in Scotland, for what it is worth, also emphasises the concentration of army activity in eastern Scotland for with one exception they all lie along Dere Street or on the east coast (fig. 30). Nine coin hoards ending with Commodus or Severus may also point to Roman activity at this time, possibly even the payment of subsidies to the northern tribes, though a variety of reasons could have led to their deposition. Nevertheless the hoards do emphasise Severan activity in this area, not least because following the Falkirk hoard of 1900 coins, collected mainly under Severus but not deposited until twenty years later, there are no more coin hoards in Scotland until the fourth century.

The length of the campaign is not known. Although minor engagements did occur, there were no major battles for the Caledonians and Maeatae employed guerilla tactics, drawing the Romans on and attempting to wear them out. Dio even states that cattle and sheep were deliberately left as a lure. The sources give the impression that the Roman advance was slow but sure for in its progress the army provided causeways through the marshes, bridged rivers, levelled hills and cut paths through the forests. The Romans reportedly suffered heavy losses, 50,000 according to Dio – surely an exaggeration. Severus did not stop until he had almost reached the end of the island, a statement which suggests that more temporary camps remain to be discovered. In spite of the difficulties of coming to grips with the enemy he forced them to accept terms and cede a considerable part of their territory to Rome. Dio records an incident which took place while terms were being discussed, of no relevance here, but incidentally demonstrating that the peace negotiations were conducted by the emperors and their advisers and the Caledonians in front of the two assembled armies. On completion of the peace negotiations Severus and Caracalla returned south. The victory was celebrated by the adoption of the title Britannicus by Severus, Caracalla and Geta in 210. Early coins of this year do not include this title but the award is recorded on coins produced later in the year and victory in Britain was also celebrated on coins in the following year.

The only certain fact about the peace treaty is that the Britons – possibly a term used here to cover both the tribes involved – ceded a considerable part of their

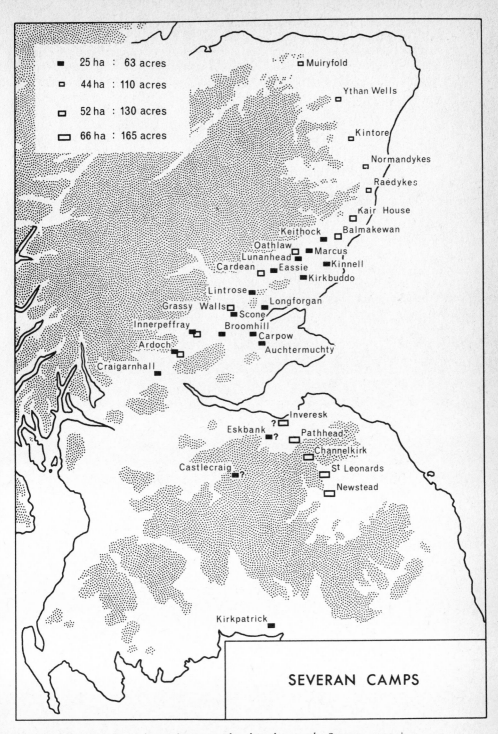

29 *Marching camps in Scotland considered to date to the Severan campaigns*

30 The distribution of Roman finds on non-military sites in Scotland in the Severan period (after Robertson)

country to Rome. This will presumably have included all or part of Strathmore, once part of the province, but may have also extended to land beyond the Mounth, the territory of the Caledonians. In the third century, in 232, a unit, *Brittones dediticii Alexandriani*, is recorded in Upper Germany. The inclusion of the word *dediticii* in the title suggests that the soldiers were conscripted into the army from recently conquered tribes, such people being officially termed *dediticii*. The most appropriate occasion for the raising of such a unit in Britain at this time would be the extension of the province by Severus in 209. Even though this was not a permanent arrangement, there may well have been time before the abandonment of Roman pretensions so far north for the raising of new units from the new provincials.

In May 210 Severus was at York, for he and Caracalla issued a rescript on 5 May from there. However, that year the Maeatae broke out in revolt. Severus placed Caracalla in charge of the army and issued instructions to the soldiers to kill everyone they met. It is possible that the route taken by this force is reflected in the second series of third century marching camps in Scotland. After the invasion had taken place the Caledonians joined the revolt. Severus now, in spite of his illness, made preparations to join his army, but before he could do so he died at York on 4 February 211. Caracalla now had different priorities. In spite of the fact that he had been co-emperor for thirteen years his first concern would naturally be to return to Rome to ensure a smooth transference of power. It is not surprising therefore that he made peace with the barbarians, gave up the new conquests, abandoning forts, and, together with his brother and mother, returned to Rome with his father's ashes.

Only two forts in Scotland are known to have been occupied at this time (fig. 31). One was Cramond on the Forth. This may have served as a link in the supply chain up the east coast, though there is no definite evidence for this. The other is the legionary base at Carpow on the south shore of the Tay, a little downstream from modern Perth. Here a fortress was constructed, 11 hectares in size. At least two legions, *II Augusta* and *VI Victrix*, helped to build the base and it is possible that the garrison was furnished by these two units. The fortress, with ramparts of turf and gates of stone, contained headquarters building, palace for the commanding officer, and granary all in stone, with timber barrack-blocks.

The exact date of construction of the site is not known, though it has produced coins of the early third century and fragments of monumental building inscriptions. One inscription has been restored to record the titles of Caracalla after he became sole emperor in February 212 when he murdered his brother Geta. Unfortunately there is some controversy surrounding the interpretation of the inscription. There is further evidence to suggest that the occupation of the site may not have been too brief. In one area of the fortress at least there were two phases of building activity. The earlier, possibly temporary, timber buildings were dismantled at about the time that the adjacent stone headquarters and commanding officer's house were erected. The date of commencement of construction work at Carpow is not known. Building may have started as part of the preparations for the campaigns recorded by the literary authorities. On the other hand this would be unusual, if not most difficult in view of the position of the fortress in or on the very edge of Maeatian territory, while the stamped tiles from the site record that *legio VI Victrix* had been awarded the title *Britannica*, which would not have occured until after the proclamation of victory in 209 at the earliest, and more likely 210 or later. On all grounds a date of 210 for the commencement of building is the most likely.

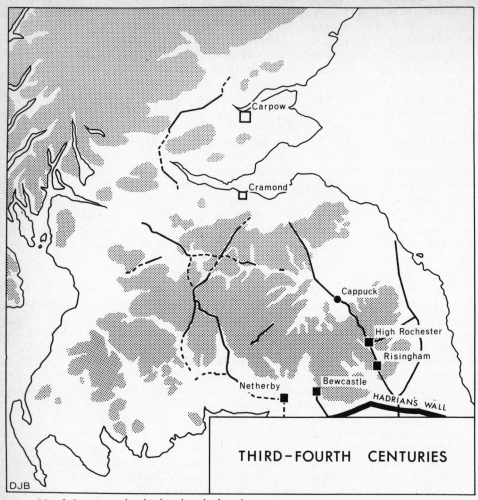

Carpow

Cramond

Cappuck

High Rochester

Risingham

Netherby

Bewcastle

HADRIAN'S WALL

THIRD - FOURTH CENTURIES

DJB

31 North Britain in the third and early fourth centuries

Whatever the date Carpow was certainly abandoned after a very short life and Cramond was presumably given up at the same time.

The reorganisation of the frontier in the late second century

It is now necessary to turn from the literary accounts of warfare in Britain to the archaeological and related material to examine the methods used by Rome to guard and patrol the northern frontier in the late second century and through the third. This evidence comes from a variety of sources, archaeological, epigraphic and documentary, and is piecemeal and sketchy. In broad outline it suggests that in the late second century important modifications were carried out to Hadrian's Wall while the outpost system north of the Wall was extended and strengthened. The effect of these changes appears to have been to reduce the importance of the Wall itself – though not the forts on the barrier – and push the real frontier northwards at least to the Cheviots. The size of the units based in the outpost forts was sufficient to patrol extensive areas north of the Wall, possibly even the whole area formerly within the province.

When the Roman army withdrew from Scotland in the 160s and reoccupied Hadrian's Wall and its hinterland forts the Wall appears to have been put back into commission with the minimum of change. The only important modification would appear to have been the addition of a road, which connected the forts, and was generally positioned between the Wall and the Vallum, though in places it ran along the north mound of the Vallum. Apart from this imposition the Vallum seems to have continued in use as before. The extra, or marginal, mound which can still be seen in places on the south lip of the ditch, between the ditch and the south mound, probably results from cleaning out the ditch at this time. However, there appears to have been no thorough attempt to dig out the rock and soil dumped at regular intervals to create crossings twenty years before. The milecastles and turrets were cleaned out and repaired and the forts regarrisoned. Where evidence survives it suggests that most forts were now occupied by units of similar size and type to those which had evacuated them on the occupation of the Antonine Wall: in one instance, Carvoran, the garrison was apparently the same.

Although the Wall was at first brought back to the state it was in when abandoned changes soon seem to have been made. Some turrets appear to have had short lives. One, 33b Coesike, seems to have had a brief period of reoccupation followed by blocking of the door and abandonment of the site. Some time later, probably in the late second century, or the early third, possibly at the time that Severus' governors carried out their repairs elsewhere, the turret was demolished down to its lowest courses and the recess into the thickness of the Wall built up. The history of other turrets seems to have been similar. The building-up of the recesses may have been necessary in order to make a walk along the top of the Wall safe through the replacement of rotting timber floors by a more substantial platform. In these years many turrets, mainly in the crags sector, were abandoned; most had been superfluous from the very beginning. Elsewhere the abandonment was more selective as if thought was given to the working of the Wall so that redundant turrets were given up while those serving a useful purpose were retained.

Milecastles too were modified, as a result of a more realistic reappraisal of their function. Excavation has revealed that many had either their north or south gate narrowed so that it could only be used for pedestrian traffic, while two (MCs 22 and 36) had their north gates blocked completely. However, only one milecastle, 27 Brunton, across the river from Chesters fort, is known to have been abandoned.

These changes extended to the structures on the Cumbrian Coast. Few mile-fortlets and towers seem to have been reoccupied in the 160s, though more than was once considered. However, only one of these sites appears to have survived in occupation till the later years of the second century, MF 5 Cardurnock, the largest milefortlet on the Coast, and a fortlet in its own right.

The major rethinking in fort garrisons appears to have been in the 180s, presumably by Ulpius Marcellus. In many cases the units garrisoning the Wall forts in the early third century were different in size and type from those recorded either by inscriptions, or, by implication, in the earlier years of the second century. The most important change was the strengthening of the cavalry component on the Wall. There were now apparently four cavalry units on the Wall line as opposed to two or three under Hadrian while at least seven of the remaining twelve forts now contained mixed units compared with four or five under Hadrian. The result would be to increase the mobility of the Wall garrison. It can be shown that three forts were provided with their new garrisons before the Severan campaigns, and in one case, Chesters, the unit was already in residence under Ulpius Marcellus. It is not impossible therefore that this governor was responsible for the complete overhaul and modification of all the fort garrisons.

These were not the only changes to fort garrisons on Hadrian's Wall. Inscriptions reveal that in the third century the normal garrison of three forts was supplemented by the addition of *numeri*. Four such *numeri* are known, garrisoning the three forts: at Housesteads the *cohors I Tungrorum* was strengthened by the addition of two units, the *cuneus Frisiorum* and the *numerus Hnaudifridi*. The date at which these units arrived is not known but it is not impossible that they were also introduced to the northern frontier by Ulpius Marcellus in the early 180s. It is possible also that Marcellus was responsible for the construction of the fort at Newcastle for recent excavation has suggested that the stone fort here may not have been built before the late second century.

The *numeri* on the Wall had their counterparts in the outpost forts to the north. However, before examining the garrisons of these forts it is necessary to examine the history of the sites from the abandonment of the Antonine system through into the third century. Most surviving archaeological evidence points to the abandonment of forts on and in front of the Antonine Wall in the 160s, c.163 being the preferred date. At this time not all forts behind the Wall were abandoned; on the contrary some were retained to serve as outpost forts for Hadrian's Wall. In the west all three Hadrianic outpost forts continued in occupation, or were reoccupied at this time: Birrens, Netherby and Bewcastle. In the east a line of forts appears to have been retained along Dere Street at least as far north as Newstead. There may also have been outposts beyond the Tweed, for several sites on the Antonine Wall have furnished evidence for occupation after the mid 160s. At Castlecary, an important fort on the watershed between the Forth and Clyde basins and apparently occupied at different times by milliary cohorts, the evidence comes in the form of an inscription. This altar, dedicated to Mercury, records the erection of a shrine or temple and a statuette by soldiers of *legio* VI Victrix who were citizens of Italy and Noricum. The most straightforward way in which these soldiers could have entered a British legion was by transfer from *legio II Italica*, raised in 165, almost certainly practically entirely in Italy, the normal area at this time for the recruitment of new legions. The inscription would have been erected within twenty-five years of 165, probably in the latter half of this period. The presence of a military establishment here receives some support from a sherd of late second-century samian ware, the only fragment of this date found on a military site north of Newstead. The other archaeological evidence for a military presence on the Forth-Clyde isthmus in the late second century is numismatic: two unstratified coins from former Antonine Wall forts, Mumrills and Kirkintilloch. No military structure of late second-century date is known at any of these sites.

The invasion of the early 180s seems to have resulted in a reappraisal of the outpost system. In the west Birrens appears to have been abandoned in the 180s and in the east Newstead: any outposts further north were presumably withdrawn at the same time if not before (fig. 31). Newstead may have been reoccupied briefly in the early third century when Roman armies were operating in Scotland, but otherwise the outpost system was now based upon the four forts at Netherby, Bewcastle, Risingham and High Rochester. These were not large forts – they varied in size from 1.6 to 2.4 hectares – but they appear to have been the bases for large forces, probably from the 180s into the third, possibly even fourth, century. Three units are attested at each of the eastern outpost forts: a 1,000-strong mixed unit, a *numerus* and a detachment of scouts. The garrisons of the western forts are not so clearly known, but Netherby, and probably also Bewcastle, was garrisoned by a thousand strong mixed cohort in the third century. According to the Antonine Itinerary the Roman name for Netherby was *Castra exploratorum*, which is certainly suggestive in relation to the garrison of the eastern outpost forts. Birrens, abandoned probably in the late 180s, was also the base for a thousand strong mixed unit in the second century. The total strength of the outpost forts in the third century will have been about 5,000 men, the equivalent in manpower of a legion.

The forts which were the nominal homes of these units were, in each instance, too small to hold even the milliary cohort alone, so it follows that many soldiers from the cohorts, *numeri* and *exploratores* must have been outposted elsewhere. Only one hint survives concerning the possible location of such an outpost. Two altars found at Jedburgh Abbey were dedicated by soldiers from the cohort and the *numerus* from High Rochester in the third century: it is possible that the stones were carried from Cappuck, 3km to the east, by the medieval masons.

The main duties of all the soldiers based in the outpost forts will have included long-range patrolling and surveillance of the tribes to the north of Hadrian's Wall as well as the protection of the province from attack. Documents from elsewhere in the empire demonstrate that such patrols could range widely in the pursuit of their duties. On the Eastern frontier of the empire one outpost, admittedly not the same as a mobile patrol, was permanently outstationed 250km from its parent unit at Dura Europos. If this was transferred to the north British frontier, it is almost exactly the distance from High Rochester to Stracathro, and suggests that Roman soldiers could have maintained watch over the whole of the territory of the former province north of Hadrian's Wall.

It has been suggested that the Ravenna Cosmography contained reference to places, *loca*, tribal meeting places, supervised by the army. However, it is possible that these are simply places north of Hadrian's Wall which did not fit into any other of the Cosmographer's categories. Nevertheless, it is probable, on the basis of parallels with other frontiers, that the army did closely supervise the activities of the tribes north of the Wall after the abandonment of the Antonine system. Cassius Dio records the arrangement made by the Roman authorities to control the tribes north of the Danube in the late second century when the Emperor Commodus (180–192) gave up the plans formulated by his father, Marcus Aurelius, to incorporate these peoples into the empire. Treaties defined the boundaries of the tribes, the size of the tribute to be paid to Rome and the tribal assemblies. The Marcomanni, for example, had to pay an annual tribute of corn and also supply weapons and soldiers, though rather less than the Quadi whose contribution was fixed at 15,000 men. They were allowed to assemble once a month under the supervision of a Roman centurion and were forbidden to make war on certain neighbouring tribes. The Buri and other tribes were forbidden to settle within 400 stades of the border of the province of Dacia. It seems probable that similar arrangements, though presumably not the restrictions on settlement, were introduced on the northern frontier as the army withdrew in the 160s.

The system of control established in the late second century, in part at least apparently as early as the 160s, seems to have lasted well into the fourth century. The historian Ammianus Marcellinus writing at that time records that in the Barbarian Conspiracy of 367 the *areani* (a term best interpreted as frontier scouts) had been bribed by the barbarian tribes to reveal the Roman positions to them. Ammianus asserts that the *areani* had been established in early times, and it seems possible that they are the descendants of the *exploratores*, and perhaps other units, placed in the outposts forts in the second and third centuries. Archaeological evidence supports the supposition arising from this, namely that the outpost forts continued in occupation into the fourth century.

Brochs, duns and souterrains

Before we move finally into the third century it is necessary to consider the intrusion of certain dwellings – brochs, duns and souterrains – more usually found north of the Forth-Clyde line, into southern Scotland. Brochs originated in the far north of Scotland in the second century BC, possible earlier. Their distribution is concentrated in the northern isles and the counties of Caithness and Sutherland, but spreading down the west coast to Skye and across to the Outer Hebrides. No brochs are known between the Firths of Moray and Tay, with the exception of three in the north shore of the Tay, but several, about a dozen, appear further south (fig. 33). Three of these southern brochs have been excavated. All have produced Roman artefacts: Torwoodlee in Tweedale samian and coarse pottery, glass, part of a glass armlet, a quern; Leckie in the Forth valley samian ware, glass, iron sword blade, quern, plough fragment, carbonised grain, sheep shears, brooch, beads, glass armlets, pins and finger rings; and at Buchlyvie a few miles west of Leckie, fragments of samian, coarse pottery, amphorae, mortaria and glass, a coin, four querns, a sickle blade, carbonised grain, whorls, pins and finger rings, brooches, lead ingots and iron slag. There is ample evidence here of contact with the Roman world; evidence too of farming communities. The farmers who lived in the brochs were not the first settlers on the site, for in all cases the broch succeeded a pre-existing structure. This is clearest at Buchlyvie where the stone tower followed a round timber house with no significant break in the occupation of the site. The occurrence of mid-second-century artefacts within the occupation levels at Torwoodlee and Leckie demonstrates that both were occupied in or after the Antonine period: at the former site pottery and glass were found beneath the broch wall. The occupation of both these brochs ended in destruction, at Torwoodlee apparently after only a short life.

The brochs probably entered southern Scotland from the west rather than the north: certainly the dun came from this direction. Two excavated duns, Castle Hill Wood in the valley of the Forth and Stanhope in Tweeddale, have produced Roman objects of second century date, including a brooch, glass and querns.

The final introduction to southern Scotland was the souterrain. This was an underground, or partially underground, passage which led off from a surface dwelling. Souterrains have been found attached to both timber and stone houses. Their function is uncertain and various possibilities have been suggested: store houses, byres, refuges, and temples. On the whole the former interpretation seems to be the best. Roman artefacts, usually of second or third century date, have been found in some souterrains in southern Scotland and one or two examples incorporated Roman stones. The main areas of distribution of souterrains in Scotland are Angus, Aberdeenshire and Caithness/Sutherland, though they also occur in the northern isles, Ireland, Cornwall and on the continent. They presumably spread south from Fife and Angus; a recently excavated example in this area, Newmill in Perthshire, was probably constructed in the first century AD and

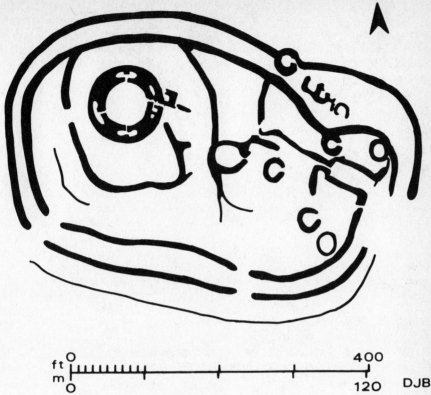

ft 0 ... 400
m 0 ... 120   DJB

32 *The broch and fort at Edinshall, Berwickshire (after* RCAHMS). *The sequence appears to be: fort; broch, which lies in the W part of the enclosure; open (Romano-British?) settlement overlying the E part of the fort*

abandoned in the late second or early third century, though the site continued in occupation for several centuries.

The distribution of all these three structures in southern Scotland is similar. On the east they reach as far south as the Tweed, with several examples of brochs and souterrains on the north bank, but none on the south. In the west the brochs and duns extend further south, for their distribution is along the coast to Luce Bay, with a single outlier in Wigtown Bay to the east. It may or may not be significant that this pattern matches closely the spread of heavy armlets, snake bracelets and Donside terrets, whose manufacture and centre of distribution was clearly in Aberdeenshire. These objects, probably mainly in the second century AD, trickled down into southern Scotland though, interestingly, they stopped at the Tweed, with the exception of four outliers, two on the Tyne (fig. 34).

Although the distribution patterns of the structures and objects in southern Scotland may be similar, and fall within the same general period, they do not all have the same point of origin. The souterrains presumably spread south from Angus and Fife, while the metal objects emanated from north-east Scotland. The duns will have entered southern Scotland from the west, and it seems possible that the brochs moved in the same direction. It seems unlikely therefore that a single influence was at work. It is difficult to use the appearance of the structures and

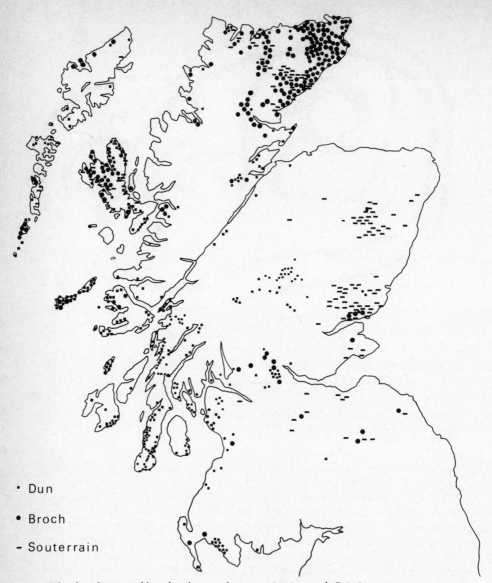

- Dun

• Broch

- Souterrain

33 The distribution of brochs, duns and souterrains in north Britain

metalwork south of the Forth to support the hypothesis that they reflect an extension of Caledonian power, or at least influence, in the second century. The situation is complicated by the appearance of so much Roman material in the brochs and duns. It would appear that the inhabitants of these sites had close contacts with the Roman world and it seems more probable that the objects were gained through trade than plunder.

The people of the land between the Tweed and the Forth, former provincial territory, were, it seems, subject to influences from the south, north and west, probably over a period of years. However, when the archaeological material can be

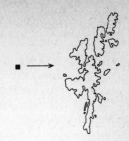

- ● MASSIVE ARMLETS
- ◆ SNAKE BRACELETS
- ■ 'DONSIDE' TERRETS

34 *The distribution of armlets, snake bracelets and 'Donside' terrets in north Britain*

closely dated most falls within the second half of the second century. For part of that period this area was, of course, part of the empire. But in the late second century, when the Roman army in Britain and the Roman empire was in turmoil, the army lost control over events in the north on at least two occasions. It may have been on either or both of these occasions, in the early 180s and the late 190s, that these southern brochs, duns and souterrains were erected and the metalwork trickled south. The new dwellings certainly seem to have been shortlived for no broch, dun nor souterrain has produced Roman artefacts of a date later than the second century. This may reflect the increased Roman control over southern Scotland from the Severan period through the third century, as seemingly recorded in the documentary sources. However, this is only a partial answer, and possibly not the correct one. The range of Roman objects found within the brochs is considerable. Buchlyvie and Leckie have each produced more finds than nearly any other native settlement in Scotland, the nearest comparison in range and number of objects being at Traprain Law. Indeed the wealth of Roman material at these two brochs is such as to hint that they were occupied while Roman forces still resided in Scotland, though it is difficult to see a context for their construction at such a time. Clearly in the present state of knowledge any definitive statement concerning the reasons and date of the construction of brochs, duns and souterrains in southern Scotland – and the entry of northern metalwork into this area – would be more than usually foolhardy.

The third century

The establishment of the system of supervision over the northern frontier in the later second century heralded an era of peace in the third. No war is known to have taken place on the north British frontier from that of Severus and Caracalla in 208–11 until the campaign of Constantius Chlorus against the Picts in 306. The reasons for this century of peace are not known. Certainly it cannot be claimed that the measures taken to control the frontier alone were responsible for they were the same as those that had not prevented the invasion of the early 180s nor the troubles of the late 190s. Perhaps events were moving in a cyclical manner: a century of disturbed conditions in north Britain was followed by a century of relative peace, a phenomenon which can be observed in other areas and at other times.

The Roman army of the early third century did not, of course, appreciate what was to come. They no doubt continued to train and prepare for war as they had done for centuries, so that, in the words of Josephus, their exercises were bloodless battles and their battles bloody exercises. Many of the training routines and exercises are known and there also survives part of the speech of the Emperor Hadrian (117–138) in which he commented on the military displays of certain units which he had just witnessed. No such evidence survives in Britain, though evidence of a different nature is preserved. A number of training areas in north Britain have been postulated. Two in particular are more certain than the others. Around the abandoned pre-Roman hill fort on Woden Law in Roxburghshire, immediately beside Dere Street, lie three lines of ramparts and ditches which have been interpreted as practice Roman siege works. More spectacular are the practice camps on either side of the long abandoned hill fort at Burnswark in Dumfriesshire, overlooking the road up Annandale (pl. 2). This seems to have been a training area for the army of north Britain. On top of the remains of the three south entrances of the hill fort targets were laid out for the soldiers to fire at. The missiles were arrows, ballista balls and sling shot. The latter are especially interesting, for they are made of lead and are thus a type of shot which went out of use elsewhere in the western provinces of the empire in the mid-first century. As many as 133 lead shot have been recovered from Burnswark and 28 from other military bases in north Britain: Housesteads, Birdoswald, Chesterholm, Corbridge and Ambleside. It would appear probable that troops came up from these sites to train at Burnswark. The date of use of Burnswark as a training area cannot be precisely determined. One practice camp, the southern, partly overlies the remains of an Antonine fortlet and the silting pattern of the fortlet ditch suggests that some time had elapsed between its construction and its infilling by the rampart of the camp. All the pottery from the site dates to the second century and the lead sling bullet from Birrens was found in a mid-second century layer. But two of the lead bullets, those from Chesterholm and Housesteads, came from levels tentatively dated to the third century, so it seems possible that the use of Burnswark as a Roman army training area may have continued from the mid-second century for some decades. It is not surprising therefore that traces of semi-permanent occupation have been discovered in one of the camps.

While the army, into the third century, no doubt continued training and patrolling, it also improved the facilities in its base forts as if realising that the days of large-scale troop movements were over. Many inscriptions record the mainten-ance of the fort or the improvement of its defences. Some inscriptions clearly state that rebuilding was necessary because the previous buildings had fallen down through old age. Thus in 205/7 at Risingham the south gate, with its walls, was restored from ground level because it had fallen in through age, while in 221 a similarly worded inscription records the restoration of an unnamed building at Chesters and another, a granary at Greatchesters in 225. This process continued throughout the third century being recorded on three other inscriptions, from Lanchester, where the headquarters and armoury was rebuilt in 238–44, Lancaster, where the baths were restored in 262/6 and in a slightly different formula at Birdoswald at the end of the century.

Other inscriptions adopt a variant wording: the building was built or restored from the ground level, or from its foundations. Thus baths were built at Chester-le-Street in 216 and at Lanchester in 238/44, while the *ballistaria*, or artillery platforms, were erected at High Rochester in 220 and restored 225/35 – perhaps a different platform. An inscription from Chesterholm specifically states that the (south) gate with its towers was restored from its foundations in 223. There is no reason to doubt the veracity of the carvers of these inscriptions. The Romans could be remarkably frank about the reasons for restoring buildings. Milestones from Cyrene record the restoration of a road which had been damaged during the Jewish revolt which broke out there in 115 while late second century inscriptions from Lower Pannonia (modern Hungary) state that the new defences were being constructed to afford better protection against bandits.

It is possible that some of the buildings which had collapsed through old age or were restored from the ground had previously lain abandoned for some years. But while that might be the case with Risingham in 205/7 it is unlikely, for example, that Greatchesters was abandoned prior to 225, or Chesterholm before 223. It may be that while certain inscriptions are recording the re-occupation of some forts or the restoration of parts of others, abandoned for perfectly acceptable reasons, others are bearing witness to the general round of maintenance carried out by the Roman army engineers.

The early third century saw not only the maintenance of existing defences and buildings but the improvement of facilities for the soldiers. Already under Commodus (180–92) an aqueduct had been constructed at Chesters. In 216 not only was the bath-house at Chester-le-Street rebuilt but a new aqueduct was laid as well and one for South Shields followed in 222. The soldiers may not altogether have approved of some of the facilities for they included the erection of a drill hall at Netherby.

This building activity, as recorded by inscriptions, continued unabated through the 220s. Thereafter it slowed in the 230s with a single later record at Lancaster in the 260s. This parallels the decline in the erection of inscriptions throughout the empire in the third century. However, it also parallels another development, the abandonment, partially or complete, of many forts in northern England in the late third century. There is considerable evidence, both literary and archaeological, for this abandonment. The 'literary' evidence lies in the pages of the *Notitia Dignitatum*. This document, probably prepared at the beginning of the fifth century, records the officials of the empire, listing in particular army units together with the rank of their commanding officer. In Britain there is a clear distinction between the names of the units on Hadrian's Wall and those behind the Wall (fig. 35). The former, with one exception, retain the form of titles found in the early empire and indeed many of the units were attested in these forts in the late second or third century. The latter, mainly, have the titles introduced in the late empire and in many cases these units replaced known third-century garrisons. It seems probable that the earlier units were withdrawn some time during the course of the third century, probably in the second half, while the new units arrived probably in the first quarter of the fourth century. Their distribution, generally on the two main roads leading north from York up the east coast and over Stainmore, suggests that their purpose was to act as a mobile reserve for the troops on the Wall.

Archaeology supports the suggestion that some forts in northern England were abandoned in the late third and early fourth centuries. However, recent excavations have emphasised that the pattern was not the same everywhere. Some forts appear to have been completely abandoned; others continued to be occupied but with a considerably reduced garrison; a third group continued in occupation seemingly at the same strength as before. Thus on Hadrian's Wall Housesteads seems to have been maintained with a full garrison through the third century, new buildings being constructed in the rampart backing apparently in an attempt to use all available space within the fort, while in the early fourth some or all of the barrack-blocks were rebuilt to a completely new design (fig. 36). At the eastern end of the Wall space was apparently not at a premium at Wallsend in the third century; and when, in the early fourth, the barrack-blocks were rebuilt to a new plan, not all the fort interior was utilised (fig. 37). Halton Chesters and Rudchester exhibit a different history. Here no barrack-blocks were built in the early fourth century; on the contrary, much of the area of the forts appears to have been abandoned for many years until buildings of a different form of construction were erected in the later fourth century. Yet the forts retained the same garrisons in the *Notitia Dignitatum* as they had in the early third century. This suggests that while the strength of the units was allowed to fall to minimal levels they were not permitted to die, but continued throughout the third and fourth centuries to be reinvigorated in the 360s. At South Shields, beyond the eastern end of the Wall, this process seems to have gone a stage further for archaeological excavations have suggested that the fort was abandoned in the late third and early fourth centuries while the *Notitia Dignitatum*

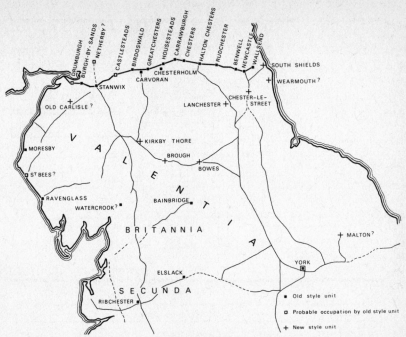

35 *Forts in northern England listed in the* Notitia Dignitatum. *A closed square denotes an old-style unit, an open square the probable site of such a unit, a cross a new-style unit. Forts considered, on archaeological evidence, to be occupied at the end of the fourth century are omitted*

records that the fort was later garrisoned by one of the new types of unit, the *numerus barcariorum*.

The differing history of these forts no doubt reflects changed conditions on the northern frontier in the third and fourth centuries. The strength of the garrisons of the outpost forts in particular, combined with the peaceful conditions apparently pertaining on the frontier during the third century, led to the withdrawal of units from many of the hinterland forts and the scaling down of the garrisons of certain forts on the Wall line. However, where strong garrisons were required these seem to have been maintained. Housesteads was such a fort, while in the west forts along the Cumbrian Coast continued to be occupied, probably to protect the west coast against raids from Ireland.

The peace of the third century appears to have led to the growth of a flourishing civil population. Little can be said concerning the rural native settlements north of the Wall, in addition to that discussed above, not least because so few have produced third- or fourth-century artefacts: this gap is a major problem in determining the relationship between Roman and native in the north at this time. Our knowledge of settlements south of the Wall is not much better. In the western zone of the hinterland the construction of roads aided the growth of the settlements in their vicinity, such farms no doubt profiting from the presence of the lucrative military market. Some of these farms, such as Ewe Close and Crosby Garret in Westmorland, grew to a considerable size, being surrounded by extensive field systems. Aerial photography in the southern part of the Solway basin has recently

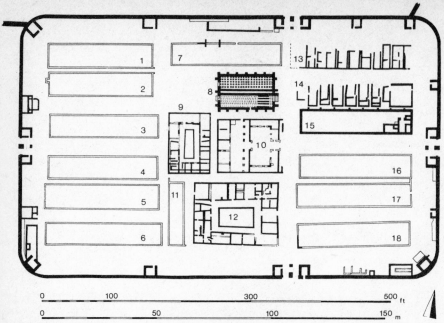

36 *The fort at Housesteads in the early fourth century. 10 headquarters building, 12 commanding officer's house, 9 hospital, 8 granaries, 13 and 14 barrack-blocks, 15 ?store-house with baths at east end. The other buildings have not been re-excavated. (Drawn by C.M. Daniels)*

emphasised the considerable number of settlements in this area, many associated with field systems, and while most are undated many no doubt are of the Roman period. There seems, on the other hand, to be rather fewer settlements on the north shore of the Solway, beyond the frontier. Taken at face value this would appear to support the view that the construction of the Wall aided the economic exploitation of the land to the south, but many factors must be taken into account in assessing this evidence and it is too soon to do more than note the possibility.

Civil settlements outside forts also continued to expand. On the Wall houses were allowed to encroach on the Vallum and spread round the forts, being constructed immediately outside fort gates. Some settlements grew to be even larger than the adjacent fort. Many must have acquired self-governing rights, though little is known of this. In addition to the inscription from Carriden on the Antonine Wall recording the existence of a *vicus* with self-governing powers there, such records survive only at Housesteads on the Wall and Old Carlisle in the western hinterland, while from Chesterholm comes a dedication erected by the *vicani Vindolandenses*. If settlements such as these were given powers to administer their own affairs, it may be presumed that similar authority was granted to the towns of Carlisle and Corbridge. Indeed the former may have been created a *civitas* in the third century, for the *civitas Carvetiorum* was then formed in the Eden valley (fig. 28). If not centred on Carlisle, then it seems almost certain that this town, the largest in the area, was established as a *civitas* in its own right. Corbridge too grew to a substantial town of about 12 hectares with walls, though it still remained a garrison town with legionaries being quartered immediately by its very centre.

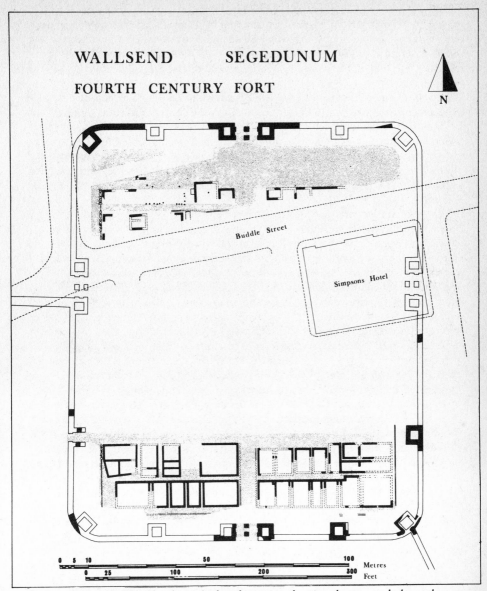

37 *The fort at Wallsend in the early fourth century showing the new style barracks. (Drawn by C.M. Daniels)*

There is a hint also at other administrative divisions in northern England: an inscription from the South Tyne valley points to the existence of the *curia Textoverdorum*, an otherwise unknown sept or administrative unit of the Brigantes, or just possibly the Votadini.

Sometimes it seems possible that the running down of the fort had an effect on the adjacent civil settlement. Thus the *vicus* at Chesterholm is now considered to have been abandoned in the 270s, possibly as a result of a similar event in the fort (pl. 12).

However, other settlements acquired a life of their own. What little evidence there is suggests that South Shields was not deserted by its townsfolk though the garrison was withdrawn: no doubt, the town owed much to its strategic position at the mouth of the Tyne. There is a hint too that the settlement at Cramond on the Forth survived for some time after the abandonment of the fort, probably for similar reasons.

It is unfortunate that so little evidence for civilian administration in the frontier area survives for Britain. In Upper Germany in the second and third centuries the military forces were reduced to a thin band stationed on the frontier, while the land behind was given over to civilian administration. It seems probable that the same process was happening in Britain at the same time, with the abandonment of the hinterland forts and the establishment of a *civitas* in the Eden valley and, one may confidently assume, another based on Corbridge, though detailed evidence is lacking.

The civil settlements had mostly, it may safely be assumed, started as shanty towns containing the dwellings of merchants and the unofficial wives and families of soldiers: Roman soldiers until at least the third century were not allowed to marry but there was nothing to prevent them contracting an unofficial union with a native woman, marrying her according to local custom, and inscriptions demonstrate that many soldiers availed themselves of this opportunity. Their sons were a valuable source of recruits for the army, which relied primarily upon local volunteers, from both town and country. This is best demonstrated by the career of Nectovelius, a Brigantian from north England who joined a unit raised originally in Thrace (modern Bulgaria), stationed at Mumrills on the Antonine Wall in the mid-second century, where he died. During the later second and third centuries many of these houses, shops and taverns were rebuilt in stone, and the villages were augmented by temples and possibly other civic buildings, while cemeteries spread beyond their boundaries (pl. 12). Sometimes the village grew to such an extent that it sprawled over the cemeteries of earlier inhabitants. While much of the life of the inhabitants of these villages centred on the activity of the soldiers in the forts, religious dedications in particular point to influences from elsewhere. Roman gods were worshipped in the fort and in the temples of the village, and in many cases these were equated with local Celtic gods. Foreign gods came from Germany, imported by soldiers drafted into the army of the Wall. New Eastern religions were brought by officers or soldiers transferred across the empire, and in the fourth century the potent mysteries of Mithraism and Christianity arrived. These must have added an element of variety to the households where father and son through the generations served in the unit garrisoned 'up the road'.

Throughout these years of peace, and on into the fourth century, little is known of the relations between the empire and its northern neighbours, as witnessed by artefacts. Few coins drifted north after the time of Severus. The Falkirk hoard of nearly 2000 coins buried in or soon after 230, though mainly collected in the Severan period, was the last known hoard of Roman coins in Scotland until the end of the century. Third century Roman pottery is scarce in barbary, but neither is it plentiful in the frontier installations. Its rarity in the north may accordingly reflect supply rather than demand. The small number of other artefacts cannot be closely dated and could fall within either the third or the fourth century: nevertheless these do not substantially affect the prevailing pattern.

Little can be said about life at, or the cultural affinities of, most settlements in southern Scotland in addition to that discussed above. However, the situation at

38 *The distribution of Roman finds on non-military sites in Scotland in the late third and fourth centuries (after Robertson)*

Traprain Law was very different. It is the only native site in southern Scotland which has furnished evidence not only of continuing occupation through the Roman period, but also occupation on a substantial scale. Little of the hill fort has been examined archaeologically and most of this work was carried out before the Second World War. As a result much doubt surrounds the chronological history of the site.

Traprain Law was a town. When the Roman forces arrived in the area it had already acquired a lengthy history, for there is evidence for human activity on the hill top over 2,000 years before AD80. The settlement may have been first fortified at the same time as many other similar, though smaller, sites in Scotland, in the earlier half of the first millennium BC. The first enclosure may have been no more than 4 hectares in area, but if so it seems probable that it was soon doubled in size by the construction of a new rampart of stone. This in turn was extended by the construction of a further stone rampart probably enclosing an area of about 12 hectares. The town achieved its greatest extent at about the time Roman armies arrived in north Britain. It is not possible to determine whether the new extension to Traprain Law took place before or after the Roman advance, though what evidence there is points perhaps to a late first or early second century date. The extension at this time took in the northern flanks of the hill and may have resulted from the pressure of increased population within the settlement. The rampart was subsequently repaired within the Roman period and again, perhaps in the late Roman period or in following centuries. It has been suggested that Traprain Law was abandoned in the late second and early third centuries, but this is uncertain.

Roman material found its way to Traprain Law from the late first century onwards. Samian ware from Gaul has been unearthed at the town in some quantity, as well as provincial pottery and crude locally produced wares. While late fourth-century pottery is absent the sequence of Roman coins continues through to the Emperor Honorius (395–423). The other objects from the site include knives, sickles, spearheads, bronze horse harness fittings, as well as items relating to clothing – dress fasteners, dragonesque, pennanular and trumpet brooches, pins and glass bangles – and personal ornaments such as finger rings and armlets. More unusual items include keys, locks, toilet instruments and a bronze folding spoon.

Traprain Law was not merely the home of a farming community. Metalworking was certainly carried out there for among the finds are portions of two-piece clay moulds for making small bronze artefacts, including a ring-headed pin and a dress fastener of a type dating to the second half of the second century. Crucibles also point towards local bronze-working at Traprain Law. It also seems possible that glass bangles were made at the town. Two inscriptions demonstrate that someone at least had a literacy of a kind. IRI on a fragment of pot was probably scratched at Traprain Law and the letters ABCD on a piece of mudstone certainly was (pl. 15).

Although much can be said about the artefacts from the site, little is known about the dwellings of the inhabitants of the town. Stone foundations have certainly been uncovered during the excavations, but whether these were for stone or timber buildings is not clear. There is, however, some indication that in one area at least the buildings were rectangular in shape rather than circular as the houses on the smaller native rural settlements. This sophistication is reflected in the discovery of keys and locks, possibly from houses, on the Law.

The wealth of material found at Traprain Law and its continuation as a defended town throughout the Roman period points to a special relationship between the Votadini and Rome. It is unfortunate that no other evidence survives to allow elaboration of this tantalising glimpse into frontier politics. Throughout the Roman period visitors from the south must have been a regular occurrence at Traprain Law. Merchants and traders certainly came there and, it may be presumed, soldiers also, though no carved name of a soldier has survived – as it has on a rock at Zinchecra, the hill fort capital of the Garamantes of the Fezzan in the Sahara desert. No matter what the strict treaty relationship between Rome and the Votadini, the army will have been concerned to keep almost as watchful an eye on their friendly northerly neighbour as on the other tribes of southern Scotland.

The Picts

If the theme of the third century was peace, that of the fourth was war. The changed situation was heralded by a chance comment at the end of the third century in a panegyric to the Caesar Constantius. The panegyricist, referring to events in 297, in passing mentioned that the Britons were only used to fighting the Picts and the Hibernians, both still half-naked enemies. This is the first reference to the Picts (and indeed to trouble from across the Irish Sea) but it is clear from later literary references that this nation was an amalgamation of earlier attested tribes. Already by the time of Septimius Severus some of the northern tribes recorded by Ptolemy had disappeared, probably incorporated into larger units. Now these tribes combined to form the Picts, a nation which, by the immediate post-Roman period, held sway over all or most of Scotland north of the Forth-Clyde isthmus (fig. 39; pl. 18–19). This process of coalescence took some time to achieve. Thus in the early fourth century a Roman writer could still speak of the Caledonians and other Picts, while the Verona list of 314 included the Caledoni and Picti (and Scotti); later in the century Ammianus Marcellinus mentioned the two divisions of the Picts, the Dicalydones and the Verturiones. This new unity may well have resulted from the adjacent presence of Rome: it was certainly a phenomenon which occurred along all the borders of the empire. The existence of a large and powerful state south of the Forth, occasionally interfering in their affairs, seems to have had the result of fusing the northern tribes together, eventually into one nation, consciously or subconsciously, in order to be able to resist the further expansion of Roman ambitions to the best of their ability.

The first known mention of the Picts in Roman sources was in 297 but it was not until 306 that war between Rome and the Picts was recorded. On 25 July of that year the Emperor Constantius Chlorus (305–6) died at York after defeating the Picts. The occasion for the war is not known, but in view of the general state of the empire and its frontiers elsewhere it is more likely to have resulted from the aggression of the Picts than the desire of the Romans to expand their empire. In 314 Constantius' son, Constantine the Great (306–37), took the title Britannicus Maximus and it seems possible that this followed a further campaign against the Picts.

The next disturbance was not for another thirty years. In the winter of 342/3 the Emperor Constans (337–50), son of Constantine, came urgently to Britain to deal with trouble apparently caused either by the Picts and Scots or by both. Then in 360 both nations, ignoring their treaty relationship with Rome, raided Britain, laying waste places near the frontier. The Emperor Julian (360–3), cousin of Constans, sent one of his generals, Lupicinus, with a small field army to the island to restore order. Four years later the writer Ammianus Marcellinus recorded further raids, this time by the Picts, Saxons, Scots and Attacotti, who were, Ammianus stated

39 *The tribes of north Britain in the fourth century*

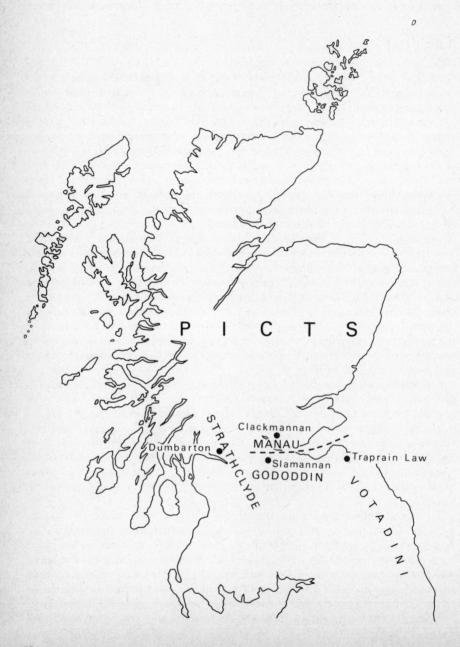

PICTS

Clackmannan

MANAU

STRATHCLYDE

Dumbarton

Slamannan

GODODDIN

Traprain Law

VOTADINI

despairingly, harrassing Britain in a never-ending series of disasters. These attacks culminated in the 'Barbarian Conspiracy' of 367. In what appears to be a concerted invasion, the four tribes of 364 were joined by the Franks, who attacked the Channel coast, all the invaders, in the words of Ammianus, 'breaking in wherever they could, by land or sea, plundering and burning ruthlessly, and killing all their prisoners'. The frontier scouts were bribed by the enemy to reveal to them the disposition of the Roman forces. Nectaridus, Count of the Saxon Shore, was killed and Fullofaudes, commander of the army, surrounded. The Emperor Valentinian (364–75), at that time in Gaul, sent at first one of his leading generals, Severus, but quickly replaced him by another, Jovinus, who carried out a strategic withdrawal demanding a larger army, before Valentinian deciding to entrust the recovery of Britain to Theodosius.

Theodosius' campaigns against the invaders lasted into 368 and possibly 369. He at first made for London and restored order in that area. He attacked the marauding bands of the enemy, putting them to flight and recapturing their booty, including prisoners and cattle, which, after taking a percentage for his soldiers, he restored to its rightful owners. Before moving on Theodosius gathered intelligence concerning the enemy, planned his campaign, brought over two new generals from the continent and strengthened his army by issuing an edict summoning deserters back to the ranks without penalty, together with those absent on leave.

Thus with his army reinforced he left London, mopping up resistence as he moved north. Ammianus states that he restored cities and forts and protected the frontier with sentries and forts. The frontier scouts, who had gone over to the enemy, were disbanded. The historian, in passing, records their duties: 'they ranged backwards and forwards over great distances to obtain information about disturbances among neighbouring nations'. Thus they were clearly the descendants of the scouts established in the outpost forts in the late second or early third century. These are the only specific actions of Theodosius recorded in relation to the northern frontier. Nothing is known of the sentries established by him and no forts rebuilt or repaired at this time are recorded by name. It is possible that the general carried the war into the enemy's camp for the poet Claudian, writing at the time of Theodosius' grandson, the Emperor Honorius (393–423), states that he pitched camp among the Caledonian frosts.

Invasions by the Picts and Scots did not cease after the successful conclusion of the 'Barbarian Conspiracy'. In 382 they again invaded the empire and Magnus Maximus, later a usurper (383–8), conducted a vigorous campaign in order to defeat them. A few years later, at the very end of the century, Stilicho, ruler of the empire for Honorius, took measures to protect the island against the Picts, Scots and Saxons, though the nature of these activities is not known.

Throughout the fourth century Rome reacted to protect the provinces of Britain from their enemies – Picts, Scots, Saxons, Franks and Attacotti. Some of the defensive measures are known through literary references, documentary sources or archaeology. The strengthening of the army of Britain by the establishment of new units on the roads leading north from York to the Wall at the beginning of the fourth century has already been mentioned (fig. 35). Possibly at the same time, certainly before the death of Constantine in 337, all the army units in northern England came under the control of a newly created official, the *dux Britanniarum*. Previously the provincial governor had been responsible for both civil and military affairs within his province. Now this responsibility was divided, soldiers being appointed to the new military commands: this must have led to an improvement in the leadership of the army.

The *dux* commanded all the units of the province of northern England, Britannia Secunda, the new province created by Constantine, who subdivided both Upper and Lower Britain. The long struggle of Constantine for sole control of the empire also led to the creation of field armies. At first these remained with the emperor(s), but by the middle of the fourth century regional field armies under the command of *magistri* had been created. It was units of the field army based at Trier in Gaul which came to Britain in 360 and 367. The next step was the creation of more local field armies. Britain does not appear to have received its field army until the end of the fourth century, possibly shortly after 395 when Stilicho was active in Britain. This small force was under the command of the *comes Britanniae*, and may well have been stationed in the midlands within easy reach of both the northern frontier and the Saxon Shore.

Another army reform introduced by Diocletian was the institutionalisation of the family traditions of military service by making it hereditary and compulsory. Hitherto the army had mainly relied upon voluntary enlistment, though conscription was, at certain times and in certain areas, a not inconsiderable source of recruits: it is mentioned twice by Tacitus in relation to Britain. The new law was in theory a considerable change, but in practice it probably had little effect on matters in northern England where the sons of soldiers would continue to enter their father's unit in ready acceptance – and probably ignorance – of the law.

While the size, organisation and command structure of the army were being reformed, repairs and improvements to the defences of the province were also put in hand. Two inscriptions have survived to demonstrate that, in the years following the recovery of the island by the central authorities in 296, rebuilding was carried out at Birdoswald and Housesteads on Hadrian's Wall. At the former the ruined commanding officer's house was completely rebuilt and the headquarters building and the bathhouse repaired: the fragmentary inscription at Housesteads does not record the nature of the renovations there. At both forts archaeological investigation has revealed other modifications at about this time. These are particularly clear at Housesteads where some at least of the barrack-blocks initially built in the second century were completely remodelled. The previous arrangement of a centurion's block and ten rooms for the men in each barrack was swept away and replaced by a new centurion's block and several separate rooms for the men: six rooms in one of the two barracks so far examined and eight in the other. This arrangement of 'chalets' has been discovered at other forts, Greatchesters, Birdoswald and Wallsend on the Wall and also at the outpost forts at Risingham and High Rochester. It seems probable that these new arrangements reflect the reorganisation of the army that was taking place at the same time. However, it is impossible otherwise to relate the two events, not least because the size of the centuries at this time is not known, while the number of men who might be expected to live in one of the new barrack rooms is equally uncertain.

Elsewhere rebuilding was more drastic. Hadrian's Wall just west of Birdoswald was rebuilt from the foundations in the fourth century, while the fort at Chesterholm seems to have been completely rebuilt. Some of the milecastles on the Wall were also remodelled, probably at this time. In the area of the River Irthing milecastles and turrets seem to have been repaired. At two milecastles, 50 and 52, the normal round arch over the gateways was replaced by monolithic masonry doorposts, presumably carrying a flat lintel. However, these appear to be isolated repairs: there was certainly no attempt to restore all the turrets and milecastles, only a few of which can demonstrate occupation continuing into the fourth century.

It is not possible to date closely any of the repairs and rebuildings discussed above. Archaeology can point only to an approximate date within the later years of the third century or the early part of the fourth century, though it may be legitimate to link many with the re-establishment of central authority over Britain in 296 when affairs in the island must have been overhauled. There is no evidence to connect them with invasion from the north, which is not attested at this time.

An imperial visit to Britain may have been the occasion for further changes on the northern frontier. Constantius Chlorus was in the north in 306 while Constantine almost certainly came to Britain in 312 in order to gather troops in preparation for his struggle against his rival emperor Maxentius. It has been suggested that this latter visit led to the abandonment of the outpost fort at High Rochester, in spite of the extensive repairs which had taken place there just a few years before, for the coin series at this site ends in the early fourth century: this suggestion is, however, incapable of proof at the present time.

The putative visit of Constantine in 314, when he assumed the title *Britannicus Maximus*, probably following a successful campaign against the Picts, may have been the time when the new, mobile units were introduced into northern England in order to strengthen the northern frontier against attacks from the north. Possibly at the same time the military dispositions on the Cumbrian Coast were also strengthened, presumably following raiding by the Scots of Ireland, who appear to have menaced the whole of the west coast of Britain throughout the fourth century. A new fort was built at Burrow Walls sometime in the century and some of the milefortlets appear to have been reoccupied: none of these events are closely dated.

The final group of changes on the northern frontier are generally related to the events of 367 and their aftermath. There is little positive evidence for destruction in the Wall forts at this time, and it is possible that the Picts attacked by sea, sailing down the east coast and ignoring the Wall. However, renovations and rebuilding at several Wall forts, dated only approximately to the late fourth century, have been associated with the statement of Ammianus Marcellinus that Theodosius restored the forts, protecting the frontier with sentries and forts. New buildings were constructed at Birdoswald and Chesterholm and further minor modifications were carried out at the latter fort and at Housesteads. The work was more striking at Haltonchesters and Rudchester, forts which had been neglected through much of the preceding century. New buildings were erected over the accumulated debris of the previous 100 years. These buildings were not of the normal stone construction, but were of timber, the main uprights being set into large stones.

The strengthening of forts on the Wall, and in particular Haltonchesters and Rudchester, was accompanied by the abandonment of the system of scouting to the north which had operated for perhaps as long as 200 years. This event, recorded by Ammianus, is reflected in the archaeological record, for there is no evidence for any of the outpost forts continuing in occupation after about 367, though it is equally possible that some were abandoned earlier. After 367, for the first time in its entire history, Hadrian's Wall itself became the frontier of the province.

This frontier was strengthened by the addition of towers along the Yorkshire coast. Five of these towers are known and others may have existed along the coast of County Durham. The towers were placed on good vantage points and were presumably designed to maintain watch over the coastal approaches and possibly also communicate with Roman naval ships at sea. The construction of the towers emphasises the danger to the province from across the sea and supports the suggestion that the Picts in 367 sailed down the east coast to attack the Romans.

The attacks of the Picts, Scots and their allies in the fourth century must have had an important effect on the people of the frontier area, but that effect is impossible to measure. Practically no evidence survives from the rural sites to determine the history of even one such settlement during this century. There is more evidence from the villages outside the forts, but even that is difficult to interpret. There is evidence from only one village, Chesterholm, for occupation after 367, and this settlement appears to have been rebuilt after an abandonment of about 100 years. It is possible that the selective excavation carried out at other sites has failed to locate the remains of the late fourth century civilian occupation. On the other hand it is possible that in these years the civilians moved inside the forts to live with the soldiers, who were in any case fathers, brothers, husbands or sons to most of the civilians. This would account for the non-military objects found within forts in the later levels – infant burials at Chesters, trinkets at Housesteads – though it must be noted that most of these objects could have entered the forts after the end of Roman rule in 410.

The pattern of contact between Roman and barbarian, or rather lack of it, continued from the third century into the fourth. A small amount of pottery and glass found its way north, and also more exotic objects such as brooches of bronze, silver or gold as well as coins. However, all types of objects are few in number and most have a coastal distribution (fig. 38, pl. 13). Several of these objects were used as grave goods: glass vessels in Aberdeenshire (pl. 14) and Orkney, stone gaming counters in Aberdeenshire. Some of the objects, such as the pottery, are most likely to have entered Scotland by way of trade, but others, the brooches and the coins, may have been plundered. This is particular true of the seven fourth century coin hoards from Scotland, though it is difficult to see what use the northern tribes could make of Roman coins. One of the late fourth century is from Traprain Law and was found with a great collection of silver treasure (pl. 16). Some of the pieces in the hoard of treasure were cut up as if the collection was not to be used for its proper purpose, but as bullion, to be divided up among the tribesmen. The problem lies in the location of the treasure at Traprain Law, the capital for three centuries of a tribe supposedly friendly to Rome. Was the treasure plunder won by a tribe which had turned against its long standing friend, or was it a payment from Rome, aimed at supporting and continuing that friendship?

In trying to determine the answer to that question, and understand the late fourth century on the frontier, a new type of evidence comes into play, the genealogies of the British kings, written down in the medieval period but referring back even into the fourth century. AD. These genealogies are partly garbled, not easy to interpret and are the subject of scholarly dispute. They demonstrate the existence of two, possibly four, native kingdoms in Lowland Scotland during the fourth century. One kingdom was centred on the Clyde and either now or later had its capital at Dumbarton Rock: this was known in later centuries as Strathclyde. Another lay in the east in the territory of the Votadini, known later as the Guotodin or Gododin, and its main power base appears to have been in the Lothians and around the head of the Forth, the area termed the Manau of Gododdin. A third kingdom may have been in south-west Scotland, while the fourth is less easy to locate.

The genealogies suggest that these kingdoms were established in the late fourth century, possibly about the decade 370–80. Attention has been directed at the Roman names of many of the early kings and their immediate followers, and in particular to the name of the first king of the Manau Gododdin, Patern or Paternus Pesrut, Patern of the Red Cloak. This garment has been considered a symbol of office, Patern being invested with it by Theodosius. It has accordingly been proposed that Theodosius established two or more kingdoms in Lowland Scotland when he disbanded the scouting system and abandoned remaining outpost forts, to govern the people and act as buffer states between Rome and the Picts. Parallels have been drawn with the operation of a similar arrangement on the north African frontier in 371 when Ammianus Marcellinus, in a statement corroborated by St Augustine, reports that after Theodosius subdued the border tribes he placed over them reliable prefects, *praefecti gentium*. Two at least of the fourth-century kings in Britain, Cinhil of the Clyde and Patern Pasrut of the Manau Gododdin, appear to have come to their kingdoms from elsewhere, the former from the Mediterranean and the latter from Kent. One other is stated to have derived his authority from Magnus Maximus (383–8) and thus this emperor is sometimes seen as the designer of the northern settlement.

However, there are problems. Not all would agree, for example, that Cinhil is really Celtic for the Latin name Quintilius. Further, while Latin names may suggest Roman influence this may do no more than reflect the prestige of Rome among the tribes on its borders. It has also been suggested that the Roman names may merely indicate that these people had adopted Christianity, the Roman religion. Patern Pesrut, moreover, may have been so called because he liked to wear a red cloak! Certainly these kingdoms and their ruling dynasties were established by the early fifth century. What is less certain is that they can be extended backwards into the fourth and that they were established by Rome.

The end of Hadrian's Wall

Little can be said about the last days of Hadrian's Wall. We have already seen that Magnus Maximus (383–8) defeated the Picts and Scots who had invaded Britain in 382, the year before he left the island to claim, unsuccessfully, the empire. Maximus' name survived for long in folk memory and in several of the British genealogies, which implies that he did more than this, but the extent of his other deeds remains unknown. In 400 Stilicho is recorded as fortifying the British provinces against the Scots and Picts, but the exact nature of his activity is likewise uncertain. Then, in the latter part of the first decade of the fifth century the situation changed dramatically. On 31 December 406 hordes of barbarians crossed the Rhine and devasted Gaul. The British army appointed their own emperor, Marcus, who they murdered, then Gratian, who suffered in similar fashion, and finally Constantine (407–11). Constantine III appointed commanders for the troops in Britain and sailed for the continent, where he attempted to restore order. In his absence Britain suffered attack and in the absence of help from Constantine III, took measures to protect itself. Even on the death of Constantine III in 411 the central authority was not able to restore its rule in Britain owing to the more important threats from other quarters. Roman rule in Britain had officially ended.

There is no evidence that Hadrian's Wall in these last years was denuded of its garrison to help the British usurpers. No sources mention the exact origin, within Britain, of the armies of Magnus Maximus or Constantine III, or the 'legion' withdrawn by Stilicho in 401/2 to help protect Italy. Presumably the main body of troops was provided by the field army established on a permanent basis in Britain between 395 and 407, but no doubt this was augmented by soldiers withdrawn from the units in the forts of north Britain. Whole units, however, do not appear to have been withdrawn, for they survive to be listed in the *Notitia Dignitatum*, compiled in about 408. The *Notitia* does record units which had previously been stationed in Britain now serving on the continent, but none from Hadrian's Wall or its hinterland. Coins indicate the continuing occupation of sites on the Wall, though not necessarily by the army. Coins of 383–410 have been found at a number of forts on the frontier (Chesterholm, Birdoswald and Maryport), towns (Corbridge and Carlisle) as well at sites which might be either civilian or military (South Shields and Chesters) and as stray finds (Heddon and Walltown). There were also five coins of 387–96 in Coventina's Well at Carrawburgh, while in the adjacent fort a hoard of coins contained issues of the Emperors Valentinian (364–75) and Valens (364–78) so worn that the hoard may not have been buried until the early fifth century. Late fourth-century coins also found their way north of Hadrian's Wall. The hoard of four coins from Traprain Law, unearthed with the silver plate, has already been mentioned, but there are also records of another 20 coins, mostly stray finds. The army is the most likely source of all these coins, not only those found in forts, but in the towns and settlements inside and outside the province.

While Britain was still part of the Roman empire pay for these soldiers would continue to arrive at these forts, though much was now rendered in kind. Sometime between 407 and 411, however, these pay chests would have stopped arriving and it is probable that only then did the situation on the frontier change. At first the soldiers may not have understood what was happening, thinking that this was only a temporary break in payment, but as the position continued unchanged realisation must have set in. It seems unlikely that many soldiers immediately left the fort or its attendant village: most had probably lived there all their lives and stayed there, though presumably changing their occupation from soldier to farmer. Others may have turned to banditry. Quite simply no evidence survives. The only local inscription of later years is the fifth century tombstone of Brigomaglos at Chesterholm. But if the evidence for continuing occupation by the Romano-Britons is absent, evidence for the intrusion of Picts, Scots or Saxons into the frontier area is equally scarce, for only Corbridge has produced Saxon artefacts. It appears that the Roman frontiers had effectively done their job and defended the Roman province from foreign incursions to the very end.

8

Roman and Barbarian

The majestic remains of Hadrian's Wall, evocative survival of a long dead empire, can too easily obscure the fact that its life, so far as that empire was concerned, was short. A Roman state lasted in some form for over 2,000 years: Hadrian's Wall was occupied for less than three of those twenty centuries. Indeed the era of frontier building and experimentation may be considered to be even shorter, lasting in Britain from the late 80s for sixty years to the mid 140s, for thereafter no new frontier was built and the army merely modified the existing structures. The strength of Hadrian's Wall, even in decline, can also blind the onlooker to the fact that it is essentially a monument to failure: the failure of the Roman empire to expand and conquer the known world. The conquest of the Caledonians and their relatives would have eliminated the necessity for a frontier in Britain and, in the long run, have been cheaper than the maintenance of a large standing army in the island. The presence of a monolithic state in the southern part of the island, with well-defended frontiers, led to a reaction in the north and the creation of a nation capable of challenging, and occasionally defeating albeit briefly, the might of Rome. In the end sub-Roman Britain was to succumb to a different enemy, but this was only possible because the reaction against Rome on the continent had produced larger and more powerful foes who were able to triumph over the empire and thereby bring about the loss of limbs such as Britain. So far as Britain was concerned the empire had a hard shell in Hadrian's Wall, but a soft centre, and the collapse of that centre led to the abandonment of Hadrian's Wall, not the other way round.

Britain is singularly lucky in possessing the visible remains of two major Roman frontiers within a distance of little more than 160km. Further, archaeological research on these remains over the last century has produced a wealth of material allowing, usually, for greater understanding. The development of Rome's artificial frontiers can be traced here, perhaps more clearly than in any other province of the empire.

Little is known, ironically, of the only first-century frontier to be specifically attested in the literary sources, that established in 81 by Julius Agricola across the Forth-Clyde isthmus. Only one structure, a small fort of about 0.4 hectares, can be considered as a possible element in this frontier. The next frontier appears to be that built through Strathallan and Strathearn, probably in the late 80s, the 'Gask frontier'. This consisted of a series of timber watch-towers placed beside an existing road and between existing forts. The purpose of the soldiers stationed at these towers appears to have been to assist the units in the forts, whose main duty was to protect the province from attack, by improving the control of movement over the frontier. The slight archaeological dating evidence points to a late first century context for this frontier so it is mainly on historical, military and logical grounds that the towers are assigned to the late 80s.

Following the abandonment of most of the forts in Scotland in the late first and early second century no clear pattern can be determined until the construction of Hadrian's Wall. However, there was clearly an attempt to improve frontier control on the Tyne-Solway isthmus in the reign of Trajan (98–117). The existing forts between Corbridge and Carlisle, at either end of the Stanegate, were strengthened by the establishment of new forts, either now or early in the reign of Hadrian (122–38), so that the distance between each was reduced to about 11km, half the normal distance, which was approximately equivalent to a day's march. In addition two other forts of a different size are known: these 'small forts' were the same size as that built earlier on the Forth-Clyde isthmus and were clearly the bases for troops stationed elsewhere, presumably employed in frontier control duties. Archaeological evidence suggests that these elements were in existence some time before the construction of Hadrian's Wall. However, new elements appear, apparently shortly before work commenced on the Wall. One such element was the erection of watch-towers. Isolated towers were built, perhaps early in Hadrian's reign, on the line later taken by the Wall and also west of Carlisle, where one at least was soon superceded by an example of the second new element, a fort. At least two new forts were built in the west between Carlisle and Kirkbride, again seemingly early in Hadrian's reign, and the garrisons of some of the existing forts may have been changed at this time.

Whatever the improvements carried out on the northern frontier in the early years of Hadrian, they do not seem to have satisfied the emperor for he ordered, probably during his visit to the island in 122, the construction of the only effective method of control, a barrier. Initially this was to consist of merely a wall, punctured by gates defended by small fortlets and provided throughout its length with watch-towers. The troops to man the barrier and defend the province were to be those continuing to occupy their forts behind the Wall on the Stanegate and in northern England: some garrisons appear to have been changed at this time and new forts built. However, before the first scheme for the Wall was completed the forts immediately behind the Wall were abandoned and new forts were built on the line of the Wall itself, wherever possible astride the barrier. The main reason for this seems to have been that the Wall not only impeded the movement of the enemy, but it also hindered the free mobility of the Roman forces: placing the units on the Wall restored that mobility. Within a short period of this move forts began to be built not astride the Wall, but wholly south of it, though still attached. There was another experiment, the Vallum, an earthwork designed to protect the rear of the Wall installations.

The reasons for the advance north at the beginning of the reign of Antoninus Pius (138–61) do not concern us here. What is interesting is that the Wall now built was planned on similar lines to the redundant Hadrian's Wall: rampart and ditch, updated but otherwise hardly revolutionary; forts for whole units at 13km intervals, thus reflecting the length of the Wall; fortlets probably at every mile; and with the hint of a system of small enclosures only now being revealed. The main differences lay in the materials of construction, turf and timber predominating over stone. The experimental Vallum was not repeated, but a new feature was added, a road. This Wall, like its predecessor, was amended before it was completed, and again this was by the addition of forts. At least ten new forts were added, bringing the total to at least 16 and possible as many as 19, and reducing the distance between each to about 3.5km.

The artificial barrier had now reached its peak. With the completion of the Antonine Wall there were more men per mile stationed on the frontier than on any

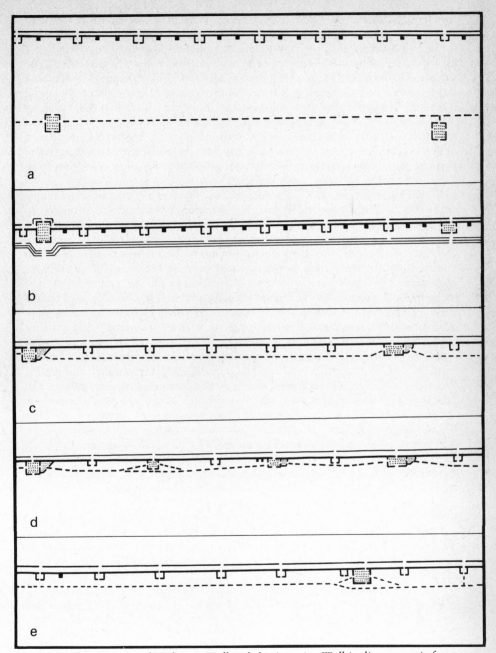

a

b

c

d

e

40 *The development of Hadrian's Wall and the Antonine Wall in diagrammatic form:*
(a) Hadrian's Wall as planned; (b) Hadrian's Wall as completed; (c) The Antonine Wall
as planned; (d) The Antonine Wall as completed; (e) Hadrian's Wall in the third
century

frontier in Britain either before or after. The relationship between fort and Wall was close with the main axis of the former being related in all but one example to the barrier. Further, the later forts on the Antonine Wall were nearly all built for detachments, sometimes composed of legionaries, rather than complete units, and this also emphasised the close relationship between Wall and forts. Nevertheless there is no hint at a change in Roman military tactics. The Antonine Wall, and Hadrian's Wall, could not prevent a major attack on the province. It could slow up such an attack, it could help prevent petty local raiding and banditry and aid the Roman administration in controlling movement across the frontier but the defence of the province now, and for many years, lay with the units based in the forts on or near the Wall and the military issue would be decided in the field and not from behind fort walls, as it was on every recorded occasion.

Within the reign of Antoninus Pius himself there is a move away from this concentration of troops on the frontier line: the pendulum starts its return swing. In the second period on the Antonine Wall one fort was abandoned altogether while the garrison of another two can be shown to have been reduced. With the return to Hadrian's Wall in the 160s there was no attempt to increase the number of troops on the Wall line to bring this barrier into step with the Antonine Wall at either its most developed state or even during its second period. On the contrary there was the start of a process which reached its logical conclusion in the later second century. Then large, mobile units supported by smaller units and scouts were established in front of the Wall, while the garrisons of several of the Wall forts were strengthened. At the same time redundant turrets were abandoned, and even occasionally milecastles, while many remaining milecastles were adapted to the realities of their situation. A road was belatedly added to aid communication. This defence in depth, combined, presumably, with supervision of the affairs of the tribes to the north, was a more effective method of defence and was to last, apparently without major modification, into the late fourth century.

This defence in depth emphasises the various factors which governed the differing positions of the political, military and physical frontiers. Today we loosely refer to Hadrian's Wall or the Antonine Wall as a frontier, yet neither was the provincial boundary, the real frontier of the empire. The boundaries of the tribes in the frontier area controlled the position of the provincial boundary. The forts were placed in relation to this frontier, though also respecting the overriding topographical considerations. But if it was political, and military, factors which governed the position of the provincial boundary, then geography primarily ordained the location of the physical barrier. Agricola's Forth-Clyde frontier, Hadrian's Wall and the Antonine Wall all utilised natural geographical features, the great isthmuses which bisect northern Britain. These were the obvious 'natural' frontiers of the province within the island. It so happened that these geographical features largely coincided with the local tribal boundaries, though this is not surprising. However, on Hadrian's Wall the two, political and physical frontiers, do not appear to have coincided exactly, and outpost forts were held to the north. Outpost forts were also occupied north of the Antonine Wall, presumably because the provincial boundary lay further north, reaching up to the edge of the Highlands, and/or because the eastern end of the Wall did not make military sense and the army required more northerly posts to better protect the province. This leads to the final consideration. Two equal powers did not face each other across the provincial boundary. In spite of whatever treaties ordered the relationships between Rome and the barbarians, through most of the Roman period in Britain the empire was so powerful that she could intervene at will beyond the province and impose her views on the location of the frontier on the tribes beyond: the frontier was truly *Rome's* frontier.

The major developments on the frontier in the second century coincided with a century of warfare in north Britain. These years too saw the service in Britain of exceptionally able governors, men like Julius Severus sent by Hadrian from Britain to Judaea to deal with the Jewish revolt because he was the most able military man of his day, or Statius Priscus who in the early 160s moved in rapid succession from Upper Moesia on the Lower Danube to Britain and thence to Cappadocia, to organise the Roman reaction to the Parthian attacks on the Eastern frontier. Great care has, however, to be exercised in considering the literary sources: the relative wealth of the documentary sources for the second century, and indeed the fourth also, may artificially heighten the successive crises of these years at the expense of the third century.

The third century seems to have been a time of peace on the northern frontier, but for no obvious reason. The system of defence in depth was insufficient to prevent either the invasion of the early 180s or the troubles of the 190s, so there is no clear reason why it should have suddenly succeeded in the third century. Nor can it be seriously argued that the defeat of the Caledonians and Maeatae by Severus and Caracalla quelled those tribes for three or four generations. Remarkably, however, the apparently sharp change in the fortunes of the northern frontier coincided with a major administrative change in the province of Britain. Severus divided the single province which had existed since 43 into two, thus reducing the number of troops at the disposal of the governor of northern Britain. Furthermore, this province, Lower Britain, was not in the top group of provincial appointments so the northern frontier ceased to receive the attention of men of such high calibre as Julius Severus or Statius Priscus. If this area had been a continuing source of trouble through the third century the capacity of the Roman army to respond would have been seriously diminished.

The rise of the Picts in the fourth century and invasions from across both the Irish and North Seas brought about a changed situation. The creation of a unified military command in Britain under the *dux Britanniarum*, probably in the early fourth century, will have helped the army respond to these new threats, as did the stationing of new units in northern England. But as improvements in military architecture came to be introduced to the island during the fourth century, there seems to have been no attempt to strengthen the defences of the northern frontier by the addition of bastions, higher and thicker walls, etc, to the existing forts. In fact while new forts containing all these defensive devices came to be built in southern England, the north, in military architectural terms, became a backwater. Whether this reflected the nature of the enemy, it is difficult to determine.

It is unfortunate that all the literary source material for the northern frontier is one-sided, presenting only the Roman point of view. The speech of Calgacus before Mons Graupius is the only attempt to look at the situation from the other side, but even this of course is by a Roman intent on making a political point as much as presenting an alternative opinion. Almost the most that can be said about the barbarians' reaction to the Roman advance is that they resisted it in the only way they knew how, by military force. In this they showed guile and cunning, as demonstrated by their tactics against Agricola – in particular the night attack on the Ninth legion and the guerilla warfare employed against the might of Severus. However, in no war were the barbarians successful. True, the Highlands were never conquered, but this was due to Roman lassitude rather than Caledonian – or Pictish – might.

The progress of Roman arms in Britain, as indeed on any frontier of the empire, depended ultimately upon the will of the emperor. The sudden and major move forward of Roman arms in the 70s was due to the interest of the Emperor Vespasian (69–79), who had previously served in the island. This advance halted abruptly in 85 when the Rhine and Danube frontiers were assailed by more serious threats: the British frontier, on the edge of the empire, far away from the centre of power and the heartlands of the empire, could be safely left while more important, indeed vital, problems were dealt with. A new emperor, Trajan (98–117), was intent to expand the empire, but characteristically chose more exotic parts to achieve his ends. The progressive withdrawal of garrisons from Scotland over the twenty years following Mons Graupius had brought the northernmost line of forts in the province, by the early second century at the latest, to the Tyne-Solway isthmus. These were strengthened in Trajan's reign by the construction of new forts and this process continued into Hadrian's reign (117–38) when the Wall was built as an addition to an existing group of installations. The position of Hadrian's Wall was governed by the prior existence of these forts, and in turn they were related to a geographical feature, the Tyne-Solway isthmus. After the Forth-Clyde isthmus, this was the most convenient line on which to halt the creeping withdrawal, indeed almost the only line. It was also the northern boundary of the tribe of the Brigantes which, since they had accepted client status in the 40s, would have been regarded as part of the empire: to retreat further then would have been to relinquish territory 'Roman' for fifty years or more. Antoninus Pius (138–61) moved the frontier forward to the best line within the island, the Forth-Clyde isthmus, though the reasons for this are far from clear and the decision, sensible though it might be seen on many grounds, was reversed by his successors Marcus Aurelius (161–80) and Lucius Verus (161–9). This was the period when the empire could most easily have solved the running sore of the British frontier by moving towards the conquest of the whole island. Instead Pius decided on a limited operation, reconquering only those tribes formerly within the province.

Septimius Severus (193–211) in the early third century returned to the question of the northern frontier. Dio states, unmistakably, that he intended to conquer the whole island and Severus did achieve the defeat of the two major tribes of the north, the Caledonians and Maeatae. The subsequent revolt of these peoples is irrelevant, for Severus amply demonstrated his intention to deal with this rebellion and there is no reason to believe that he would not have succeeded. His purpose was frustrated by his death and Rome never again was in the position to take the offensive against the northern tribes and attempt to incorporate them into the empire. The absorption of an area as large as Britain was almost bound to be piecemeal, while the haphazard interest of the emperors ensured that the progress of Roman arms would be erratic. The conquest of Spain, a not unfair parallel especially in view of its mountainous fastnesses, in the unsettled conditions of the Republic took two centuries to achieve and was only completed under the single-minded directorship of Augustus. Conditions on the frontier in Britain for the first 150 years of the life of the province were almost equally unsettled, though in a different way, and two centuries after 43 Rome was no longer able to devote sufficient resources to the completion of the conquest of Britain. This, combined with the lack of interest shown in expansion through much of the second century, was to decide the issue. Furthermore, Britain suffered from its position on the edge of the empire. There was no particular need to press ahead because even if there was a major attack from the north Rome and the immediately adjacent provinces would not be affected. Yet there is every reason to believe that, given a series of emperors who viewed the British frontier through the same eyes as Vespasian, or even longer lives for certain emperors, or a lack of crises elsewhere, Rome would have proceeded north until she had reached the end of the island and then been able to reduce the garrison of the province to a token force, as she did, eventually, in Spain.

The main events on the northern frontier can be charted with a certain degree, sometimes a high degree, of accuracy and, at least on the Roman side, the main participants can be brought to life through the surviving literary or documentary records; but the more intimate details are less clear. Sometimes an occasional fragment, such as the negotiation of the treaty between Severus and the Caledonians, is preserved, but little else of the details of the relationships between the two armies. The Romans did not generally indulge in indiscriminate killing and it may be assumed that if they could take over a tribe without a fight they would. If the tribe resisted but then surrendered after defeat, they would be treated honourably. Trajan's Column reveals some of the actions undertaken by the army to achieve that surrender: not only hand-to-hand fighting but the burning of enemy villages and crops, the capture and enslavement of its people. If, after surrender, the enemy then rebelled, it was subject to harsher treatment, in theory extermination, though that can hardly having been carried out thoroughly. Nevertheless following the rebellion of the Ordovices, just before his arrival in Britain, Agricola led the ruthless suppression of the revolt and in 210 Severus, when the Maeatae revolted, ordered his soldiers to march against them and kill everyone they met.

Of embassies and personal communication between the Romans and the barbarians we know nearly nothing. The only recorded embassy was that sent by the northern tribes to Severus in 208 offering terms for surrender, which were refused. Nevertheless the accounts of the campaigns of Agricola and Severus demonstrate that there was more knowledge of the plans and movements of the other side – Roman or barbarian – than is often realised: there is a level of contact here of which we know little.

Our knowledge of the diplomatic relations between Roman and barbarian is much greater elsewhere, though still imperfect and patchy. Such records make clear that at all times and on all frontiers the Romans were prepared to stoop – in modern eyes – to immoral methods in order to secure their own ends: the imprisonment and murder of ambassadors, the assassination of foreign kings, the encouragement of inter-tribal feuding, if necessary by the payment of bribes. . . . The list is long and even otherwise honest and upright Romans indulged in such dealings. This picture was not one-sided and many similar deeds were perpetrated by the opponents of Rome, though retold by Romans to best effect. There is no reason to assume that the Romans and barbarians who acted out the events recorded briefly in the historical record for north Britain were any different, though little evidence for such dark deeds survive. One action may bear repeating: the treacherous deceit of the frontier scouts in 367 when they were bribed by the barbarians to reveal the Roman military dispositions. There is a record too of the payment of bribes by the Romans for Virius Lupus, governor of Britain 197–200, had to buy peace from the Maeatae for a considerable sum because he did not have the military strength to deal with them: in return Lupus also regained a few captives. There is even a hint in Dio's account of the troubles of 197 that Rome tried to play the Caledonians and Maeatae off against each other in the time honoured manner. Certainly the existence of a treaty relationship with the Caledonians in 197 demonstrates the extent of Roman influence in north Britain even when the frontier lay on Hadrian's Wall.

The Roman method of obtaining a *casus belli* is also worth examining, for in spite of their power and ability to intervene without having to justify their actions to anyone, they still liked to be able to say that they were fighting a just war. Thus, in considering intervention in Ireland in his fifth campaign, Agricola gained a justification by taking into his retinue a fugitive Irish prince. The following year the threatening activity of the Caledonians was given as the excuse for the Roman invasion of the tribes north of the Forth! The situation is not so clear at the beginning of the third century, but it seems probable that the intention of Severus to campaign in the grand manner in Scotland was occasioned more by personal desires than any real need so far as the safety of the British frontier was concerned. The garbled account of Pausanias concerning the appropriation of part of the territory of the Brigantes by Antoninus Pius might be an excuse for the action of that emperor in moving the frontier forward.

Yet all was not governed by dark events. Most Romans tried to rule fairly and when officials did misbehave, as for example, in the prelude to Boudica's rebellion, they were not applauded by the historians and writers. On the whole no doubt most governors and procurators were content to keep the peace. Tacitus waxes eloquently on the desire of Agricola to root out injustices and encourage the Britons adopt the manners and practices of Rome: how far he was representative of the normal governor is a matter of debate. Except during the great campaigns there is no record of provincial governors visiting the northern frontier. One provincial governor in the 130s, following its submission to Hadrian, published the report of his tour of inspection of the forts under his command on the Black Sea coast. While carrying out this tour Arrian, the governor, gave directions for the improvement of fort defences where necessary. Similar tours of inspection will presumably have been made on the north British frontier, though no reports survive. On a higher plane, Hadrian, during his visit to Britain in 122, will no doubt have inspected the provincial army as he did six years later in north Africa: the difference is that part of the record of that tour of inspection survives on inscriptions. In this whole area, which could be extended to the annual unit reports to provincial headquarters, or the relations between the auxiliary commanders on the frontier and the legionary legate in York, and his superior in London, no evidence from Britain survives. This major gap in our local knowledge has to be filled by evidence by analogy from the other frontiers of the empire.

One such area lies in the composition of the Roman army. Throughout the empire men from beyond the empire came willingly to join her army. Thus Arminius, the great enemy of Rome, had previously served in the Roman army, while his brother fought on the Roman side in the German revolt of AD 9. In the fourth century most of the field armies were composed of Germans from beyond the empire: Stilicho, virtual ruler of the empire in the late fourth century, was a Vandal. There are plentiful references to the service of Germans in the army of Britain from the Usipites at the end of the first century, through Notfried's regiment at Housesteads in the early third century to Fraomarius and his Alamanni in the late fourth century. In the second century there were also the Sarmatians sent to the island in 175 after their surrender to Marcus Aurelius. It seems probable that Caledonians, possibly even Hibernians, also joined the Roman army, though no undisputed record survives.

Yet even if this was the case it is unlikely that it would help to account for the

Roman artefacts found beyond the empire in both Scotland and Ireland from the first to the fifth century. The documents are uniform in stating that very few recruits from beyond the empire ever returned home, even after the completion of their term of service in the army. On retirement they would usually settle down, like other veterans, in the villages outside the fort in which they had served. These objects are mute testimony to contact of some nature between Roman and barbarian. The paucity of material of any century found beyond the Highland Line seems to point to relatively little contact. It may be assumed, on faith rather than firm evidence, that most objects found their way north through trade. Such might include the fine glass vessel from Aberdeenshire dating to the second century (pl. 14). Plunder must have accounted for some at least of the artefacts, while the payment of subsidies or bribes will have brought not a few of the Roman coins into Scotland. What is remarkable, however, is not the paucity of material in the north, but the few objects of third or fourth century date in the Lowlands. Nearly every Roman period farmstead between Tyne and Forth, on excavation, produces at least one object of second century date, but very rarely one of the succeeding years.

Nevertheless certain objects particularly emphasise the close relationship between Roman and native in southern Scotland. Glass bangles, mainly dating to the late first and second centuries, are common to both military and civil sites in the Borders, and stretch down into northern England, with few found either north of the Forth or south of the Mersey. The significance of this object, however, would be greater if it were known who wore it and how it was worn; whether it was manufactured locally before the Romans arrived or whether it was a southern import. Another such object is the so-called dress fastener, more usually found on Roman and native sites in the military north than further south. This did have pre-Roman antecedents but, like the glass bangle, its function is still uncertain. The number of finds of fasteners at military installations suggests that they were items of military equipment, but their manufacture at Traprain Law and discovery elsewhere points to another, uncertain dimension.

Such gaps in our knowledge, on the military, civil and native sides, and in the relationship between all three, can only be solved, if at all, by further excavation. Over the last decade archaeological research has made great strides on the northern frontier. The first Agricolan fort on the Forth-Clyde line has been discovered. An important new dimension has been added to Hadrian's Wall by the detection of Hadrianic and pre-Hadrianic frontier works behind and beyond the west end of the Wall. The implications for the Antonine Wall of the discovery of five new fortlets and three examples of a wholly new structure, the one-sixth of a mile enclosure, are considerable. Also on the Antonine Wall much of a complete fort has been examined archaeologically for the first time in over forty years, while on Hadrian's Wall almost the whole of Wallsend fort is being excavated in a rescue operation, revealing important information concerning, in particular, the layout of the fort in the second and fourth centuries and the history of the site. At Chesterholm large-scale excavation has uncovered, for the first time, almost a complete civil settlement with most important results and implications far beyond that particular site, while the chance discovery of the writing tablets has brought into existence a wholly new strand of evidence for northern Britain, while revealing the large element of luck which plays such an important part in archaeology. Further north, also for the first time, the existence of civil settlements outside forts in Scotland has been confirmed by excavation, while two brochs with important Roman connections have been examined. In a different field judicious small-scale excavation has allowed the elaboration of theories concerning the function of the camps at Burnswark with more confidence. In many areas methodical work has produced no wide implications, but has rather added a little flesh to the still very bare bones of the history and life of the northern frontier and its people.

This more eye-catching work in the field has been accompanied throughout by its counterpart, examination and analysis in the study. The range of new books, articles, papers and lectures is too numerous to enumerate there, but attention may be directed to the date of publication of many of the works cited in the bibliography. There is no doubt that excavation and research will continue and will result in fresh discoveries and the solving of old problems as well as the creation of new.

References and Bibliography

General

A.R. Birley, 'The Roman governors of Britain', *Epigraphische Studien* 4, (1967) 163–202

A.R. Birley, *The People of Roman Britain*, London, 1979

E. Birley, *Roman Britain and the Roman Army*, Kendal, 1953

D.J. Breeze, *Roman Scotland: A guide to the visible remains*, Newcastle upon Tyne, 1979

D.J. Breeze and B. Dobson, *Hadrian's Wall*, Harmondsworth, 1978

R.G. Collingwood and J.N.L. Myres, *Roman Britain and the English Settlements*, Oxford, 1937

C.M. Daniels, 'Problems of the Roman northern frontier', *Scottish Archaeological Forum* 2, 1970, 91–101

B. Dobson (ed) The Tenth Pilgrimage of Hadrian's Wall, Kendal, 1979

S.S. Frere, *Britannia*, London, 1974

J.P. Gillam, 'The frontier after Hadrian – a history of the problem', *Archaeologia Aeliana* 5 ser. 2 (1974) 1–15

B.R. Hartley, 'Some problems of the military occupation of the north of England', *Northern History* 1 (1966) 7–20

B.R. Hartley, 'Roman York and the northern military command', in R.M. Butler (ed), *Soldier and Civilian in Roman Yorkshire*, Leicester, 1971, 55–69

E.N. Luttwack, *The Grand Strategy of the Roman Empire from the First Century AD to the Third*, Baltimore and London, 1976

J.C. Mann (ed), *The Northern Frontier in Britain from Hadrian to Honorius: Literary and Epigraphic Sources*, Newcastle upon Tyne, nd. [1971]

J.C. Mann, 'The frontiers of the principate', in H. Temporini (ed), *Aufstieg und Niedergang der Römischen Welt* II, i, Berlin, 1974, 508–33

J.C. Mann, 'Power, force and the frontiers of the empire', review of E. Luttwack, *The Grand Strategy of the Roman Empire from the First Century AD to the Third*, Baltimore and London, 1976, in *J. Roman Studies* 69 (1979) 175–83

J.C. Mann and R.G. Penman, *Literary Sources for Roman Britain* (= Lactor II), 1977

S.N. Miller, *The Roman Occupation of South-western Scotland*, Glasgow, 1952

T.W. Potter, *Romans in North-West England*, Kendal, 1979

I.A. Richmond, *Roman Britain*, London, 1963

I.A. Richmond (ed), *Roman and Native in North Britain*, London, 1958

A.L.F. Rivet and C. Smith, *The Place-Names of Roman Britain*, London, 1979

A.S. Robertson, 'Roman Finds from non-Roman sites in Scotland', *Britannia* 1 (1970) 198–226

A.S. Robertson, 'The Romans in North Britain: The Coin Evidence', in H. Temporini and

W. Haase (edd), *Aufstieg und Niedergang der Römischen Welt* II, iii, Berlin, 1975, 364–426

A.S. Robertson, 'The circulation of Roman coins in North Britain: the evidence of hoards and site-finds from Scotland', in R.A.G. Carson and C.M. Kraay (edd) *Essays presented to Humphrey Sutherland*, 1978, 186–216

P. Salway, *The Frontier People of Roman Britain*, Cambridge, 1965

J.K. St Joseph, 'Air Reconnaissance in Roman Britain, 1969–72', *J. Roman Studies* 63 (1973) 214–46

J.K. St Joseph, 'Air Reconnaissance of Roman Scotland, 1939–75', *Glasgow Archaeological J.* 4 (1976) 1–28

J.K. St Joseph, 'Air Reconnaissance in Roman Britain, 1973–76', *J. Roman Studies* 67 (1977) 125–61

L. Thoms (ed), *Scottish Archaeological Forum* 7 1975, Edinburgh, 1976

D. Young, *Romanisation in Scotland, an essay in perspective*, Tayport, n.d. [1955?]

1 Romans

Ancient sources

Caesar, *The Gallic War*

Cassius Dio, *History of Rome*, 19–23; 62

Florus, *Epitome of Roman History*, 4, 12

Velleius Paterculus, *Compendium of Roman History*, 2, 90–131

Tacitus, *The Annals of Imperial Rome*

Tacitus, *Agricola*

Modern works

H. Schönberger, 'The Roman Frontier in Germany: an archaeological survey', *J. Roman Studies* 59 (1969) 144–97

G. Webster, *The Roman Imperial Army*, London, 1969

C.M. Wells, *The German Policy of Augustus*, Oxford, 1973

2 Barbarians

Ancient sources

Bede, *A History of the English Church and People*, 1

Caesar, *The Gallic War*

Cassius Dio, *History of Rome*, 76

Herodian, *History of Rome*, 3

Ptolemy, *Geography*

Tacitus, *Agricola*

Modern references

L. Alcock, 'Was there an Irish Sea Province in the Dark Ages?' in D. Moore (ed), *The Irish Sea Province in Archaeology and History*, Cardiff, 1970, 55–65

B. Cunliffe, *Iron Age Communities in Britain*, London, 1978

J.G. Evans, *The Environment of Early Man in the British Isles*, London, 1975

K. Jackson, *Language and History in Early Britain*, Edinburgh, 1953

G. Jobey, 'Homesteads and settlements of the frontier area', in C. Thomas (ed), *Rural Settlement in Roman Britain*, London, 1966, 1–14

M. MacGregor, *Early Celtic Art in North Britain*, Leicester, 1976

V. Megaw and D.D.A. Simpson, *British Prehistory*, Leicester, 1979

G. and A. Ritchie, *Edinburgh and South-east Scotland*, London, 1972

G. and A. Ritchie, *Scotland, Archaeology and Early History*, London, 1981

A.L.F. Rivet (ed), *The Iron Age in Northern Britain*, Edinburgh, 1966

A.L.F. Rivet and C. Smith, *The Place-names of Roman Britain*, London, 1979

A. Ross, *Pagan Celtic Britain*, London, 1967

A. Ross, *Everyday Life of the Pagan Celts*, London, 1970

3 Agricola and the first frontier in Britain

Ancient sources

The basic text, with commentary, of the *Agricola* is:

R.M. Ogilvie and I.A. Richmond (ed.), *Cornelii Taciti, de vita Agricolae*, Oxford, 1967

There is also a translation in the Penguin classics series.

Modern works

Two fundamental, though differing, discussions of Agricola's career and achievements are:

E. Birley, 'Britain under the Flavians: Agricola and his predecessors', in *Roman Britain and the Roman Army*, Kendal, 1953, 10–19

I.A. Richmond, 'Gnaeus Julius Agricola', *J. Roman Studies*, 34 (1944) 34–45

Scottish Archaeological Forum 12, 1980, forthcoming, will be devoted to Agricola, containing papers by D.J. Breeze, B. Dobson, S.S. Frere, W.S. Hanson, V.A. Maxfield and G.S. Maxwell

A.R. Birley, 'Agricola, the Flavian Dynasty, and Tacitus', in B. Levick (ed), *The Ancient Historian and his Materials*, Farnborough, 1975, 139–54

A.R. Birley, 'The date of Mons Graupius', *Liverpool Classical Monthly* 1, No. 2 (1976) 11–4

D.J. Breeze and B. Dobson, 'A view of Roman Scotland in 1975', *Glasgow Archaeological J.* 4 (1976) 124–43

J. Clarke, 'Roman and Native, AD 80–122', in I.A. Richmond, *Roman and Native in North Britain*, Edinburgh, 1958, 28–59

R.W. Davies, 'The investigation of some crimes in Roman Egypt', *Ancient Society* 4 (1973) 199–212

W.S. Hanson, 'The first Roman occupation of Scotland', in W.S. Hanson and L.J.F. Keppie (edd), *Roman Frontier Studies 1979* (= BAR International Series 71), Oxford, 1980, 15–43

W.S. Hanson and G.S. Maxwell, 'An Agricolan *Praesidium* on the Forth-Clyde Isthmus (Mollins, Strathclyde)', *Britannia* 11 (1980) 43–9

J.C. Mann, review of R.M. Ogilvie and I.A. Richmond (edd), *Cornelii Taciti, de vita Agricolae*, Oxford, 1967, in *Archaeologia Aeliana* 4 ser. 46 (1968) 306–8

N. Reed, 'The fifth year of Agricola's Campaigns', *Britannia* 2 (1971) 143–8

4 The retreat from total conquest

The Gask Frontier

Ancient sources

Tacitus, *Histories*, 4, 64 (Tencteri)

Tacitus, *Germania*, 41 (Hermanduri)

Modern works

D. Christison, 'Excavation undertaken by the Society of Antiquaries of Scotland of earthworks adjoining the "Roman Road" between Ardoch and Dupplin, Perthshire', *Proc. Soc. Antiq. Scot.* 35 (1900–1) 15–43

C.M. Daniels, 'Problems of the Roman northern frontier', *Scottish Archaeological Forum* 2, 1970, 91–101

A.S. Robertson, 'Roman "Signal Stations" on the Gask Ridge', *Trans. Perthshire Society of Natural Science*, Special Issue (1973) 14–29

E. Ritterling, 'Legio', in Pauly-Wissowa, *Real-Encyclopödie der Classischen Altertumswissenschaft* XII, 2

J.K. St. Joseph, 'Air reconnaissance in Roman Britain, 1969–72', *J. Roman Studies* 63 (1973) 218

J.K. St. Joseph, 'Air reconnaissance in Roman Britain, 1973–76', *J. Roman Studies* 67 (1977) 135–9

H. Schönberger, 'The Roman frontier in Germany: an archaeological survey', *J. Roman Studies* 59 (1969) 144–97

The abandonment of Scotland

E.B. Birley, 'The fate of the Ninth Legion', in R.M. Butler (ed), *Soldier and Civilian in Roman Yorkshire*, Leicester, 1971, 70–80

D.J. Breeze and B. Dobson, 'A view of Roman Scotland in 1975', *Glasgow Archaeological J.* 4 (1976) 124–43

J. Clarke, 'Roman and Native, A.D. 80–122', in I.A. Richmond (ed), *Roman and Native in North Britain*, Edinburgh, 1958, 28–59

B.M. Dickinson and K.F. Hartley, 'The evidence of potters' stamps on samian ware and on mortaria for the trading connections of Roman York', in R.M. Butler (ed), *Soldier and Civilian in Roman Yorkshire*, Leicester, 1971, 128–42

W. Eck, 'Zum Ende der *legio IX Hispana*', *Chiron* 2 (1972) 459–62

B.R. Hartley, 'The Roman occupation of Scotland: the evidence of samian ware', *Britannia* 3 (1972) 1–44

The Stanegate 'frontier'

E. Birley, *Research on Hadrian's Wall*, Kendal, 1961, 132–50

R. Birley, *Vindolanda*, London, 1977

C.M. Daniels, 'Problems of the Roman northern frontier'. *Scottish Archaeological Forum* 2, 1970, 91–101

G.D.B. Jones, 'The western Stanegate', in B. Dobson (ed), *The Tenth Pilgrimage of Hadrian's Wall*, Kendal, 1979, 27

G.D.B. Jones, 'The hidden frontier', *Popular Archaeology* 2, 1 (July 1980) 14–7

5 Hadrian's Wall

Ancient sources

Scriptores Historiae Augustae, Hadrian, 5 and 11

Cornelius Fronto, *Letter to Marcus on the Parthian War*

Modern works

General

E. Birley, *Research on Hadrian's Wall*, Kendal, 1961

D.J. Breeze and B. Dobson, *Hadrian's Wall*, Harmondsworth, 1978

J.C. Bruce, *Handbook to the Roman Wall*, 13th edition by C.M. Daniels, Newcastle, 1978. This contains a detailed bibliography of each structure on the Wall

D. Charlesworth, 'The turrets on Hadrian's Wall', in M.P. Apted, R. Gilyard-Beer and A.D. Saunders (edd), *Ancient Monuments and their interpretation*, London, 1977, 13–26

Ordnance Survey, *Map of Hadrian's Wall*, 1st edition 1964; 2nd edition 1972, Chessington

G. Simpson (ed), *Watermills and Military Works on Hadrian's Wall: Excavations in Northumberland 1907–1913 by F.G. Simpson*, Kendal, 1976

Cumbrian coast

See the series of papers by R.L. Bellhouse in the *Trans. Cumberland Westmorland Antiquarian and Archaeological Soc.* 2 ser. from 54 (1954) to 70 (1970)

N.J. Higham and G.D.B. Jones, 'Frontier, forts and farmers: Cumbrian aerial survey', *Archaeological J.* 132 (1975) 16–53

G.D.B. Jones, 'The western extension of Hadrian's Wall: Bowness to Cardurnock' *Britannia* 7 (1976) 236–43

G.D.B. Jones, 'The development of the coastal frontier', in B. Dobson (ed), *The Tenth Pilgrimage of Hadrian's Wall*, Kendal, 1979, 28–9

G.D.B. Jones, 'The hidden frontier', *Popular Archaeology* 2, 1 (July 1980) 14–7

T.W. Potter, *Romans in North-West England*, Kendal, 1979

T.W. Potter, 'The Cumbrian coast defences and Ravenglass', in B. Dobson (ed), *The Tenth Pilgrimage of Hadrian's Wall*, Kendal, 1979, 24–8

T.W. Potter, 'The Roman frontier in Cumbria', in W.S. Hanson and L.J.F. Keppie (edd), *Roman Frontier Studies 1979* (=BAR International Series 71), Oxford, 1980, 195–200

The function of Hadrian's Wall

E. Birley, 'Hadrianic frontier policy', *Carnuntina* 3 (1956) 25–33

D.J. Breeze and B. Dobson, 'Hadrian's Wall: some problems', *Britannia* 3 (1972) 182–93

R.G. Collingwood, 'The purpose of the Roman Wall', *Vasculum* 8 (1921)

The building of the Wall

P.S. Austen and D.J. Breeze, 'A new inscription from Chesters on Hadrian's Wall', *Archaeologia Aeliana* 5 ser. 7 (1979) 115–26

B. Dobson and D.J. Breeze, *The Building of Hadrian's Wall*, Newcastle upon Tyne, 1970

B. Heywood, 'The Vallum – its problems restated', in M.G. Jarrett and B. Dobson (edd) *Britain and Rome*, Kendal, 1966, 85–94

J. Hooley and D.J. Breeze, 'The building of Hadrian's Wall: a reconsideration', *Archaeologia Aeliana* 4 ser. 46 (1968) 97–114

R. Hunneysett, 'The milecastles of Hadrian's Wall: an alternative explanation', *Archaeologia Aeliana* 5 ser. 8 (1980) 95–107

V.A. Maxfield and R. Miket, 'The excavation of turret 33b (Coesike)', *Archaeologia Aeliana* 4 ser. 50 (1972) 145–78

C.E. Stevens, *The Building of Hadrian's Wall*, Kendal, 1966

B. Swinbank and J.E.H. Spaul, 'The spacing of the forts on Hadrian's Wall', *Archaeologia Aeliana* 4 ser. 29 (1951) 221–38

6 The Antonine Wall

The move north

Ancient sources

Scriptores Historiae Augustae, Antoninus Pius, 5

Pausanias, *Description of Greece*, 8, 43

Eumenius, *Panegyric Constantio Caesari*, 14

Modern references

A.R. Birley, *Marcus Aurelius*, London, 1966

A.R. Birley, 'Roman Frontiers and Roman Frontier Policy. Some Reflections on Roman Imperialism', *Trans. Architect. Archaeol. Soc. Durham Northumberland* 3 (1974) 13–25

D.J. Breeze, 'The abandonment of the Antonine Wall: its date and implications', *Scottish Archaeological Forum* 7, 1975, 67–80

J.G.F. Hind, 'The "Genounian" part of Britain', *Britannia* 8 (1977) 299–34

B. Swinbank, 'The activities of Lollius Urbicus as evidenced by inscriptions', *Trans. Architect. Archael. Soc. Durham Northumberland* 10, Pt 4 (1953) 382–403

The Antonine Wall

General

G. Macdonald, *The Roman Wall in Scotland*, Oxford, 1934

Ordnance Survey, *Map of the Antonine Wall*, Chessington, 1969

A.S. Robertson, *The Antonine Wall*, Glasgow, 1979. This contains a detailed bibliography of all structures on the Wall.

R. Feachem, 'Six Roman Camps near the Antonine Wall', *Proc. Soc. Antiq. Scot.* 89 (1955–6) 329–39

J.P. Gillam, 'Possible changes in plan in the course of the construction of the Antonine Wall, *Scottish Archaeological Forum* 7, 1975, 51–6

L.J.F. Keppie, 'The Building of the Antonine Wall: Archaeological and Epigraphic Evidence', *Proc. Soc. Antiq. Scot.* 105 (1972–4) 151–65

L.J.F. Keppie, 'Some rescue excavation on the line of the Antonine Wall, 1973–6', *Proc. Soc. Antiq. Scot.* 107 (1975–6) 61–80

L.J.F. Keppie, *Roman Distance Slabs from the Antonine Wall*, Glasgow, 1979

G.S. Maxwell, 'The building of the Antonine Wall', *Actes du IXe Congrès international d'etudes sur les frontières Romaines*, Bucharest, 1974, 327–32

I.A. Richmond, 'The Roman frontier in Scotland', *J. Roman Studies* 26 (1936) 190–4

A.S. Robertson, *An Antonine Fort: Golden Hill, Duntocher*, Glasgow, 1957

RCAHMS, *An Inventory of the Prehistoric and Roman Monuments in Lanarkshire*, Edinburgh, 1978

K.A. Steer, 'The Antonine Wall 1934–1959', *J. Roman Studies* 50 (1960) 84–93

K.A. Steer, 'The nature and purpose of the expansions on the Antonine Wall', *Proc. Soc. Antiq. Scot.* 90 (1956–7) 161–9

Antonine Scotland

Ancient sources

Tacitus, *Agricola*, 19

Tacitus, *Annals*, IV, 72: Frisii.

Modern Works

D. Baatz, *Kastell Hesselbach (Limesforchungen 12)*, Berlin, 1973

A.K. Bowman, 'Roman Military Records from Vindolanda', *Britannia* 5 (1974) 360–73

R.W. Davies, 'The Roman Military Diet', *Britannia* 2 (1971) 122–42

J.H. Dickson, C.A. Dickson and D.J. Breeze, 'Flour or bread in a Roman military ditch at Bearsden, Scotland', *Antiquity* 53 (1979) 47–51

J.H. Dickson, 'Exotic Food and Drink in Ancient Scotland', *Glasgow Naturalist* 19, pt 6 (1979) 437–42

J.C. Ewart, 'Animal Bones', in J. Curle, *A Roman Frontier Post and its People, The Fort of Newstead*, Glasgow, 1911, 362–77

W.S. Hanson, 'Croy Hill', in D.J. Breeze (ed.), *Roman Scotland: Some Recent Excavations*, Edinburgh, 1979, 19–20

N.M. McQ. Holmes, 'Excavations at Cramond, Edinburgh 1975–78', in D.J. Breeze (ed.), *Roman Scotland: Some Recent Excavations*, Edinburgh 1979, 11–4

C. Jobey, 'Homesteads and settlements of the frontier area', in C. Thomas (ed), *Rural Settlement in Roman Britain*, London, 1966, 1–14

C. Jobey, 'Notes on some population problems in the area between the two Roman Walls, I', *Archaeologia Aeliana* 5 ser. 2 (1974) 17–26

W.H. Manning, 'Economic influences on land use in the military areas of the Highland Zone during the Roman period', in J.G. Evans, S. Limbrey and H. Cleere (edd), *The Effect of Man on the Landscape: The Highland Zone*, London, 1975, 112–6

G.S. Maxwell, 'Early rectilinear enclosures in the Lothians', *Scottish Archaeological Forum* 2, 1970, 86–90

G. Thomas, 'Inveresk Vicus, Excavations 1976–77', in D.J. Breeze (ed), *Roman Scotland: Some Recent Excavations*, Edinburgh, 1979, 8–10

S.N. Miller (ed), *The Roman occupation of south-western Scotland*, Glasgow, 1952

I.A. Richmond and K.A. Steer, '*Castellum Veluniate* and Civilians on a Roman Frontier', *Proc. Soc. Antiq. Scot.* 90 (1956–7) 1–6

The abandonment of the Antonine Wall

D.J. Breeze, 'The abandonment of the Antonine Wall: its date and implications', *Scottish Archaeological Forum* 7, 1975, 67–80

J.P. Gillam, 'Sources of Pottery found in Northern Military Sites', in A. Detsicas (ed), *Current Research in Romano-British Coarse Pottery*, London, 1973, 53–62

B.R. Hartley, 'The Roman occupation of Scotland: the evidence of samian ware', *Britannia* 3 (1972) 1–55

G.S. Maxwell, 'Excavations at the Roman fort of Crawford, Lanarkshire', *Proc. Soc. Antiq. Scot.* 104 (1971–2) 147–200

I.A. Richmond, 'Excavations at the Roman Fort of Newstead, 1947', *Proc. Soc. Antiq. Scot.* 84 (1949–50) 1–37

7 War and Peace

Ancient sources

Scriptores Historiae Augustae, Marcus Aurelius, 8 and 22

Scriptores Historiae Augustae, Commodus, 6 and 81

Scriptores Historiae Augustae, Pertinax, 2 and 3

Scriptores Historiae Augustae, Severus, 19, 22 and 23

Cassius Dio, *History of Rome*, 71–77

Herodian, *History of Rome*, 3

Modern Works

A.R. Birley, *Septimius Severus*, London, 1971

A.R. Birley, 'Virius Lupus', *Archaeologia Aeliana* 4 ser. 50 (1972) 179–89

M. Brassington, 'Ulpius Marcellus', *Britannia* 11 (1980) 314–5

B. Dobson and D.J. Breeze, 'Hadrian's Wall: some problems', *Britannia* 3 (1972) 200–6

J.D. Leach and J.J. Wilkes, 'The Roman military base at Carpow, Perthshire, Scotland; summary of recent investigations (1964–70, 1975)', in J. Fitz (ed), *Limes: Akten des XI Internationalen Limeskongresses*, Budapest, 1977, 47–62

R. Reece, 'Coins and frontiers: The Falkirk hoard reconsidered', in W.S. Hanson and L.J.F. Keppie (edd), *Roman Frontier Studies 1979* (= BAR International Series 71), Oxford, 1980, 119–29

N. Reed, 'The Scottish campaigns of Septimius Severus', *Proc. Soc. Antiq. Scot.* 107 (1975–6) 92–102

A.S. Robertson, 'The bridges on Severan coins of AD 208 and 209', in W.S. Hanson and L.J.F. Keppie (edd), *Roman Frontier Studies 1979* (= BAR International Series 71), Oxford, 1980, 131–9

C.J. Simpson, 'Ulpius Marcellus again', *Britannia* 11 (1980) 338–9

R.P. Wright, 'Carpow and Caracalla', *Britannia* 5 (1974) 289–92

The reorganisation of the frontier in the late second century

J.P. Gillam, 'Calpurnius Agricola and the northern frontier', *Trans. Architect. Archaeol. Soc. Durham Northumberland* 10, pt 4 (1953) 359–75

J.P. Gillam, 'The frontier after Hadrian – a history of the problem', *Archaeologia Aeliana* 5 ser. 2 (1974) 1–12

J.P. Gillam and J.C. Mann, 'The northern British frontier from Antoninus Pius to Caracalla', *Archaeologia Aeliana* 4 ser. 8 (1970) 1–44

M.G. Jarrett and J.C. Mann, 'Britain from Agricola to Gallienus', *Bonner Jahrbucher* 170 (1970) 178–210

I.A. Richmond, 'The Romans in Redesdale', *Northumberland County History* 15 (1940) 82–106

A.S. Robertson, *Birrens (Blatobulgium)*, Edinburgh, 1975

K.A. Steer, 'The Severan reorganisation', in I.A. Richmond (ed), *Roman and Native in North Britain*, Edinburgh, 1958, 91–111

Brochs, duns and souterrains

E. Mackie, 'Excavations at Leckie, Stirlingshire', in D.J. Breeze (ed), *Roman Scotland: Some Recent Excavations*, Edinburgh, 1979, 52–5

L. Main, 'Excavations at the Fairy Knowe, Buchlyvie, Stirlingshire', in D.J. Breeze (ed), *Roman Scotland: Some Recent Excavations*, Edinburgh, 1979, 47–51

S. Piggott, 'Excavations in the broch and hill-fort of Torwoodlee, Selkirkshire, 1950', *Proc. Soc. Antiq. Scot.* 85 (1950–51) 91–117

R.B.K. Stevenson, 'Metal-work and some other objects in Scotland and their cultural affinities', in A.L.F. Rivet (ed), *The Iron Age in Northern Britain*, Edinburgh, 1966, 17–44

F.T. Wainwright, *The Souterrains of Southern Pictland*, Edinburgh, 1963

T. Watkins, 'Excavation of a settlement and souterrain at Newmill, near Bankfoot, Perthshire', *Proc. Soc. Antiq. Scot.* 110 (1980), 165–208

The third century

R.E. Birley, *Civilians on the Roman Frontier*, Newcastle upon Tyne, 1973

R.E. Birley, *Vindolanda*, London, 1977

C.M. Daniels, 'Excavations at Wallsend and the fourth-century barracks on Hadrian's Wall', in W.S. Hanson and L.J.F. Keppie (edd), *Roman Frontier Studies 1979* (=BAR International Series 71) Oxford, 1980, 173–93

J. Dore and J.P. Gillam, *The Roman Fort at South Shields*, Newcastle upon Tyne, 1979

J.P. Gillam, 'Excavations at Halton Chesters, 1961', *University of Durham Gazette*, n. ser. 9, no 2.

J.P. Gillam, R.M. Harrison and T.G. Newman, 'Interim Report on Excavations at the Roman fort of Rudchester', *Archaeologia Aeliana* 5 ser. 1 (1973) 81–5

G. Jobey, 'Traprain Law: a summary', in D.W. Harding (ed), *Hillforts*, London, 1976, 191–204

G. Jobey, 'Burnswark Hill', *Trans. Dumfriesshire Galloway Natural History and Antiq. Soc.* 53 (1977–8) 57–104

G.D.B. Jones, 'Invasion and Response in Roman Britain', in B.C. Burnham and H.B. Johnson (edd), *Invasion and Response, The case of Roman Britain* (=BAR British Series 73), Oxford, 1979, 57–70

J.C. Mann, 'The northern frontier after AD 369', *Glasgow Archaeological J.* 3 (1974) 34–42

P. Salway, *The Frontier People of Roman Britain*, Cambridge, 1965

D.A. Welsby, 'Roman building inscriptions, recording buildings collapsed through age or destroyed by the enemy?', *Archaeologia Aeliana* 5 ser. 8 (1980) 89–94

The Picts

Ancient sources

Panegyric Constantio Caesari

Panegyric Constantino Augusti

Anonymous Valesianus, 2.4

Ammianus Marcellinus, *History of Rome*, 20; 26–28

Claudian, *On the fourth consulship of Honorius*

Claudian, *On the first consulship of Stilicho* 2

Modern Works

P.J. Casey, 'Constantine the Great in Britain – the evidence of the coinage of the London mint, AD 312–14', in J. Bird *et al* (edd), *Collectanea Londiniensia: studies in London archaeology and history presented to Ralph Merrifield*, London, 1978, 181–93

P.J. Casey and M. Savage, 'The coins from the excavations at High Rochester in 1852 and 1855', *Archaeologia Aeliana* 5 ser. 8 (1980) 75–87

D.V. Clarke, D.J. Breeze and G. MacKay, *The Romans in Scotland*, Edinburgh, 1980

K. Jackson, 'The Britons in southern Scotland', *Antiquity* 114 (June 1955) 77–88

J.C. Mann, 'The northern frontier after AD 369', *Glasgow Archaeological J.* 3 (1974) 34–42

J.C. Mann, 'What was the Notitia Dignitatum for?' in R. Goodburn and P. Bartholomew (edd), *Aspects of the Notitia Dignitatum* (= BAR Supplementary Series 15) Oxford, 1976, 1–9

J.C. Mann, '*Duces* and *comites* in the fourth century', in D.E. Johnston (ed), *The Saxon Shore*, London, 1977, 11–15

J. Morris, *The Age of Arthur*, London, 1973

F.T. Wainwright, 'The Picts and the problem', in F.T. Wainwright (ed), *The Problem of the Picts*, Edinburgh, 1955, 1–53

The end of Hadrian's Wall

Ancient Sources

Claudian, *On the first consulship of Stilicho*

Claudian, *On the Gothic War*

Notitia Dignitatum Occ. XL

Modern works

J.P.C. Kent, 'Coin evidence and the evacuation of Hadrian's Wall', *Trans. Cumberland Westmorland Antiq. Archaeol. Soc.* 2 ser 51 (1951) 4–15

8 Roman and Barbarian

A. Alföldi, 'The moral barrier on Rhine and Danube', in E. Birley (ed), *The Congress of Roman Frontier Studies 1949*, Durham, 1952, 1–16

D.J. Breeze and B. Dobson, 'The development of the mural frontier in Britain from Hadrian to Caracalla', *Proc. Soc. Antiq. Scot.* 102 (1969–70) 109–21

D.J. Breeze and B. Dobson, 'The development of the northern frontier in Britain from Hadrian to Caracalla', *Actes du IXe Congrès international d'etudes sur les frontières Romaines*, Bucharest, 1974, 321–6

J.P. Gillam, 'Roman and Native, AD 122–197', in I.A. Richmond (ed), *Roman and Native in North Britain*, Edinburgh, 1958, 60–90

J.C. Mann, 'The frontiers of the principate', in H. Temporini (ed), *Aufstieg and Niedergang der römischen Welt II*, i, Berlin, 1974, 508–33

R.B.K. Stevenson, 'Romano-British Glass Bangles', *Glasgow Archaeological J.* 4 (1976), 45–54

Index

Index